W9-AEY-603

LOST AIRMEN

LOST AIRMEN

The Epic Rescue of WWII U.S. Bomber
Crews Stranded behind Enemy Lines

CHARLES E. STANLEY JR.

REGNERY
HISTORY
Washington, D.C.

Copyright © 2022 by Charles E. Stanley Jr.

All rights reserved. No part of this publication may be reproduced or transmitted in any form or by any means electronic or mechanical, including photocopy, recording, or any information storage and retrieval system now known or to be invented, without permission in writing from the publisher, except by a reviewer who wishes to quote brief passages in connection with a review written for inclusion in a magazine, newspaper, website, or broadcast.

Regnery History™ is a trademark of Salem Communications Holding Corporation
Regnery® is a registered trademark and its colophon is a trademark of Salem Communications Holding Corporation

Cataloging-in-Publication data on file with the Library of Congress

ISBN: 978-1-68451-262-1
eISBN: 978-1-68451-282-9
Library of Congress Control Number: 2021949800

Published in the United States by
Regnery History, an Imprint of
Regnery Publishing
A Division of Salem Media Group
Washington, D.C.
www.RegneryHistory.com

Manufactured in the United States of America

10 9 8 7 6 5 4 3 2 1

Books are available in quantity for promotional or premium use. For information on discounts and terms, please visit our website: www.Regnery.com.

With gratitude to
Reverend James B. MacGee, OMI,
mentor

CONTENTS

CHAPTER 1

The Making of a Pilot

A forlorn Army Air Forces private sat alone in the back pew of an unadorned chapel. It was a Friday night, and most of his fellow aviation students at the University of Buffalo were out on the town blowing off steam. He had opted to attend this religious retreat instead.

The private yearned to be a pilot, but he knew the odds were against him. Half his classmates would "wash out" and be relegated to lesser duties. He worried that he might fail too, as he found his coursework difficult and uninspiring and felt he was floundering. Yet if he won his wings, the private faced a far greater problem: he would have to survive the most terrible war in history. The six-month Guadalcanal campaign had just proven the Japanese would be a tenacious foe. In eastern Europe, Hitler's Germany and Stalin's Soviet Union squared off across a thousand-mile front stretching from Leningrad to the Caucasus Mountains. Meanwhile, British and American forces battled the Germans in northern Africa.

The Normandy D-Day invasion remained over a year away. For now, the air war served as the second front against Hitler's Fortress Europe. It held perils beyond the private's imagination. The casualty rate for

American airmen was worse than among the Marines in the Pacific—the life expectancy of U.S. Eighth Air Force crews was fourteen missions. Just one quarter of its personnel survived a full twenty-five-mission tour. The struggle for air supremacy had become a war of attrition, and replacements were desperately needed.

The private was eager to become one of them. Six months before, he had been a twenty-year-old civilian facing two options: he could wait to be drafted, or he could volunteer for one of the specialized service branches. He did not want to spend the war marching through muddy battlefields, and the Navy was out of the question as he hated water and did not know how to swim.

Aviation, however, held a certain romance. World War I aces, barnstorming daredevils, and aeronautical record-setters lived fresh in memory. Only fifteen years had passed since Lindbergh's solo transatlantic flight. Magazines showcased handsome fliers being admired by pretty girls. In contrast, the nickname for the common infantryman—dogface—spoke for itself. If a young man wanted high status, good pay, and a sharp uniform, enlisting in the Army Air Forces was just the ticket.[1]

■   ■   ■

So far, however, the private's experiences had not lived up to his expectations. He passed the qualifying examinations with ease, but boot camp in wintertime Atlantic City had been awful, beginning with his quarters in an unheated hotel designed for summer tourism. His lightweight, short-sleeved uniform offered little protection against the elements. The inductees received a battery of inoculations. As each recruit filed through, a doctor held up a needle to capture his attention. Then a second doctor jabbed him from the opposite side. When the victim turned his head toward the pinprick, the first doctor stabbed the other arm. Some fainted on the spot.

The unit's drill sergeant spewed profanities as he drove the recruits up and down the boardwalk. When heavy uniforms arrived, he refused to let them drill in their overcoats, marching them in sub-zero temperatures to the point of frostbite. The private thought the sergeant must be insane.

For exercise, the recruits formed a circle and took turns breaking out through the group's interlocked arms. One scrum had injured the private's left knee, but he hid his limp as best as he could for fear of washing out.

To add to his troubles, his girlfriend, Mary, had just broken up with him. It was small consolation she had jilted him to enter a convent. Now a novice, she still corresponded with him. "Just around the corner," she predicted in her most recent letter, "is a darling girl who's sweet enough and good enough to share with you your heart and home. I know she'll make you very happy."

Now, seated in the quiet chapel, the private didn't realize he was being watched from above. Mary Alice Schmitz, a freshman at Buffalo's State Teachers' College, stood perched in the front row of the choir loft with her friends Janice and Lorraine. They had volunteered to help run the religious retreat sponsored by their school's Newman Center, a ministry organization for Catholics attending secular colleges. Between hymns, the trio checked out the male contingent below. A dozen smartly uniformed soldiers were interspersed among the assembly of worshipers. Per custom, they had removed their Army caps. One head of wavy black hair stood out. Lorraine, a pretty blonde, pointed at him. "Did you see the cute one?"

"I don't like cute boys!" snapped Mary Alice. She had indeed noticed the handsome private at the registration table, but boys with his kind of looks never seemed interested in bespectacled, serious girls like her. Besides, she volunteered regularly at the local USO and knew how visiting soldiers could be.

Saturday evening found the private at the chapel again. As that day's portion of the retreat ended, everyone lined up for confession to prepare their souls for Communion the next day. The private entered the confessional, knelt, and murmured, "Bless me Father, for I have sinned." He usually disliked confession, and he especially hated sharing confidences with priests he did not know. This time, however, his confessor was Father Dempsey, the jovial moderator of the retreat. Something about the priest's manner helped the words come out. The private confessed more than his sins; he revealed his loneliness and admitted self-doubt. Father Dempsey listened, gave the private his penance, and encouraged him to be more assertive. God would be with him wherever he went.

The private emerged from the confessional with a renewed spirit. A medical student from the university named Charlie Bauer had promised to give him a ride back to his quarters across town, but Bauer was nowhere to be found, even outside in the wintry March air. The private retreated to the sanctuary of the church. There he spotted a young lady making her way down the line of penitents awaiting their turn in the confessional.

What a pretty girl, thought the private. Her glasses didn't bother him a bit. He had noticed her selling raffle tickets earlier in the day.

Father Dempsey had asked Mary Alice to take a count for breakfast the next morning. Only one soldier remained. Drawing closer, she took in his square chin, steel-gray eyes, and wavy black hair. He was the "cute one" from the evening before. She swallowed and asked if he would attend.

The private said yes, he would be present. His name? "Charles Stanley." Would she be there tomorrow, too? She would. Normally laconic, the private began to blather away, sharing random thoughts— anything to keep the conversation going. Mary Alice wondered if she would ever be able to break away and finish her duties. Mercifully, Charlie Bauer materialized to take Private Stanley off her hands.[2]

■   ■   ■

The next morning, after the retreat's closing Mass, Charles sat down to breakfast as promised. He had not seen Mary Alice all morning. Just when he was about to give up, she took a seat at the opposite end of his table and began chatting with some of the soldiers. Charles ate his French toast, sipped his tomato juice, and beat his brains out trying to think of something to say to her.

The moderator began a speech and the table quieted down. Charles stole a look at Mary Alice. She caught his glance and smiled. He winked at her, surprised he could be so bold. She did not seem to mind, but refocused her attention on the speaker. He must talk to her again—but how? He needed an entrée, an excuse to begin the conversation.

The program finished and the crowd broke up. Off to one side, Charles spotted Mary Alice talking to Charlie Bauer, again his ride back to the university. Charles strode up and joined them. It happened that Bauer and Mary Alice lived in the same neighborhood and knew each other's families well. Bauer asked if she wanted a ride home. Mary Alice, who otherwise faced a long bus ride, accepted gladly. By the time the ride was over, Charles had arranged to take her to lunch.[3]

Mary Alice and Charles saw each other at every chance over the next several weeks. Often, they went to the movies. On Sundays, they returned to her home for dinner. Afterward, as her family listened to Jack Benny and Charlie McCarthy on the radio, Mary Alice and Charles snuggled behind the Sunday funnies.

Mary Alice's mother did not object when they took a half hour to read a single page. Charles was a teetotaling, well-mannered young man in the service of his country and—most important—a fellow Catholic. Mrs. Schmitz fed him her best meals and plied him with his favorite treat, ice cream. Despite wartime rationing, the family grocery business ensured there were no food shortages in the Schmitz household.

One Sunday afternoon, Mary Alice and Charles rode a bus to nearby Niagara Falls, where Charles kissed her for the first time. They had been dating for a month.

When Charles finished his final week at the university, he took Mary Alice to his graduation dance. The band played a new tune, "Wait for Me, Mary," seemingly written just for them. Charles whispered, "I love you," took off his high school ring, and asked Mary Alice to wear it. She said she would because she loved him too.

When the day arrived for Charles to ship out, Mary Alice went to the campus to see him off. After he left, she returned home and threw herself on her bed, sobbing uncontrollably. The next day she would turn eighteen.[4]

■   ■   ■

Charles's next stop was the Army Air Forces (AAF) Classification Center in Nashville. There the Army tested its officer candidates and matched their aptitudes and personality traits to one of three specialties: pilot, navigator, and bombardier. Unsuitable candidates were dropped to the enlisted ranks.

The AAF asked each candidate his preference for placement. Charles listed pilot as his first choice. He assumed pilots needed the highest scores, though this was not necessarily the case. Sometimes navigators needed better marks than pilots due to the required mathematical skills.

Charles's first hurdle was a day-long battery of exhausting paper-and-pencil tests. Toward afternoon, his head fogged and his vision blurred. By the end, simple arithmetic became difficult. The next day Charles confronted four more hours of written exams, followed by several tests on apparatuses designed to measure his coordination and ability to multitask. The Army had designed these tests to be both challenging and frustrating, so the candidate's aptitude and attitude could be evaluated simultaneously. Finally, he met with a psychologist on the lookout for emotional disorders. One in ten candidates failed such interviews. Anyone exhibiting homosexual tendencies was disqualified.

The doctor asked Charles whether he got along with his family and if he smoked, gambled, or drank. Yes, no, no, and no. Did he like girls? Charles happened to have a girlfriend in Buffalo. The psychologist finished by wishing him good luck. Charles took this as a good sign.

He faced his AAF physical exam the next day. The exam, the most stringent in the Army, included a critical set of eye examinations. Poor eyesight generated more disqualifications than any other factor. Charles was more concerned that the doctors would discover his bad knee, but he need not have worried. He possessed the exact physical qualities needed by the AAF. His eyesight, reflexes, and hand-to-eye coordination proved to be exceptional. Even among the elite aviation students, he rarely lost at his favorite pastime, ping-pong.

Four days after the tests, an envelope arrived for Charles. He was to train as a pilot.[5]

Charles now belonged to Army Air Forces Class 44-B. He was part of the most rapid—and successful—expansion of any nation's military the world had ever known. In June 1939, the Air Corps mustered only 13 B-17 heavy bombers and 22,287 personnel. As war approached, American industry mobilized to produce tens of thousands of fighters, bombers, and transports. An unprecedented number of pilots were needed to man them, along with hosts of other skilled specialists. The Army Air Forces transformed itself into the largest educational institution on earth. By 1944, at 2.4 million personnel, the AAF comprised one-third of the United States Army.

Only eighteen months were allotted for pilot training. Slow learners faced elimination. The war would not wait. First, Charles entered the "Pre-Flight" program at Maxwell Field, Alabama. There he would receive the technical and physical training required of every AAF officer.

Maxwell Field's history coincided with that of manned flight. The Wright brothers had opened a flying school on the site in 1910. Eventually, it hosted the Air Corps Tactical School (ACTS), the first military aviation academy in the world.

The faculty at Maxwell had refined schools of aerial thought that were introduced in the 1920s by Italian fascist Giulio Douhet and General William "Billy" Mitchell. Douhet believed air superiority would win future wars. He held that civilian workers contributed to the war effort as much as soldiers and were therefore legitimate objectives for long-range bombers. Moreover, they would be more easily cowed than uniformed personnel. Mitchell agreed with Douhet on the importance of air power, but he focused more on the enemy's transportation and industrial targets.

Casualties might occur among civilian workers, but only as a necessary side effect. At first the U.S. Army rejected these revolutionary theories and relegated the newborn Air Corps to a supporting role for ground troops. Eventually, however, the Air Corps adopted the doctrines developed at Maxwell. Strategic bombing, not tactical support for infantry, became the Air Corps' core mission, and the long-range heavy bomber became its main instrument.

Students at Maxwell Field learned that future wars would be won by attacking the enemy's key industries: steel, electric power, oil, and railroads. Precision bombing would also minimize civilian casualties—an important political consideration for the Western democracies even in wartime.

Strategic bombing became more than a theory when war broke out in Europe. Germany attempted to implement Douhet's precepts during the Battle of Britain but failed to subjugate the British population. In turn, Britain's Bomber Command experimented with day raids against German industries but reverted to nighttime attacks against population centers when losses proved too costly. The AAF picked up the mantle of daylight precision bombing and sustained heavy losses, but still failed to achieve air superiority. The efficacy of the Maxwell theories remained in doubt.[6]

Pre-Flight's physical conditioning regimen was another innovation developed at Maxwell Field. Its routines, including calisthenics, parallel bars, and dumbbells, were designed to improve coordination and build the muscles associated with flying. Most cadets, including Charles, viewed the newfangled exercises as strange and silly, though they were certainly exhausting.

The most distinctive workout at Maxwell, however, was the legendary "Burma Trail," a pretzel-shaped cross-country running course. Although one cadet estimated it to be "exactly 77,098,675,233 miles in length," in actuality the trail featured three miles of diabolical torture better suited for mountain goats. The trail opened with an innocent-looking footpath and swept across a ravine riddled with trees, bushes, and jagged rocks. After climbing a sharp slope, it enjoyed a brief, level sprint before breaking to the left and tripping down steep grades. Up sprang hairpin turns through woods, unnavigable streams, and a staircase hewn out of rock. Traversing a deep ditch, the trail escaped the forest and flattened into a dusty savanna exposed to the hot Alabama sun. Just as all trespassing legs had transformed into wobbly lead weights, it teased around an easy curve, confronted one last impossibly steep incline, and staggered flaccidly across the finish line.

Much to his surprise, Charles thrived on the exercise. He even ran the Burma Trail voluntarily to stay in top shape. He had gained thirty pounds since enlisting, and for the first time, he began to think of himself as a man rather than a boy.[7]

■   ■   ■

Maxwell's academic program proved just as rigorous as its physical training. The cadets could hardly believe the pace of their regimen. Legend had it that a cadet once dropped his pencil in math class and missed a year of algebra.

Charles breezed through the academic subjects, but his other courses—Aircraft Recognition, Naval Recognition, and Radio Code—were another story. Cadets were required to identify Allied and Axis aircraft silhouettes in one-fifth of a second, replicating a fighter pilot's need to distinguish friend from foe at four hundred miles per hour. Radio Code was even more feared. Each cadet had to master the "dits" and "dahs" at eight words per minute or face elimination.

Charles grappled with these perceptional subjects. His inability to transcribe Morse code gnawed at his nerves. The tension impacted his other studies, and his fragile self-confidence waned.

As usual, Charles sought solace from his two main sources of support: his faith and Mary Alice. These had become intertwined. Mary Alice had attended Catholic schools since kindergarten and knew more about their religion than he did. She instructed him in the Act of

Contrition so he would go to heaven if he died without going to confession. They exchanged religious pamphlets and arranged to pray the rosary simultaneously at 9:30 p.m. at every chance.

Now, in his time of crisis, Charles paid a lengthy visit to the chapel. He also wrote a letter to Mary Alice, his longest since leaving Buffalo.

Somehow, the pressure diminished. Over time Charles's aircraft recognition improved, and even Radio Code came easier. His favorite song, "Comin' in on a Wing and a Prayer," auspiciously struck #1 on the *Your Hit Parade* radio program. He graduated from Maxwell with high marks.[8]

■   ■   ■

Charles felt more in his element once he reached flight school. He soloed after only eleven hours in the air. The next question was whether he would choose single- or multi-engine aircraft. He flirted with fighters but ultimately opted for multi-engine training. That way, he could branch into either bombers or transports. He already planned to make a life with Mary Alice after the war, and there might be a post-war demand for commercial pilots.

Working with multiple engines, however, meant Charles would have to command a crew. He had never supervised anyone. The AAF offered little instruction in leadership. It assumed its carefully selected men would become natural leaders once they survived flight training.

Charles's closest brush with leadership training came when his instructors taught him how to give orders—that is, how to yell at his subordinates. Shouting for effect made him feel self-conscious and embarrassed. His superiors berated him for not barking his orders stridently enough. He confessed in a letter to Mary Alice that he doubted his leadership potential. She would have none of it. In her mind, Charles already was a leader; he just did not realize it yet. She promptly set him straight with a long letter denouncing loudmouths and praising his quiet moral strength.

Mary Alice's note had its intended effect. Charles's leadership rating increased. The letter became his favorite, and he carried it constantly as a reminder of her faith. He never doubted his ability to become a leader of men again.

Charles received only a single, one-hour lecture on parachute jumping during his flight training. His female instructor assured the cadets that their chute would not fail them as long as they treated it with the appropriate care. The cadets took no practice jumps—there was too much risk of injury after the AAF's large investment in the men. Instead, the apparently expendable woman made a demonstration jump, landed in a swamp, and nearly drowned. Unimpressed, the lieutenant in charge of the group declared that anyone who parachuted from a perfectly good airplane ought to have his head examined.

"I'll stick to the plane, thanks," commented Charles in a letter to Mary Alice.[9]

After a gestational nine months, Second Lieutenant Charles Stanley graduated from flight school on February 8, 1944. Forty percent of his class had washed out. Stanley's graduation was the realization of his most fervent ambition, and—just as important for his morale—meant he got a ten-day pass. First, he traveled home to rural Pennsylvania. Growing up, he had been educated in a one-room schoolhouse, progressing through his lessons so rapidly that he graduated from high school at sixteen. Still growing, he had been too underdeveloped for athletics and shy with girls despite his good looks. Now everyone in town greeted the smartly uniformed soldier as a hometown hero. The kid who had spent his youth in obscurity was now a *pilot*.

Stanley hoped that Mary Alice would visit, but she could not take time off from school, so he boarded a bus for Buffalo after only a few days at home. They had not seen each other since the prior May. Most of their courtship had been by correspondence. Stanley knew Mary Alice kept a practical eye on their relationship. Had she decided their long-distance romance was hopeless? Was she still the person he remembered?

There had been bumps along the way. The written word had its limitations, and misunderstandings could take weeks to resolve. In one letter, Mary Alice commented that "soldiers are not to be trusted too far away from home." Stanley bristled when he read it and responded acerbically. He was a soldier far from home. Did she consider him untrustworthy? Mary Alice responded, explaining that she was merely repeating her mother's warnings about the soldiers she met at the USO. She had taken for granted that her boyfriend was not that kind and failed to see he might be insulted.

Mary Alice suffered her own qualms. "If we're honest," she wrote, "we'll have to admit that we aren't the same two people who said goodbye." Maybe their feelings had changed too.

When they reunited, however, their doubts melted like the morning mist. Soon they talked as comfortably as before. Stanley joked about the tradition that women could propose marriage on the upcoming leap-year day. "I'll never have to propose to you," he teased. "You'd better!" Mary Alice quipped. It was the perfect time to pop the question, but Stanley chickened out.

After three days, Stanley left for his next phase of training. He considered calling Mary Alice long-distance to ask her to marry him, but again he got cold feet. He never liked talking on the telephone anyway. Instead, he would use his usual medium, a letter. "I guess there is an understanding between us for after the war," he wrote, "but I feel I owe you more than that—that I should offer you a real ring in place of my graduation ring."

Stanley dropped the note at the base's post. With that, he could only sweat it out while he awaited her reply.[10]

■   ■   ■

Happily, the AAF granted Stanley's request to be assigned to heavy bombers and sent him to Smyrna, Tennessee, for transition training. He was less pleased that he had been assigned to fly the B-24 Liberator. Stanley's first impression was that it must be the ugliest airplane in the AAF.

Despite its homeliness, by many measures the B-24 was the most successful bomber of the war. More airmen flew aboard B-24s than any other airplane. Employed by both the Army and the Navy, it was the only American bomber that served in every theater of operation. Over a thousand Liberators were exported to the British, Canadian, and Australian air forces.

The key was the aircraft's versatility. Its range and speed exceeded that of the more glamorous B-17, making it an ideal craft not just for raids deep into enemy territory, but also for reconnaissance and submarine-hunting missions. Occasionally, it even served as a transport.

Nevertheless, the B-24 had its drawbacks. The pilots' small windows provided a limited view. The blunt nose turret featured on later models caused its nose to wander in flight. The B-24's powerful engines could bully through the choppiest air, but flying it demanded strength, endurance, and attentiveness. Due to the aerodynamic, narrow design of its wings, the plane needed high speed to stay aloft. It glided like a rock. If a wing took a direct hit from a flak shell, it often collapsed or broke off, leaving the crew little time to bail out.

The plane's real Achilles' heel was its fuel system. It sprang leaks easily, making the aircraft susceptible to fires and explosions. Fuel transfers from reserve tanks to the mains were tricky, and it was difficult to get a true reading on the fuel gauges.

Airmen were fond of disputing the merits of the B-24 versus the B-17. Liberator pilots sneered there were only four things wrong with the B-17—its engines. Motorheads agreed that the B-24's Pratt and Whitney engines topped the B-17's Wright Cyclone motors. Cyclones rattled; Pratt and Whitneys purred.

On the other hand, B-17 pilots boasted of their bomber's superior handling, ability to fly at higher altitudes, and legendary capacity to endure battle damage. In addition, the B-17 had one unquestioned advantage: its broad, low wings offered a much higher survivability factor during crash landings. Ditching at sea was close to suicidal in a Liberator. The plane would often break up and sink before the crew could escape.

Regardless, one thing was for certain: the B-24 was the far more challenging aircraft to fly, particularly during an emergency. Any mediocre aviator could fly a B-17. A B-24 commander had to be a good pilot, or he was a dead one.[11]

■　　■　　■

A week after Stanley mailed his proposal to Mary Alice, her response arrived in the morning post. She kept him waiting until the fourth page. "The answer is 'yes' my darling," she wrote. "I want to wear your ring and I'll be proud to wear it." They would not marry until after the war—assuming Stanley survived.

Stanley grinned all day long, but there was little time for celebration. His busy schedule would not allow it.[12]

■　　■　　■

At first, Stanley had found learning to fly the B-24 to be somewhat daunting. The controls were more complex than any he had operated before. Moreover, as he was a budding aircraft commander, the AAF expected him to know nearly as much about each crewman's station on the plane as he did. Some of his future crew might be assigned to his B-24 without having trained in one, and it would be his job to complete their instruction.

Now, however, Stanley believed he could surmount any challenge. He still welcomed Mary Alice's daily letters of encouragement, but they were not as essential as before. With her help, he had developed into the self-assured pilot the AAF expected him to become. He felt confident he would be designated as a first pilot—the aircraft's commander—rather than a copilot. In due course, he proved to be correct.

Stanley grew to appreciate the B-24. An awkward, ugly duckling on the ground, it revealed a surprising elegance once aloft. Like many, he learned that to fly a Liberator was to love it.[13]

■   ■   ■

Passing through the AAF processing point at Lincoln, Nebraska, Stanley drew his first crewman, a husky bombardier named Edward Seaver. "Big Ed" seemed friendly, capable, and eager to learn. Stanley hit it off with him right away. They soon transferred to Biggs Field near El Paso, Texas, where Stanley would meet the rest of his men and shape them into a crew.

Soon Stanley's copilot, Robert Plaisance, arrived with a pretty wife and small son in tow. Plaisance stood six foot one but looked thin as a rail. Stanley doubted he would be strong enough to help much in the cockpit. Maybe his slight build had consigned him to the position of copilot.

To Stanley, everything about Plaisance, from his sandy blond hair to his loud sports jacket and his jaunty convertible, just reeked of his native California. He even listed his home address as Hollywood. When Plaisance smiled, his hollow-cheeked, tanned face revealed bright, conceited teeth. His audacious blue eyes sparkled with mischief. His legs stretched languidly like Gary Cooper's. Stanley wondered if he had been in the movies.

Since Plaisance lived off-base with his family, Stanley hardly got to know him. He never suspected that Plaisance, who was six years older than his straitlaced pilot and considerably more worldly, thought he should command the aircraft in his place.

Other crewmen straggled in. The plane's flight engineer and top enlisted man would be Corporal Forrest Smalley, one of the few men on base who had previously worked on B-24s. Smalley was the oldest member of the crew at twenty-nine, and Stanley hoped his maturity would set a good example for the rest.

Staff Sergeant Darrell Kiger manned the radio. A former pre-veterinary student, Kiger had washed out as a pilot when he contracted jaundice and could not make up the lost sick time. He switched to radio school, where he became captain of his training class.

Nose gunner Albert Buchholz and tail gunner Sam Spomer were both German-speakers whose parents had immigrated from pre-Nazi Germany. Otherwise, they were as different from each other as their opposing positions on the plane. Buchholz, a burly, rough-looking man, hid his gentility behind a gruff exterior. Spomer, younger and delicately featured, seemed purposeful and willing to please.

Waist gunner Claude Tweedale, the baby of the crew, had been a fireman. His occasional mustache grew with a red tint that clashed with his sandy brown hair and never quite filled in.

Peter Homol took the Sperry ball turret. A stocky five foot six, Homol was large for the position but possessed the steady nerves it took to fly suspended under the plane in a tiny Plexiglas sphere.

In mid-June, a group of navigators arrived, and Leo Cone, a lean six-footer from Montana, joined the crew. Cone promptly demonstrated impeccable navigation. His calm presence helped the crew jell. Plaisance flew better and Ed Seaver often dropped his bombs within five hundred feet of the bull's-eye, an excellent mark. The gunners peppered their targets with accuracy.

By the main criteria set by the AAF—the speed at which they earned their proficiency ratings—they were a fine crew. They ranked third among twenty-eight crews at the end of their first month.[14]

■   ■   ■

Regardless of their rating, only one factor would earn Stanley the crew's respect: they needed to have complete faith in his flying skills. Like all of them, Stanley was learning on the job. It was his first time flying the turret-nosed version of the B-24. Always self-critical and honest with himself, he knew better than anyone that some of his flights were less than perfect.

One evening, Stanley and Cone happened to be outdoors practicing celestial navigation when they spotted two planes flying toward nearby Mount Franklin, a seven-thousand-foot peak. *They'll turn*, Stanley thought. But the lead plane flew straight into the mountainside and dissolved in a ball of flame. The second plane barely veered off. The fire could be seen for miles. Eight men died in the crash.

The accident reminded the crew that their lives were in Stanley's hands. His test came when he was forced to make a nighttime landing in a blinding rainstorm. Stanley executed the difficult landing flawlessly, convincing his men that he could get them through the war in one piece. The forming of the crew was complete.[15]

■   ■   ■

With their flight training concluded, the crew was granted a seven-day leave. It was their final chance to see their loved ones before they went off to war.

Once again, Stanley faced the dilemma of limited time and the desire to see both his family in Pennsylvania and his fiancée in Buffalo. Mary Alice solved the problem by traveling to the Stanley home, bringing her mother along as chaperone.

The Stanley family, like Mary Alice's, had been unscarred by the Great Depression. His father worked as the chief engineer of a pump station for a natural gas pipeline. Their house stood with a half dozen others on the station's grounds, far out in the country forty miles north of Pittsburgh.

Mary Alice had never seen a farm before. Cows grazed within view of the Stanleys' front porch, and the smells were far different from those of the city, as were the noises—or the lack of them. Even the constant *pockita-pockita* from the pumps sounded muffled. Mary Alice found the experience to be as exotic as a journey to the far side of the world.

On Saturday, his last night before going off to war, they stayed up all night on the porch swing. Charles's head rested on Mary Alice's lap while her fingers twirled the dark waves of his hair. After a time, they had said everything there was to say. They sat awake in silence until dawn.

Behind them, in the Stanleys' front window, hung a white flag with a red border and a single blue star in the middle. The blue star represented Charles. A gold star would replace it if he were killed. Charles assured Mary Alice he would return, but both knew there were no guarantees.

After Sunday Mass, Mary Alice accompanied Charles to the train station. On the platform, a pit grew in her stomach until she thought she might lose her breakfast. A train whistle startled her, and she nearly collapsed.

Perhaps it was the lack of sleep, but there were no dramatic farewells. Stanley felt numb. Mary Alice could not find the words. She fought tears and worried she might lose control if she hugged him. They kissed, said goodbye, and he boarded.

Mary Alice waved ferociously, hoping in vain for a last glimpse. The train was gone and so was he.[16]

CHAPTER 2

Shot Down Twice

After a long sea voyage, Stanley and his men arrived in southern Italy and joined the Fifteenth Air Force. The Fifteenth, while not as large or famous as the Eighth Air Force based in Great Britain, was playing a key role in the air war over Europe.

After Italy surrendered to the Allies, the benefits of stationing bombers there had been too great to be ignored. Much of the Third Reich's most vital strategic asset, its oil supply, lay within range. The AAF also hoped—erroneously—that "sunny Italy" would offer better flying weather than England.

In April 1944, the Fifteenth began attacks on the vast Ploesti oil complex. Raids against central and southeastern Europe continued over the next several months. The losses were appalling. Almost 500 of its heavy bombers went down between April and June. In July alone, the Fifteenth lost another 318 bombers. Meanwhile, luckier crews completed their tours and went home. Stanley's crew, with hundreds of others, rushed in as replacements.[1]

Stanley's men were assigned to the 464th Bomb Group at Pantanella. They took residence in two hilltop tents, one for the four officers and one

for the six enlisted men. Stanley's abode offered a view of the twin runways in the valley below but little else. It had no heat and no water. The
base featured no hot showers. The nearest town lay thirty miles away.

Nevertheless, morale remained high. The Red Army had just overrun
Ploesti, removing the Fifteenth's nastiest target. The Russians had also
liberated thousands of downed airmen from Romanian prisoner-of-war
camps. Shortly after Stanley's arrival, seventy-nine recently freed POWs
returned to the base. Although the men looked ragged and hungry, the
sight of them reassured everyone that being shot down was not a death
sentence.

Stanley's first mission, during which he served only as an observer,
came on September 17, a raid against Budapest. Several missions leading
his own crew followed. Eventually, he was assigned a regular aircraft,
a tired-looking B-24 called the *Fertile Turtle* after an Ogden Nash
poem: "The turtle lives 'twixt plated decks, which practically conceal
its sex. I think it clever of the turtle in such a fix to be so fertile." The
plane's nose art featured a turtle excreting bomb-like eggs from its rear.
The plane suffered from chronic mechanical maladies, but Stanley
developed an attachment to it equal to the devotion a sea captain feels
toward his vessel.

The *Turtle* exhibited its usual troubles on an October 7 mission to
Ersekujar, Hungary. Stanley was forced to land her on three engines. He
took this as a positive sign. If he could coax the *Turtle* to make a good
landing absent an engine, she must be a good and a lucky ship. Ersekujar,
however, was a near milk-run. No one could tell how the plane might
perform over more dangerous targets.[2]

■   ■   ■

On October 13, 1944, a duty officer woke Stanley at 3:30 a.m. The
pilot, in turn, roused his tentmates. Leo Cone lit the heating contraption
he had devised—a stove fed by 100 octane aviation fuel. The four officers
donned their flight suits and stepped out into the pre-dawn bleakness.

Below, silhouettes of twin-finned B-24s brooded on either side of the twin runways.

After a breakfast of powdered eggs, blackened toast, and pancakes smothered with lardy butter, they finished their cups of hot GI coffee and shuffled to Group Headquarters. Inside, they took seats on empty ammo boxes. Most of the men puffed away at cigarettes, and a smoky haze obscured the curtained map dominating the front of the room. It was Friday the 13th. Moreover, today would be the thirteenth mission for the crews led by pilots Lt. William Price and Lt. Raymond Borg. Superstition abounded.

Bob Plaisance had been lobbying for a chance to become a first pilot for weeks. The brass had scheduled a veteran pilot to check him out, but the man finished his tour before it could happen. Frustrated, Plaisance braced for another day in the copilot's chair.

The adjutant strode in and barked, "Ten-hut!" The room snapped to. The CO, Colonel Schroeder, entered and gave a perfunctory "Be seated, gentlemen. Smoke 'em if you got 'em." An aide unveiled the mission map. Their target would be Blechhammer, a synthetic oil refinery at the far end of their range. Groans settled. It would be a long, tough, dangerous day.[3]

■   ■   ■

Hitler had lacked petroleum even when he controlled Ploesti. Germany did, however, possess a plentiful coal supply that could be converted to synthetic gasoline. Hitler's production czar, Albert Speer, built several conversion plants in eastern Europe outside of the range of the Eighth Air Force. They produced most of the Reich's high-octane aviation fuel. The plants were Hitler's Achilles' heel, and only the Fifteenth could reach them.

The twin refineries at Blechhammer North and South served as Germany's largest synthetic complex. The Fifteenth had bombed the site six times since July. Now slave laborers from the nearby Auschwitz concentration camp had brought it back to life. Reflecting the complex's significance, the Germans had increased the number of flak guns protecting it by 25 percent.

The chaplain closed the briefing with a prayer. Pilots collected flimsies—detailed instructions printed on edible paper—while navigators picked up charts and bombardiers received aerial photos of the target. Everyone drew an escape kit containing nylon maps, gold-backed dollars, a compass, and other survival gear. Then trucks carried them to their awaiting planes.[4]

The 464th took off, formed up, and joined several other bomb groups over the Adriatic. Hundreds of warbirds filled the vast expanse. Every flight stirred Stanley's pride that his country could launch an armada of this scale and power.

The *Turtle* flew merrily across Hungary. A hundred barges floated on the Danube just west of Budapest. A few ineffective flak shells whizzed skyward. An hour later, the formation found the initial point (IP) for the bomb run and turned toward the target.

The sky ahead shone an azure blue. Below, German smoke generators created thick black ground cover. Flak gunners pumped shells skyward. At their appointed elevation, each casing burst into 1,500 deadly pieces of shrapnel. Every airplane within 200 yards would take hits. The barrages carpeted the skies over Blechhammer North and South.

The 464th penetrated the thick gauntlet. Black puffs belched jagged, razor-sharp steel fragments. Booming concussions rocked the planes. A cliché claimed that flak could be "thick enough to walk on." This looked more like an impenetrable wall. No one recalled having seen worse. The shrapnel did not discriminate between officers and enlisted men, nor between the virtuous and sinners. Either one of them had their name on it or not.

A cluster of shards found *No Excuse*, piloted by Lt. William Price. The plane spiraled to the right and passed out of sight at ten thousand feet. Just then Lt. Raymond Borg's plane—the optimistically named *Be Comin Back*—took direct hits and winged over. Eight chutes emerged.

The B-24 passed through plumes of smoke and transformed into a giant fireball against the ground. Neither Price nor Borg would return from his thirteenth mission. More fragments struck *Yellow Oboe*. Its pilot, Lt. John Suber, dropped out of formation. Gaps formed all over the sky as more B-24s fell in flames.[5]

The *Turtle* rocked as a shell ripped through its right outboard engine. Half a dozen bursts flayed the aircraft with jagged steel, perforating the waist section. Voices yelled, "We're hit!" over the interphone. "Bombs away!" cried Ed Seaver.

The *Turtle* plummeted. Stanley was not sure he could stabilize her. The stricken propeller windmilled limply. Stanley tried to feather it—lock it into place with the blade turned into the wind—but the mechanism failed. The other engine on the right side had lost its supercharger and could not function at the high altitude. Gasoline sieved everywhere.

Out of the blue, the right inboard propeller kicked alive, but only at reduced power. The aircraft had fallen low enough that the engine could work without the supercharger.

Stanley leveled the plane off and made a quick survey. The damage was bad, but no one was hurt. High-octane fumes pervaded the air. One spark could blow the *Turtle* to smithereens. Darrell Kiger felt as if his skin was on fire from the soaking gasoline.

The pilots discussed their next move. Plaisance wanted to head for home. Stanley disagreed. Italy lay 650 miles away, across Hungary, Yugoslavia, and the Adriatic Sea. If they attempted to cross the Adriatic and failed, the results would be fatal. He had not become a pilot to drown.

The only sure landing spot in Yugoslavia, the British fighter base on the Island of Vis, lay on the far side of the country, thirty miles off the Dalmatian Coast. Even if they could get that far, landing on its runway—half the length of a typical B-24 airfield—was notoriously tricky.

The conventional move would be to head east toward the Russian lines in Poland, but danger lurked there. Trigger-happy, often drunken Russian pilots frequently fired on unfamiliar Allied aircraft. Only a month ago, a plane from their bomb group had been downed by a Soviet fighter. The crew was lucky no one was killed. Moreover, the Warsaw Uprising had just occurred. Stanley hated that the Red Army had paused outside the city limits to let the Nazis crush the Polish resistance.

Romania was four times as distant, but its battlefront was less intense. One of the freed POWs back at base had mentioned a U.S. mission in Bucharest that repatriated American fliers. Stanley consulted with Leo Cone. He agreed Romania was the best bet—if the plane could hold out long enough.

The pilot decided: they would try for Romania. Cone gave the pilots a new heading.[6]

■   ■   ■

The *Turtle* did not want to fly straight. Only the two propellers on the left side spun as they should. Stanley countered the asymmetrical propulsion by increasing power to the left inboard engine while decreasing that of the outboard. He compensated for the lost thrust by elevating the pitch of the propellers. He pressed against the left rudder pedal with all his might. After half an hour, as his leg trembled with fatigue, he spelled it by crossing his right leg to the pedal. When that leg gave away, Stanley jammed both feet against it. When cramping and exhaustion set in, Plaisance took over. Eventually, he too became exhausted and gave the controls back to Stanley.

Per standard procedure, Stanley ordered the crew to lighten the plane. They scurried to throw out every loose item—flak jackets, helmets, and even the waist guns and ammunition.

For two hours the pilots maintained altitude at nine thousand feet above a dense layer of clouds. The undercast blinded Leo Cone to any geographical reference point, forcing him to navigate by dead reckoning—an artful combination of mathematical precision and educated guesswork. Plotting a straight line to Romania would have been relatively easy, but he had to estimate where the flak-defended cities were, direct the pilots around them, and then recalculate the path toward safety. To make matters worse, Cone did not know exactly where the Russian lines were. No American or British flier did, as the Soviets would not disclose their locations.

At last Cone announced they had probably passed the Russian front. The pilots looked for a break in the clouds to regain their bearings and locate a place to land. An opening appeared, and Stanley banked into it. A rivulet of Transylvanian mountains loomed below. Landing was impossible. They had to bail out, preferably over a valley.

They were down to their last gallons of fuel. Stanley ordered the bomb bay doors to be opened. Suddenly a panicked voice filled his earphones. Five fighter planes—maybe German Fw 190s—were taking off from an airstrip below.

Fear seized the crew. They had dumped their waist guns and most of the ammunition. A machine gun chattered. Maybe Spomer had fired from the tail turret. Thinking they were under attack, Stanley swooped into a protective cloud bank and emerged over a saw-toothed ridge.

The fighters followed. Ed Seaver identified them as Russian Yaks. He was about to notify Stanley when the *Turtle* lurched as though someone had punched it in the nose. The right inboard engine had given out. Stanley feathered it and pressed the button on his throat mic. "We have two minutes of flying time left," he cautioned. The *Turtle* veered starboard, below the peaks of the surrounding mountains. They were out of time. Stanley rang the bailout buzzer.

Al Buchholz, crouching behind Forrest Smalley at the bomb bay, heard the signal. Moments passed, but Smalley remained in his way. Buchholz itched to give him a good shove. They were a thousand feet off the ground—barely enough room for their parachutes to billow. Just as the nose gunner readied to give him a hard push, Smalley leapt. Buchholz followed and pulled his rip cord. Now he understood Smalley's hesitation. They had just cleared a sheer mountain crest. If Buchholz had heaved Smalley out, his chute would not have had time to open.

Leo Cone came to the cockpit and reported that the crew had jumped. Stanley struggled to prevent the aircraft from winging over. Another sharp rise loomed ahead.

"For God's sake," cried Plaisance, "get us over that ridge!"[7]

■   ■   ■

Four planes from the 464th Bomb Group failed to return that day—those piloted by Stanley, Borg, Price, and Suber. Down to three engines, Suber headed for the short emergency landing strip on the Island of Vis. His attempt to land the crippled aircraft failed. All ten crewmen died.

Overall, the Fifteenth Air Force lost sixteen heavy bombers that day. It was a high toll for five precious minutes over the target. Reconnaissance photographs showed that most of the bombs had fallen wide of the mark. The mission had been a failure.[8]

■   ■   ■

Seventeen days later, a glum envoy delivered a telegram to Stanley's mother. Every serviceman's parent dreaded this moment. Her son was either wounded, missing in action, or dead.

She dropped onto a chair and opened the horrid yellow envelope. The message read, "The Secy. of War desires me to express his deep regret that your son Lt. Chas. E. Stanley has been reported missing in action since thirteen Oct. over Germany." She wept. Charles might still be alive. She jotted a quick note to Mary Alice:

Charles has been missing in action over Germany since Oct 13. I'll let you know further information as soon as I receive it. Sixty percent of the missing are later reported safe, so let's pray harder than we ever did before that he will turn up and that it is God's will to return him safely to us. This is an awful shock even though I have been expecting it since I didn't hear from him. I can't write any more.

With love, Mrs. Stanley

The note stunned Mary Alice, though the news was not unexpected. Charles had not written in ten days. She did not cry until she telephoned a Dominican monastery of cloistered nuns to ask them to pray for Charles. Then the dam burst. No consolation from her family could stop the tears.

Night came. She wanted to write her usual letter to Charles but realized the futility and instead retreated to bed. Sleep would not come. She wondered if she could have helped him more. Perhaps she should have gone to confession and Mass more often. Couldn't she have written more letters? What did life hold for her if Charles were dead? He was her whole future.

At last, she dropped off. Her mother stayed awake all night.[9]

■   ■   ■

The *Fertile Turtle* scraped over the mountain ridge with mere feet to spare. Leo Cone let the pilots know he was leaving, retreated to the bomb bay, and rolled out. The pilots had seconds to follow; one of them had to go first. Plaisance offered to stay. Maybe the copilot meant well, but Stanley's temper flared. As pilot, he would leave the ship last. This was no time to argue. Stanley jerked his right thumb over his ear: "Out!"

Plaisance obeyed. He leapt, cleared the plane, and popped his parachute open. He twirled once before the *Turtle* smashed into a hillside. He was sure that Stanley's mangled body lay inside. Plaisance hit the ground. Searing pain shot upward from his left foot.

He pulled himself up with curses and groans. An open-mouthed peasant and his wife materialized. Plaisance beckoned them forward, but they stood transfixed. He unbuckled his chute and yelled at the top of his lungs; perhaps a more sharp-witted soul lived nearby. In response, a smiling young boy approached. Plaisance pointed up the mountainside toward the crash site. The boy allowed Plaisance to put his arm around his shoulder. Together they hobbled upward.

When they were halfway there, Stanley appeared over a ridge. Plaisance gasped, shocked that he had survived. Plaisance had bailed out at three hundred feet, well below the recommended thousand-feet minimum. Stanley had jumped from less without a scratch.

Reunited, they grinned and shook hands. Plaisance asked how he had managed it.

Stanley had yanked his rip cord even before he cleared the bomb bay. The bursting parachute stopped him in midair. He had felt the heat rise when the *Turtle* crashed, and he landed close by, crouching on all fours. Flame engulfed the wreckage. His first thought had been to ensure that the top-secret bombsight did not fall into enemy hands, but the fire ignited loose ammunition like lethal popcorn. The plane's nose was embedded in the hillside. The bombsight must certainly have been destroyed.

Stanley's gamble of flying to Romania had paid off—just barely. If the aircraft had given out mere minutes earlier, the crew would have gone down behind enemy lines. The two pilots agreed to stay near the plane and see what came. Romania had been a German ally until just six weeks before. Hopefully, the civilians would not be hostile.

Dozens of curious people approached. Once they realized the airmen were Americans, they welcomed them with open arms. One peasant offered fresh milk, raw bacon, and black bread. Another man fashioned a cane for Plaisance. A few indicated the pilots should follow them.

Off they trudged along the mountain ridge, hampered by Plaisance's lame ankle. Soon Sam Spomer caught up with them. After a few miles, they bumped into a Romanian gendarme who guided them to a farmhouse, where they spent the night.

Plaisance awoke to severe stomach cramps and diarrhea. The gendarme borrowed a two-wheeled horse-drawn cart and carried him into the nearest town, Campeni. Soon the other crewmen straggled in.

Over the next week, life became so comfortable that the crew pressed Stanley to extend their stay. Their hosts treated them with kindness and generosity, the Transylvanian countryside was beautiful, and the local cuisine provided a welcome respite from Army chow. The war could wait.

Stanley overruled them. It was their duty to return as soon as possible. Besides, their position seemed dicey. The money in their escape kits was running low, and the occupying Russians glowered at them with Slavic suspicion. Most important, the crew's loved ones must have received missing-in-action telegrams by now. They must be worried.

At last, transport was arranged. The trip aboard an open Romanian army truck offered a behind-the-scenes view of the Eastern Front rarely witnessed by Americans. Columns of Russian soldiers bounded toward battle aboard American-made Lend-Lease trucks. The white stars on the vehicles had been repainted red. Whenever one broke down or ran out of gas, the troops simply piled out and walked on. Female military police officers directed traffic—a novelty to the Americans.

Bucharest was half-destroyed. There the colonel in charge of Operation Reunion, the American mission to repatriate the recently liberated POWs, put them on a flight to Italy.

Relief turned to disappointment once they reached Pantanella. Other crews now occupied their tents. Leo Cone's ingenious heating apparatus was gone, and scavengers had stolen their cigarettes, candy bars, and shaving kits. Smalley and Buchholz had been turned down for promotions because they were absent.[10]

■   ■   ■

Mary Alice had learned that her fiancée was missing on Halloween, spoiling her fun with the trick-or-treaters. The next morning, despite an ache in her side and a lingering head cold, she decided to go to school. It was All Saints' Day, a holy day of obligation, and she needed to attend Mass anyway.

A letter from Charles awaited when she returned home. He had parachuted over a friendly country. Her prayers, he said, had "helped bring us all through safely."

A happy exhaustion set in. Mary Alice's appetite returned, and her pain vanished. By evening it all seemed like a bad dream. Her worries had lasted just twenty-four hours. How, she wondered, could she have stood it if it had gone on much longer? And what if the news had been the worst?

Mary Alice's mother realized the Stanley family might not have heard that Charles was safe. Since the Stanley family did not have a phone, she called one of their neighbors. The woman rushed over to Stanley's home shouting the news. Charles's mother slumped onto the nearest chair.

"If we never have another nightmare like that," Mrs. Stanley confided in a letter to Mary Alice, "it will be plenty soon enough."[11]

■   ■   ■

The AAF, knowing that breaks from the stress of combat were essential, had established a series of rest camps to restore the airmen's bodies and spirits. The Stanley crew set off for Capri without Bob Plaisance, who was confined to the base hospital with amoebic dysentery.

The enlisted men settled into one hotel and the officers another. The officers' quarters offered spectacular views over a sheer, dizzying cliff. The room featured a bidet, a fixture they had never seen before. A hot bath was the greatest luxury of all.

Everything was inexpensive in Capri, including wine, brandy, and gin mixed with seltzer. The men vastly outnumbered the female delegation of WACs, nurses, and Red Cross workers. If a local young lady attended a dance, she always came protected by a chaperone. Nevertheless, some fliers pursued wine, women, and song to such an extent that they returned to action in worse shape than when they began.

Stanley spent most of his evenings in Capri reading, watching movies, or beating all comers at ping-pong. During the day, he and kindred spirit

Leo Cone hiked Capri's many mountain trails. At the peak of one path, they found the ruins of the palace of the Roman emperor Tiberius. Across the bay, Mount Vesuvius brooded over the ruins of Pompeii.

No trip to Capri was complete without a trip to the famous Blue Grotto. On their last day, Stanley and Cone rode a *funicolare,* a small wooden cable car, two thousand feet down to sea level and hired a boatman. Inside the grotto, their tiny craft glided on a luminous pool of silver. Stanley was glad to have seen it but even happier when he reached dry land.[12]

■　　■　　■

On November 19, the crew flew their first combat mission since being shot down—a foray against Linz. Plaisance still felt too weak to carry his share of the flying, so Stanley picked up the slack. Everyone felt on edge. All illusions of invulnerability had vanished.

Over the target, a shell exploded close enough to their belly to push the plane upward. A chunk of steel missed Leo Cone's head by inches. Another shard penetrated the radio compartment, ricocheted, and struck Kiger in the back of his flak jacket. Fortunately, the fragment was spent, and everyone returned to base in one piece.

Three days later, the crew joined a massive raid against the Munich rail yards. Plaisance had departed for his overdue vacation at Capri, so another copilot substituted. Ed Seaver was also excused. Leo Cone would act as togglier, dropping bombs on the mark of the lead bombardier.

The formation encountered thick clouds over the Austrian Alps. Pilots could barely see the planes next to them. The bombers climbed, but the pea soup lingered. Planes scattered to avoid collisions. Stanley found himself alone above Bavaria. Skiers dotted the slopes below.

Berchtesgaden, Hitler's personal retreat, lay close at hand. Stanley felt tempted to bomb it but reasoned the brass would not approve of an unauthorized attack. Leo Cone suggested Spittal, Austria, a small rail center, instead. They found a train sitting in the yard. Cone released the bombs using pure guesswork. Sam Spomer reported a direct hit from his perch in the tail, but Cone doubted it.

Less than half of the 550 heavy bombers reached Munich that day. Bad weather thwarted accurate bombing. The 459th Bomb Group called the raid "the most mixed up and confusing mission this group ever participated in." It had not been the Fifteenth Air Force's finest hour.[13]

The following day, Thanksgiving, the 464th enjoyed a holiday dinner highlighted by real turkey straight from the good old U.S.A. The men agreed that the cooks had outdone themselves—everyone but Stanley, who was too ill with a stomach ailment to get anything down. It was his third Thanksgiving away from his family. Worse, there was no mail from home or Mary Alice.

Stanley's mood did not improve when bad news came a few days later. When he had arrived in Italy, the quota for returning home was fifty missions. Sorties deep into the Third Reich, such as those to Blech-hammer, had received double mission credits. Now those operations counted for only one mission, and everyone had to fly thirty-five sorties before going home. The new system effectively increased the required number of combat flights. The men grumbled; they thought it unfair that the rules had been changed midway into their tours.

Stanley did not mention the discouraging news to his mother or his sweetheart in his next notes, which he wrote on December 1. Ed Seaver sat across the tent from him writing his own letter. He expected a promotion to first lieutenant to come soon and told his parents to prepare for a big surprise.[14]

■   ■   ■

The next morning, Stanley found his copilot for the day, Lt. William "Don" Baker, at their pre-dawn briefing. They had slightly known each other stateside at Biggs Field. Baker had the day off but volunteered for this flight to pick up the mission credit.

An adjutant called the room to attention, and the briefing officer pulled back the curtain to reveal the target. The red line on the map led all the way to Blechhammer. *Blechhammer? Again?*

Colonel Schroeder brought the men up to date. Allied successes against other oil targets had enhanced Blechhammer's importance. Intelligence reports indicated the south complex would resume production within two weeks. The 464th would drop delayed-action bombs and propaganda leaflets along with the usual high-impact and incendiary bombs. The leaflets explained that the time bombs were intended to delay repairs. The attacks would continue until the people broke with the Nazis. Of course, the slave laborers working at the site had no choice in the matter.

New information had also arrived regarding possible bailout areas. Marshal Tito's Partisans controlled a safe zone in central Bosnia. If a plane could not return to Italy—or reach the emergency airstrip on the Island of Vis—airmen stood a good chance of evading capture there.[15]

Stanley's crew boarded the silver-hued *Yellow Love*—yellow being the color for Stanley's 777th Squadron, love being radio code for the yellow "L" painted on the plane's waist. Coincidentally, it was a B-24 "L" model with a light "stinger" gun replacing the tail turret. It also lacked the lower ball turret of earlier B-24s. Peter Homol, who normally manned the ball, took a waist gun instead. Once in the air, Stanley judged the B-24L to be the finest, most nimble model he had ever flown. He was also pleased that Baker proved to be an able pilot.

An undercast obscured Yugoslavia. Red-tailed P-51s from the 332nd Fighter Group, the famed Tuskegee Airmen, buzzed around reassuringly.

A supercharger acted up over Hungary. Stanley pushed the engines to their limits to keep pace with the formation, burning extra gasoline. Blechhammer already lay at the far limit of their range. If there were any more problems, he might not have enough fuel to return to Italy.

Fifteen miles from the target, the clouds dispersed. The Liberators had an open sky for a visual run at 23,500 feet. The Germans fired up their smudge pots to obscure the target. The flak gunners took aim;

they manned even more cannon than before. The bombers usually spent four to five minutes over the field of fire—this time they would take a full seven.[16]

■   ■   ■

The 460th Bomb Group led the way. The sky filled with black and red bursts as hot, jagged shards spewed in all directions. One of the planes took a direct hit and lumbered leftward toward the Russian lines.

Thirty-one B-24s from the 465th came next. One of its box leaders erupted in flames, careened into a headlong spin, and dissolved in a ball of fire.

The 464th passed over the target in the unenviable Tail-End Charlie position. Flak gunners always honed their skills on the front of the pack, saving their best aim for those in the rear. Slowed by its defective super-charger, Stanley's *Yellow Love* trailed even them.

The broad expanse resonated with thunderous explosions. The air teemed with screaming steel. Just ahead, *Red Jig* retched as a flak shell burst next to its right side. A man flew out of the gaping hole in the waist and popped his parachute open. The plane limped toward home, its tail swaying like a fish.

Ed Seaver cried, "Bombs away!" as *Yellow Love* dropped its load. A flak shell burst in front of nearby *Yellow How*. Parachutes streamed from all exits.

Stanley's wheel trembled in his hands. The plane yawed. Shrapnel darted past Al Buchholz's head. Gasoline fumes filled the frigid air.

They managed to reach clear sky, and Stanley asked for a damage report. A shell had punched a melon-sized hole in the left wing. It was too large for the self-sealing gas tank. Baker and Smalley hustled to transfer the remaining fuel but could not save much; the leaking gas had flooded the two port engines. Stanley feathered them to prevent a fire.

Yellow Love was in nearly as much trouble as the *Fertile Turtle* had been six weeks before. That time the two right engines had been damaged. This time it was the ones on the left. Stanley decided to follow the formation as far as he could. He ordered the crew to open the bomb bay doors, the nose wheel doors, and the camera hatch to let out the fumes. Freezing wind swirled through. Everyone shivered as they cast loose items out.

They soon lost sight of the formation. *Yellow Love* stumbled onward for ninety minutes, every moment a noisy, cold test of the crew's nerves. Stanley and Baker took turns fighting the uneven thrust. An undercast obstructed Leo Cone's view of the ground through Hungary and into Yugoslavia, but at last he determined they had reached the Partisan-held pocket shown on his maps.

He moved to the cockpit and shouted the news. At first, Stanley resisted ordering a bailout. *Yellow Love* was not quite a perfectly good aircraft, but two engines were running. Shouldn't they fly closer to the coast? No, argued Cone. Partisans controlled the territory below, but the area ahead was unsure. The crew should jump now, while they had plenty of altitude. Stanley was forced to agree and ordered the crew to prepare.

Everyone donned their parachutes. When the bailout bell rang, they tumbled out the bomb bays like seasoned paratroopers. Satisfied that everyone else was gone, Leo Cone let the pilots know and jumped himself. Baker left his seat and moved toward the bays. Stanley followed.

At the precipice, Baker paused. It was not easy to trust one's fate to a parachute. He blocked Stanley's exit. Any moment, *Yellow Love* would wing over, trapping them both inside. Stanley needed to get Baker out, and fast.[17]

■   ■   ■

Albert Buchholz hit the ground and tumbled rearward. Rough-clothed women and children surrounded him. He decided not to try his German. The group led him to a humble two-story farmhouse. Ed Seaver lay inside on a simple bed. He had cracked his coccyx on landing.

A few hours later, armed men arrived sporting red stars on their caps. Two of them supported a barely conscious Sam Spomer. Nothing seemed broken, but Spomer felt too concussed to walk. The peasants shared lamb soup and corn bread before the Americans bedded down. Partisans stood vigil all night, rifles at the ready. Perhaps the area was not safe after all.

The next morning, Seaver's back was so stiff he could hardly walk. Spomer still felt woozy. Buchholz helped them onto a horse-drawn cart. The Partisans guided them to a house where Homol, Kiger, Smalley, and Tweedale had spent the night. Soon Leo Cone joined them. The navigator's parachute had failed to open on the first yank, and he had tumbled several thousand feet while he worked his chest pack open. It was a good thing he had jumped from a respectable height.

Only the pilots remained missing.[18]

■   ■   ■

Stanley stepped next to Don Baker and pointed out the bomb bays. As Baker's eyes focused below, Stanley stepped back and shoved him out. Stanley followed as soon as he saw Baker's parachute blossom. His own silk opened with a nice thwack. The clouds passed peacefully.

Near the ground, Stanley relaxed his legs to roll with the impact. His face slammed into the earth anyway. He sat up and caught his breath. *How strange*, he mused. He had done better before with far less altitude and no experience. He gathered his chute and set off to find the others.

Before long he came across an isolated farmhouse. A bearded old codger sat by the barn. The man seemed nonplussed, as though American flyboys dropped onto his farm every day. "Partisans? Partisans?" repeated Stanley. The man nodded and invited him into his home.

In the morning, Partisans guided Baker to the same house. Soon a horse and buggy carried the two pilots to Prijedor, a Partisan command center.

The rest of the crew joined them in town the next day. All were stunned by the signs of war. Miasmic ruins smoldered. Putrid smells wafted about. Ragged refugees huddled around open fires. The guerillas seemed armed to the teeth. A few had Partisan uniforms, but more were dressed in various items of captured German clothing. Most wore neglected civilian garb. Only the red stars on their caps marked their allegiance.

An officer briefed them on their situation through a translator. A battle raged in nearby Banja Luka, just twenty miles to the southeast; Prijedor was unsafe. The crew would be transported to a town called Sanski Most, the gathering point for the airmen downed in the area.

Around midnight, the Americans boarded a boxcar attached to an antique miniature steam engine. The narrow-gauge railroad track, just over two feet wide, looked half the size of those in America. The Austro-Hungarian Empire had built the Steinbeisbahn line before World War I to service its forestry industry. It still served as the region's main transportation link.

The sleepless airmen arrived in Sanski Most after a night-long ride. They checked their maps and realized they were not much farther from the fighting than before. Everyone hoped the Partisans knew what they were doing.[19]

CHAPTER 3

Churchill's Choice

Yugoslavia was engulfed in a vicious war of extinction without parallel even in this bloodiest war in history. Although the Germans instigated the slaughter, most casualties were the result of Yugoslavs killing Yugoslavs. After the Axis powers conquered the country in 1941, four simultaneous and overlapping wars followed. The occupying Germans and Italians battled against two resistance groups, the Royalist Chetniks and the Communist Partisans. Meanwhile, Croatian extremists, Muslim militias, and Serbians engaged in a genocidal civil war. The worldwide war between the Axis and Allied powers overarched them all. Finally, the bitter feud between the Chetniks and Partisans decided who would rule the country after the Axis-Allied war ended. At least a million Yugoslavians died.

It was a maelstrom of bloodshed and shifting alliances that had been in the making for centuries. Bosnia, the area in which the Stanley crew found sanctuary, lay at its epicenter.

The history of Bosnia was rife with upheaval, religious and ethnic rivalry, and an endless quest for independence. The area, surrounded by greater powers, had been subject to conquest since ancient times. It also stood at the nexus of three great contending religions: the Roman Catholic Church, Orthodox Christianity, and Islam.

Modern Bosnian history began when the Ottoman Turks invaded in 1463. After a series of campaigns, the Austrian Habsburg Empire conceded most of Bosnia to the Ottomans in 1533. The Ottomans provided strong incentives for their new subjects to convert to Islam. Christians could not bring lawsuits against Muslims or testify against Muslims in court. Slaves could apply for freedom only if they converted to Islam. Muslims paid fewer taxes than Christians.

Sometimes Christian families offered their sons to the empire to improve their lot in life. Tens of thousands of Bosnian boys were packed off to Istanbul, where they converted to Islam and returned to their homeland as troops, servants, or administrators. As a result, most Bosnian Muslims were ethnic Slavs, not Turkish settlers.

Paradoxically, Orthodoxy flourished under the Ottomans. While Catholics took religious direction from Rome, Orthodox authority came from Constantinople, the seat of the Ottoman Empire. Many Catholics fled, partially depopulating the country. Over time, Orthodox believers became the plurality.

Austria regained Bosnia from the Ottomans in 1878. Many Muslims emigrated, and an influx of Catholics began. Even so, in 1910 Catholics remained the smallest of the three groups at 23 percent of the population. Since 37 percent of the population was Orthodox and 29 percent was Muslim—other minorities comprised another 10 percent—no single group dominated. Less than 1 percent of the population was Jewish.

World War I began in Bosnia's capital, Sarajevo, when a Bosnian Serb assassinated the Austrian archduke Franz Ferdinand. As members of the Austro-Hungarian Empire, Bosnians fought against neighboring Serbia during the war.

When peace came, Bosnians had no desire to be dominated by the Orthodox Serbs to the east, nor did they want to be subsumed in a Catholic "Greater Croatia" from the west. Most Bosnians considered themselves people with their own identity and culture rather than Croats or Serbs.[1]

After World War I, Serbia, Bosnia, Croatia, Slovenia, and other regions united into a new country, officially named Yugoslavia—"the land of the Southern Slavs"—in 1929. Despite its multi-ethnic name, Serbs dominated Yugoslavia's government. The Serbian king, Alexander, was assassinated in Paris in 1934 by an agent of the extremist Croatian nationalist movement, the Ustashe. Since Alexander's son, Peter II, was underage, governance of Yugoslavia fell to a regency council headed by Prince Paul, a cousin of the murdered king.

Yugoslavia remained backward and weak. Its economy suffered from the worldwide interwar depression. Eighty percent of the population lived off the land. The literacy rate remained low, especially among Muslim women. Resentments from the Great War festered as veterans found themselves countrymen of their recent enemies. Most Serbs favored a strong, central, Serbia-dominated government. Croats, Slovenes, Macedonians, and Albanians pushed for regional autonomy or even independence. Religious differences simmered among Catholics, Muslims, and Orthodox Christians.

Visceral tensions gnawed at Yugoslavia's innards. In 1937, the British author Rebecca West toured Yugoslavia and wrote her classic travelogue, *Black Lamb and Grey Falcon*. Her description of Zagreb might have been apt for any part of the country:

> Were I to go down into the market-place, armed with the powers of witchcraft, and take a peasant by the shoulders and whisper to him, "In your lifetime have you known peace?" wait for an answer, shake his shoulders and transform him into his father, and ask him the same question, and transform him in his turn to his father, I would never hear the word "Yes," if I carried my questioning of the dead back for a thousand years. I would always hear, "No, there was fear,

there were our enemies without, our rulers within, there was prison, there was torture, there was violent death."

Milovan Djilas, the Partisan commander and historian, expressed a similar view: "Vengeance, the breath of life one shares from the cradle with one's fellow clansmen in both good fortune and bad, vengeance from eternity. It was centuries of manly pride and heroism, survival, a mother's milk and a sister's vow, bereaved parents and children in black, joy and songs turned into silence. It was all, all."

Ancient battles rang fresh in the national consciousness. No defeat was forgotten or forgiven. The last war was never over. Now the Second World War brought new opportunities for bloody retribution.[2]

■   ■   ■

A glance at a map disclosed Yugoslavia's strategic importance. By early 1941, Yugoslavia was virtually surrounded by Germany and its allies. Its only non-Axis neighbor, Greece, had been invaded by Italy in October 1940. The invasion had turned into a debacle for the Italians, eventually prompting the Germans to intervene.

Hitler wanted to secure his southern flank in the Balkans before he invaded Russia. In March 1941, Hitler forced the Yugoslavian regent, Prince Paul, to join the Axis. In response, Serbian nationalists—likely supported by British agents—staged a bloodless coup, declared seventeen-year-old King Peter II to be of age, and rejected the pact.

Enraged by such impudence, Hitler gave orders to attack Yugoslavia "with merciless brutality." "Operation Punishment" began without a declaration of war on Palm Sunday, April 6. Axis troops soon overwhelmed the Yugoslavian army. Young King Peter fled to London.

Hitler dismembered the country. Slovenia was split mostly between Germany and Italy. Italy occupied Montenegro and annexed some of the Dalmatian Coast. An emasculated Serbia came directly under

German control. In a rare fit of veracity, the Nazis named it the "Serbian Residual State."

Croatia was enlarged to include Bosnia and parts of Serbia and renamed the Independent State of Croatia (the NDH). Ante Pavelić, the leader of the brutal, fascist Ustashe, became its ruler. Pavelić soon initiated a genocidal program to eliminate the large Serb minority, as well as Jews and Roma. He set up concentration camps, including the infamous Jasenovac complex, the only non-German extermination site in Europe. Ustashe militia bands roamed the countryside murdering hundreds of thousands of civilians.

The Ustashe reign of terror unleashed ancient hatreds. Serbian units rose, first in self-defense and then in revenge. They called their wholesale reprisals against the Croat and Muslim populations "ethnic cleansing," a term that would be revived during the Bosnian War of 1992–95.

Even the Nazis balked at the chaos unleashed by the Pavelić regime. Eventually, Hitler prompted his Italian allies to rein in the terror bands. For a time, the situation stabilized. With Yugoslavia seemingly secured, the Germans transferred several divisions to the Eastern Front and left the Balkans to the Italians. The few remaining German troops guarded key cities, mines, and railway lines. Neither the Germans nor the Italians controlled the mountainous countryside.[3]

■　　■　　■

Several Yugoslavian army officers wanted to carry on the fight. One of them, Colonel Dragoljub (Draža for short) Mihailović, came to lead a Serbian-based resistance movement known as the Chetniks. Mihailović's Chetniks were named after nineteenth-century rebels who had sought Serbian independence and expansion. Their descendants in the Balkan Wars of 1912 and 1913, World War I, and now World War II carried on the tradition.

King Peter II and his government-in-exile recognized Mihailović as their military commander in Yugoslavia. Mihailović viewed his Chetniks

as successors to the Royal Army and the sole legitimate resistance movement. Nevertheless, many Chetnik units scattered about the country
obeyed him only when it suited them.

As a symbol of their Orthodox abandonment of vanity, most Chetniks vowed they would not shave their beards until the country was
freed. Long, heavy beards became an important image associated with
the Chetnik cause.

Mihailović's conservatism dictated a cautious military approach. He
issued an order in August 1941 that his commanders should "avoid
clashes both with the Italians and the Germans for as long as possible."
His vision was one of restoration, not revolution. He concentrated his
efforts in Serbia, where he could best find support and refuge.

A directive attributed to Mihailović called for support for the monarchy, an expansionist Greater Serbia that included Montenegro and
Bosnia-Herzegovina, the expulsion of the minority populations in both
territories, and rejection of collaboration with the Communists. While
some historians claim the document may have been a forgery, Mihailović
never repudiated it.

Regardless, the directive was consistent with the Chetnik attitude
toward the Muslim minority. To them, the Muslims were "Turks," remnants of the long rule of the Ottomans, and Greater Serbia could never
be rid of Turkish colonization until they were eradicated. The Chetniks
practiced mass terror against Muslims, though often in retaliation for
Muslim attacks against Serbs.

Britain, clutching at straws in desperate times, supported the Yugoslavian government-in-exile and its commander in the field, Mihailović.
British propaganda invented stirring stories about his adventures and
hailed him as a heroic freedom fighter. It helped that Mihailović had
won the Victoria Cross, the highest British military honor, during
World War I.

Britain's recognition elevated Mihailović's stature. By spring 1942,
London had made him the face of the resistance movement not just in
Yugoslavia, but in all occupied countries. American media followed suit.

The *New York Times* carried fabricated stories that spoke of the Chetniks creating "one vast battlefield." Soon Mihailović graced the cover of *Time* magazine billed as "the greatest guerilla leader of Europe."[4]

■   ■   ■

The Chetniks' main competitors for the loyalty of the Yugoslavian peoples were the Communist Partisans led by Josip Broz, better known as Tito. Tito was half-Croat, half-Slovene, although he kept his ethnicity a secret for much of the war.

Communist ideology and Soviet ties shaped Tito's strategy. He had served in the Bolshevik army during the Russian Civil War and held several posts in the Communist International Committee in the 1930s. He spoke fluent German and Russian, married a Russian woman, and fathered a son who served as an officer in the Red Army.

In 1939, Germany and the Soviet Union signed the Molotov-Ribbentrop Non-Aggression Pact, which made the Nazis and the Russians near allies. Per the International Communist party line, Tito took no action when the Germans invaded Yugoslavia in March 1941. His resistance began only after Hitler broke the pact and invaded the Soviet Union the following June.

Tito sought change, not restoration. Upheaval was part of his revolutionary plan. German reprisals did not daunt him. Their atrocities only added to his base of supporters. In contrast to Mihailović's passive approach, Tito was under Moscow's orders to attack ferociously and relieve pressure on the Soviets.

Far more than the Chetniks, Tito's Partisans focused on winning the hearts and minds of the people. Over time, Tito's guerilla forces grew and evolved into an army. They presented their cause as a war against invasion. Their enemies were the Fascist invaders, the Ustashe, and the Chetniks—not always in that order.

While the Partisans were hardly averse to terror, their targets were not based on ethnicity. They attracted a broad base of support by being the sole faction committed to a multi-ethnic Yugoslavia. Jews were welcomed and became important contributors to the cause.

The Partisans were also the only faction to enlist women. Most were rear guard supporters, radio operators, couriers, nurses, and cooks, but all carried weapons and ran the same risks as men. Several served in combat brigades. Analysts estimate that 100,000 women served in the Partisan army and that over 20 percent of them became casualties.

The Partisans had several other advantages over the Chetniks. Veterans of the Spanish Civil War formed the backbone of a capable officer corps. Years of interwar clandestine activity had taught them how to develop and manage a secret organization. They were hierarchical and disciplined. There were no rogue Partisan commanders.

In contrast, Mihailović had no interest in broadening base beyond his Royalist Serbian roots. His Chetniks were led by former regular army officers who thought conventionally. They underestimated the Partisan irregulars and failed to grasp that the guerilla war was as much a political struggle as it was a military one.[5]

■   ■   ■

When the Partisans began their guerilla campaign against the Axis powers, Mihailović thought he had better follow suit. The Germans called in reinforcements and declared they would slay one hundred Serbs for each soldier killed by the resistance. They executed thousands of Serbian men and boys, far beyond their stated quota. Mihailović began to worry his people might be wiped out. The uprising failed, and the Chetniks retreated with heavy losses. Mihailović himself barely avoided capture.

Tito initiated meetings with Mihailović on September 19 and October 27, 1941, to discuss uniting their forces. The pair reached only short-lived, minor accommodations.

Mutual suspicions abounded, with good reason. Two days after the October 27 meeting, Mihailović approached the Germans and asked them for arms to fight the Partisans. As a gesture of good faith, he attacked Tito's men on November 1. Nevertheless, the Germans spurned Mihailović's offer. They already had a puppet government and did not need him. Moreover, ardent Nazis regarded Serbs as historical enemies and racial inferiors.

In January 1942, the Partisans and the Chetniks occupied a joint front in eastern Bosnia. When the Germans and their Ustashe allies attacked, Mihailović ordered the Chetniks off the line. His betrayal cost the Partisans many lives. Open fighting broke out between the two factions. For much of early 1942, Mihailovic's forces in eastern Bosnia collaborated with the Italians and raided Croat and Muslim villages. They also allowed German troops free transit across Chetnik-held territory to attack the Partisans. When the Chetniks approached the Germans for even closer cooperation, however, the Germans balked again.

The British caught wind of Mihailović's double-dealing. Their agent in his camp, Captain Bill Hudson, reported on November 15, 1942, that the general refused to fight and was likely collaborating with the enemy. The British had portrayed Mihailović as a heroic resistance leader. Now their man in the field reported otherwise. They took their first steps down the long path to disillusionment.[6]

Mihailović, frustrated by what he perceived as a lack of British material support, vented his feelings in a speech that followed a christening celebration on February 28, 1943. Colonel S. W. Bailey, who had become the chief British liaison to the Chetniks, reported that the general ranted

> that the Serbs were now completely friendless; that the British
> to suit their own strategic purposes, were pressing them to
> engage in operations without any intention of helping them,
> either now or in the future; that the British were trying to
> purchase Serb blood at the cost of a trivial supply of muni-
> tions, that he need no further contact with the western democ-
> racies, whose sole aim was to win the war at the expense of
> others... nothing the Allies could do or threaten, could divert

the Serbs from their sacred duty of annihilating the Partisans, that as long as the Italians comprised his only source of help generally, nothing the Allies could do would force him to alter his attitude toward them…that his enemies were the Ustashe, the Partisans, the Croats, and the Muslims; that when he had dealt with these, he would turn to the Germans and the Italians.

Mihailović had made a grave mistake. Winston Churchill dashed off a threatening rebuke to the Yugoslav prime minister: "You will, I am sure, appreciate that unless General Mihailović is prepared to change his policy both towards the Italian enemy and toward his Yugoslav compatriots who are resisting the enemy, it may well prove necessary for His Majesty's Government to revise their present policy of favouring General Mihailović to the exclusion of the other resistance movements in Yugoslavia."

Mihailović understood the warning. He promised to resist the Axis powers and reassured the British he would fight the Partisans only if they attacked him. Yet the damage was done.

In May 1943, Churchill appointed a close friend, Captain Frederick William Deakin, to be his envoy to Tito. Deakin reported the Partisans fought to the death with no quarter given or asked.

Meanwhile, Colonel Bailey grew increasingly disillusioned with the Chetniks. In early 1943, he intercepted a message from Mihailović to Pavle Đurišić, the Chetnik commander in Montenegro, ordering him to refrain from most anti-Axis activity. Mihailović also instructed Đurišić to withhold important intelligence reports from the British.

British code breakers learned that the Wehrmacht counted 5,697 Partisan dead from the most recent German offensive, but only 15 among the Chetniks. Moreover, Captain Deakin discovered that a division of crack German troops had passed through Chetnik territory unmolested. In August 1943, he reported the Chetniks were engaging in "close, constant, and increasing" collaboration with the enemy. His reports deeply impressed London.

Mihailović vehemently denied any collaboration. He claimed such reports were Communist lies and propaganda. He admitted to temporary agreements with the Axis powers that benefited his struggle against the Partisans, but he believed such "uses of the enemy" stopped short of betraying the Allies.

Each disclosure became another blow against Mihailović's credibility and prestige in London. The British had once considered him to be the best rallying point for a united Yugoslavian resistance. Now he was merely regarded as the only alternative to the Communists.[7]

■　　■　　■

Italy surrendered to the Allies in September 1943. The Partisans disarmed thirteen of the fifteen Italian divisions in Yugoslavia, gaining great stores of arms and equipment. Many Partisan troops became properly armed for the first time. These supplies tipped the scales in Tito's struggle against Mihailović. Still, Tito fumed that the Allies had not given him notice of the upcoming surrender. If they had, he could have captured even more Italian stores.

Although the Germans tried to retain as much Italian-held territory as possible, pressures on other fronts prevented a full occupation. By the end of 1943, the Germans controlled only the rail links, mines, and a few key cities, including the large ports on the Adriatic coastline. For the time being, they left the Chetniks and the Partisans to fight over the rest of the country.

The surrender of Fascist Italy had another key effect on Yugoslavia. The British had long viewed Yugoslavia as a place where Allied supplies could contribute to the defeat of the Axis powers at minimal cost. Previously, Allied aid to the resistance groups had to be airlifted from North Africa. Now far more supplies became available, and they could be transported from new Allied bases in southern Italy. But who should receive this new aid, the Chetniks or the Partisans?

For a time, the British tried sending material to both sides on the condition that neither would use it against the other. They also dispatched a brigadier general to each: Fitzroy Maclean to the Partisans and Charles Armstrong to the Chetniks. British Special Operations Executive (SOE) agents soon reported that the Chetniks and the Partisans were killing each other using Allied-supplied arms. A united front was impossible. The British would have to pick one side or the other.

London struggled with the issue. The Partisans were the only indigenous force actively fighting the Axis. They offered the stronger forces. Still, Mihailović might better serve British interests after the war. Winston Churchill defined the question with his usual aplomb. The bottom line became who was killing more Germans? Winning the war must come first.[8]

General Maclean sent an analysis to Churchill, who was en route to Tehran for his first summit with President Franklin Roosevelt and Soviet leader Joseph Stalin. Maclean recognized the Partisans were Communists oriented toward Moscow, but he argued that they presented a powerful fighting force that would be even more effective if given help. They were certain to become an important political force after the war whether the British aided them or not. Helping the Chetniks, Maclean argued, was counterproductive since they used the arms mainly against the Partisans. He recommended giving sole support to Tito to secure the maximum military benefit and possibly salvage postwar influence in the area.

Armed with the Maclean and Deakin reports and reinforced by intercepts of German radio transmissions, Churchill argued at Tehran that the Partisans should receive all the Allied aid. Stalin's reaction was lukewarm. He did not want a strong indigenous force in the country, even if it was a Communist one. His priority was a second front in northern France, not the sideshow in the Mediterranean. He said he did not object to the western Allies providing supplies to the Partisans if it did not interfere with the cross-channel invasion. Roosevelt and Churchill agreed.

Maclean met with Churchill in Egypt after the Tehran Conference. Maclean again cautioned that the Partisans were Communists likely to set up a Soviet-style government.

"Do you intend," Churchill asked, "to make Yugoslavia your home after the war?"

"No, sir," replied Maclean.

"Neither do I," said Churchill. "And, that being so, the less you and I worry about the form of government they set up, the better. That's for them to decide. What interests us is, which of them is doing the most harm to the Germans?"[9]

■　　　■　　　■

It was one thing to throw the bulk of British support to Tito. It was another to dump Mihailović publicly. The British needed a strong rationale to discard someone they had built up as the greatest resistance leader in Europe.

As time went on, however, Mihailović's true attitude became increasingly transparent. In late November 1943, the British learned from ULTRA intercepts that four of his commanders in Serbia had reached agreements with the Germans. The terms gave the Chetniks a ceasefire, arms, and freedom to act against the Partisans. There was no proof linking Mihailović to the pacts, but Captain Deakin concluded it was "very possible" he was "conniving" behind the scenes. London agreed. It was hard to conceive that four of Mihailović's main lieutenants would independently and simultaneously reach agreements covering much of Serbia without his consent.[10]

In May 1944, Mihailović issued a message to his corps commanders:

> German forces have not interfered with us in this last operation even though we do not have any contact or agreement

with them. So that we will not [jeopardize] operations against the Communist group, it is necessary to stop all operations against the Germans....Let it be known that we have a large number of enemies. We cannot fight against all simultaneously. Now, the most important enemies are the Communists.[11]

This was the final straw. On May 24, 1944, Churchill told Parliament that Mihailović "has not been fighting the enemy, and, moreover, some of his subordinates have made accommodations with the enemy." All British liaisons were withdrawn from Chetnik camps. The Americans followed suit reluctantly.

Eventually, King Peter recognized Tito as the commander of all Yugoslavian forces. The Chetniks, who had fought for the monarchy for three years, were denounced by their king as traitors and collaborators. Morale plummeted and desertions abounded. Mihailović fought on, but mostly against the Partisans.

Maclean and Churchill's assessment of the military situation in Yugoslavia had proven to be correct. Tito's army now boasted 200,000 to 300,000 troops, compared to perhaps 30,000 men in the Mihailović camp. The Partisans possessed a far more formidable force than the Chetniks, and thus the capacity to kill more Germans. Meanwhile, the Wehrmacht presence in Yugoslavia increased from 110,000 troops in 1942 to 530,000 troops in 1944. The strategy to divert German resources from other fronts was a resounding success.[12]

■   ■   ■

A few revisionist writers attribute Britain's abandonment of Mihailović to pro-Soviet infiltrators in the Cairo office of the SOE, especially Major James Klugmann, an unabashed Communist. History says otherwise. A recent study, based on declassified British intelligence reports, concluded, "The simple fact is that the material upon which

Churchill and the Chiefs (the British Chiefs of Staff) based their 1943 decisions did not involve Klugmann even remotely."

Churchill received his information from multiple sources. Most of his information came from German communiqués intercepted by ULTRA code breakers. Personal reports from William Deacon, Fitzroy Maclean, and Churchill's own son, Randolph—whom the prime minister had sent to Tito's camp in January 1944—merely confirmed the ULTRA accounts. A succession of British liaisons in Mihailović's camp independently concluded the Chetniks were not committed to fighting the Germans, had collaborated with the Italians, and that some of them were even collaborating with the Germans. The British Joint Chiefs, the Vice Chiefs, MI3b (military intelligence, Balkan region), and the British Joint Intelligence Committee all concluded that the Partisans were fighting Germans and the Chetniks were not. Churchill's decision was based on a consensus of his highest-level advisors, not a low-level, boastful Communist in faraway Cairo.[13]

It is also incorrect to assume that Tito and Stalin always shared common interests. Stalin's relationship with Tito was always rocky. Early in the war, Stalin said he would rather deal with a known figure like King Peter than an "adventurer" like Tito. The Soviets never supplied arms to the Partisans. Tito owed Stalin nothing and could not be controlled.

Moreover, the Soviets did not want a strong, independent Tito to rule postwar Yugoslavia—for good reason, as Tito's 1948 break with them later proved. Tito never displayed the subservience Stalin desired from local Communist leaders; in fact, Tito's communiqués to Moscow verged on the impudent. One telegram included the phrase "if you cannot help us, at least do not hamper us," causing Stalin to literally stomp his feet in rage.

Stalin was not consulted when the Anti-Fascist Council for the People's Liberation of Yugoslavia (AVNOJ) declared itself, rather than the king, to be the legitimate government of Yugoslavia in November 1943. Tito was named premier and "marshal" of the military. Stalin regarded the declaration to be a "stab in the back." He feared it might prompt Britain and America to land troops in the Balkans, a move that would threaten Russian interests and possibly even delay the long-awaited invasion of western Europe.

Stalin thawed when the British and the Americans failed to react. He finally opened the first Soviet mission with the Partisans on February 23, 1944. Even then, Stalin sent Lieutenant General N. V. Korneyev as chief of the delegation. Korneyev had fallen out of favor in the Kremlin and had been eased out of his prior job. Stalin regarded him as a drunkard.

Korneyev entered Tito's camp complaining about the lack of accommodations for a man of his standing. According to Fitzroy Maclean, Korneyev expected to take over the Partisan movement from Tito. Regardless, their relationship began poorly.

Tito could not have missed the contrast between the Russian and British overtures. Stalin had sent him a second-class emissary. Churchill had sent him his only begotten son, Randolph—a gesture of biblical symbolism.[14]

■   ■   ■

Meanwhile, the Americans became less content with the dominant British role in Yugoslavia. In March 1944, they sent U.S. Office of Strategic Services (OSS) and AAF liaisons to Tito. Soon after, U.S. air transports delivered their first cargoes. By August, the OSS had stationed ten teams in Partisan camps, and American supplies far exceeded British aid.

Nevertheless, American relations with Tito soured when the AAF bombed Belgrade on Orthodox Easter Sunday, 1944. Stray bombs killed hundreds of civilians just as the faithful were leaving church. Coincidentally, the bombing occurred near the third anniversary of the German bombing of the city, also a Sunday. The timing could not have been worse.

Eventually, the Americans learned Mihailović was harboring downed U.S. airmen. On July 14, 1944, they formed an Air Crew Rescue Unit (ACRU) under the command of Colonel George Kraigher. Two

American teams were dispatched to the Chetniks. The first, code-named HALYARD, coordinated the rescue of the downed airmen. The other, code-named RANGER, gathered intelligence. Neither mission was supposed to offer political or military support. Regardless, the move was certain to further aggravate Tito.[15]

■   ■   ■

In September 1944, eight German divisions remained in Greece and sixteen in Albania. The only evacuation route lay through Yugoslavia. If the Fifteenth Air Force and the Partisans could cut key rail lines, the Germans would be forced to retreat via narrow mountain roads or along the coast. Either way, they would be vulnerable to further attacks. Allied commanders devised a plan, code-named RATWEEK, to disrupt the German retreat. The air assaults, combined with Partisan raids on the ground, caught the Germans on the move.

RATWEEK's success emboldened Tito's operations against the Chetniks. RANGER reported that Tito sometimes directed American planes to attack Chetnik positions and used American arms against them. OSS agents embedded with Tito detected a new, colder attitude among their counterparts.

Mihailović barely escaped the Partisan offensive. Abandoned by the Allies and disowned by his king, he never recovered as a national force.[16]

■   ■   ■

Tito traveled to Moscow in secret on September 21. Two days later, he issued an order limiting the movements of British and American liaisons stationed at his headquarters. The western Allies assumed that Tito wanted no witnesses when he used their supplies against the Chetniks.

Tito had traveled to Moscow to negotiate with Stalin regarding the entry of Soviet troops into Yugoslavian soil. He needed Soviet tanks and troops to take Belgrade, but he did not want to sacrifice Yugoslavian independence as the price for their help. He struck a deal stipulating that the Red Army would advance no farther than Belgrade and would leave the country once the city fell. In return, Tito promised that if the western Allies tried to land in Yugoslavia—as Churchill was still proposing—he would treat them as invaders. Soviet troops were now free to advance through Hungary into Germany without worrying about their southern flank.

Partisan and Soviet divisions liberated Belgrade on October 20, 1944. The Red Army treated Yugoslav civilians like a conquered people, causing a rift with the Partisans. Nevertheless, Stalin kept his word. The Red Army turned north toward Budapest, leaving Yugoslavia to Tito.[17]

■   ■   ■

Whatever his deficiencies, Mihailović protected hundreds of Allied airmen from enemy capture. The HALYARD mission eventually evacuated 417 men by air, including 343 Americans. Several high-ranking Chetniks were also brought out. Mihailović hoped they might persuade the Americans to reverse their pro-Partisan policy.

Tito correctly feared that the HALYARD and RANGER missions rendered secret aid to the Chetniks, especially after Colonel Robert H. McDowell, the head of RANGER, made indiscreet pro-Chetnik statements. Against orders, the ACRU dropped a cargo of shoes, clothing, and medical supplies to Mihailović on the night of August 5–6, 1944. Additional supplies were dropped on Christmas 1944.

The Allied command, unaware of the surreptitious aid, assumed Tito's protests were groundless. Nevertheless, Tito's furious objections prompted the Americans to withdraw RANGER on November 1 and HALYARD on December 27, 1944. No liaisons were sent to Mihailović again.[18]

■   ■   ■

As winter settled in, the Germans still occupied northwestern Yugoslavia. Mihailović clung to an enclave inside their territory. With the

Germans on the run and the Chetniks as good as defeated, Tito felt free to distance himself from the British and the Americans. The Allies' huge investments in military and political capital had yielded minimal influence.

On December 2, the day the Stanley crew bailed out over Partisan territory, Churchill sent Tito a letter complaining about Tito's lack of cooperation and the rude treatment British liaisons were receiving from Partisan commanders. The Partisan actions, he declared, "can scarcely fail to hinder the attainment of our common objective." The same day, the Allied Combined Chiefs of Staff assured Tito that major Allied forces would not be deployed in the Balkans.

Meanwhile, AAF bulletins bemoaned that airmen bailing out over Yugoslavia remained ignorant of the complex political situation they faced. Sometimes they undid months of diplomacy with their unwitting insults toward their hosts.

So it was that Allied relations with the Partisans had deteriorated nearly to the breaking point even as dozens of American fliers jumped into the imbroglio and gathered in Sanski Most. None of the airmen understood the culture or the complex struggles in which they were enmeshed. They had not been briefed on how to comport themselves with the Yugoslavian people. It was a situation rife with the potential for disaster.[19]

CHAPTER 4

Following Tito's Footsteps

On November 16, 1944, the Strategic Evaluation Board for the Fifteenth Air Force met to discuss targets for the next day. The weather forecast looked excellent. The sky over southern Germany would be clear enough to allow visual bombing against oil installations for the first time in a month. The Germans took four to six weeks to restore bombed-out plants. It was time for a fresh strike.[1]

Blechhammer would be pilot Charles "Scotty" Prescott Stewart's target for his thirteenth sortie. Self-assured, intelligent, and athletic, Stewart had attended Harvard University for a year and a half before volunteering for the AAF.

Despite his stellar qualifications, Stewart had to pass his physical and mental examinations and earn his way through flight school just like everyone else. He began his basic military training at Atlantic City at the same time as Private Charles Stanley. They shared the same inglorious introduction to Army life: unheated hotel rooms, barking drill sergeants, and constant marching in the freezing February wind. He won his wings in March 1944.

Stewart possessed a pilot's panache. He enjoyed drinking good whiskey with his Ivy League friends. Several female acquaintances wrote frequently. He indulged in the forbidden practice of buzzing—flying his B-24 so close to the ground that earthbound mortals ducked their heads—to pay noisy calls on girlfriends and his mother.

Stewart had been lucky enough to be assigned to fly a brand-new plane overseas from the States. As a farewell present, his father had given him three cases of Schenley whiskey, a rare prize during the war since distilleries had been converted to military use. Stewart mischievously labeled his stockpile as "medical supplies" and stashed the boxes aboard the plane.

Stewart had been even luckier when the 485th Bomb Group allowed him to keep the fresh plane when he joined the unit in Venosa, Italy.

Stewart's luck held when his first mission turned out to be a milk run to northern Italy. His second was supposed to be equally undemanding—an attack against the railroad marshaling yards at Salonika, Greece (modern-day Thessaloniki). To take advantage of this easy run, a pilot with forty-nine mission credits—needing just one more to complete his tour—took the copilot's seat. A major from headquarters also joined Stewart's crew as an observer to pad his mission total.

After the plane reached sufficient altitude, Stewart's lower ball turret gunner, Sgt. Powell Robinson, lowered himself into his position. Robinson's winsome good looks appeared youthful even for nineteen. The AAF had disqualified him from Officer Candidate School due to poor eyesight. How, he wondered, could his vision be deemed insufficient for pilot training but good enough to hit speeding enemy fighters?

Manning the lower ball turret required special courage. Isolated from the rest of the aircraft, it was the loneliest position on the plane. The ball felt claustrophobically small, yet it offered an unparalleled view of incoming dangers. Only a strap and some Plexiglas separated the gunner from a thirty-thousand-foot fall to earth. The potential for being trapped in the ball during an emergency was unsettling. While the B-17's ball turret was fixed in place, the B-24's ball turret gunner trusted his comrades in the fuselage to retract the ball during flight. If the turret jammed, he faced the prospect of being stuck under the plane while landing.

Despite the position's drawbacks, Powell Robinson felt safe there. The ball had its own escape hatch, so he could bail out by releasing two trapdoor handles over his ears. Many ball turret gunners did not wear a parachute due to the cramped space. Robinson was small enough to fit a parachute on his back and still squeeze his body into his position.[2]

■   ■   ■

The Grecian sky filled with thick puffs of exploding black clouds as the formation began its run over the target. It was the crew's initiation to flak, and it was heavy, accurate, and intense. The veteran pilot's eyes widened. The major from HQ blanched.

Just after bombs away, a tremendous explosion blew the B-24 next to Stewart's into three fiery pieces. Two parachutes popped out. The aircraft behind tried to avoid the debris but failed and went down too. Two planes were gone, and several men were dead.

Stewart's crew had barely had time to register the disaster when jagged shrapnel riddled their aircraft. The Plexiglass in the lower ball turret pulverized. Wind shrieked in. Wiping powdery glass from his eyes, Powell Robinson saw nothing but crimson. "I'm hit! I'm hit!" he yelled. "Oh God, I'm bleeding!"

Stewart kept calm. "Everybody stay put until we get out of here," he ordered. Tense minutes later, the aircraft passed out of the flak zone, and crewmates lifted Robinson out of the ball. Red liquid soaked his flight suit, and he seemed to be in shock. Harry Carter, the crew's lanky navigator and bombardier, probed his body. "Where are you hit?" asked Carter. "Where does it hurt?" Dazed and frozen, the gunner remained mute. Gradually, Carter realized Robinson was barely scratched. The red stuff was hydraulic fluid from a ruptured line.

The crew reached base with the vast relief of those who are shot at and missed. Surveying the damage, Stewart's ground chief was amazed the plane had made it home.

Word got around that Salonika had unexpectedly hosted retreating German anti-aircraft batteries. The crew dubbed their aircraft *Salonika Sal* in honor of their survival.[3]

■   ■   ■

Trusty *Salonika Sal* saw Stewart and his men through another ten tough missions. On the morning of November 17, however, she was assigned to a crew finishing its tour. Stewart would fly a war-weary aircraft called *Dottie the New Hampshire Troubadour*. The plane's original name, *Dottie the Whore*, had been changed by the unit commander for propriety's sake.

Veteran pilot First Lt. Richard H. Boehme would sit in the right-hand seat usually reserved for the copilot. Only a month before, Boehme had survived bailing out over the Yugoslavian coast and had been awarded the Silver Star. Stewart surmised that Boehme, a rising star in the squadron, was aboard to evaluate his potential as a flight leader.[4]

Nothing about the mission went right. Getting into formation over the Adriatic took too long, so half the 230 bombers were diverted to the less distant Gyor rail yards in Hungary. Stewart's 485th Bomb Group, however, approached Blechhammer just after noon. Ahead, a cloud of explosions hovered over the target. "Holy Christ!" swore Harry Carter. "We have to go through that?" He had never seen thicker flak.

Carter had taken an instant dislike to Scotty Stewart when they first met. They had both grown up in Connecticut, but on opposite sides of the tracks. Stewart's father was a Harvard-educated Pratt and Whitney executive. Carter's father had been a small shop owner who went bankrupt when the Depression struck. Shamed and disillusioned, Carter's father took to alcohol and died at age fifty-nine. Stewart had attended the prestigious Milton Academy prep school. Carter had risen at dawn every day before high school to deliver fruits and vegetables to support his family. Carter called Stewart "Charlie"—not "Scotty"—to cut him down to size. Nevertheless, Carter never doubted his pilot's ability to fly. If anyone could get him through that field of flak, Stewart could.

Shrapnel buzzed through the air like hornets. *Dottie* blundered through the greasy black splotches. Carter released her payload. The worst seemed over, but it was still a long way back to Italy.

Over Hungary, Powell Robinson spotted two German fighters to the stern. Not daring to attack the formation, however, they pursued a crippled bomber and faded from view.

Stewart flew *Dottie* with her nose slightly up—"on the step," as it was called—to increase the lift of the wings and conserve gasoline. The fuel gauges, however, could only be read while the plane flew level. Every fuel reading cost precious gas, so Stewart took them sparingly.

Just after two o'clock, Stewart decided it was time. He leveled the plane at eighteen thousand feet and asked his flight engineer, John Elmore, for a fuel check. Elmore grabbed an oxygen bottle and left the top turret. Gunner Joe Sedlak moved from the waist to take his spot.

Elmore discovered that the main tanks were nearly empty, so he needed to transfer gas from the auxiliaries. The high altitude would make the transfer difficult. Stewart radioed the flight leader and dropped out of formation. He swooped *Dottie* down to twelve thousand feet, and the crew removed their oxygen masks. They smelled gas—a terrible sign. Stewart ordered Elmore to begin the transfer. Minutes passed, but Stewart's fuel pressure gauge registered no change.

"Where is it?" he called out.

"I turned it on," Elmore replied.

"Well, I don't have any," retorted the pilot.

Robinson, nestled in the ball turret, spotted gasoline streaming out of the starboard wing and reported the leak to Stewart. That explained it. They would soon be out of gas.[5]

Stewart pushed the button on his throat mic. "Prepare for bailout. We're not going to make it home."

Elmore passed over the catwalk and entered the waist to make sure everyone was ready. Carter opened the bomb bay doors and strapped on his chute.

Robinson could bail out directly from the ball turret, but he climbed back into the waist anyway. He retrieved his GI shoes and tied them to his harness. He also used the relief tube. The other crewmen, concerned only with survival, thought he was crazy. To Robinson, it made perfect sense; he had been stuck in the ball for hours.

The men in the waist lined up and jumped out the rear hatch. Robinson pounced out, wondering if his backpack parachute would open. He found his answer as soon as he pulled the rip cord. He had failed to cinch his harness tightly against his thighs. The nylon burst out, yanking the straps between his legs with a vengeance. It was a long, slow, painful descent.

Harry Carter walked out on the catwalk and dropped out feet first. He felt the slipstream and then nothing. There was no sense of falling. On three, he pulled the rip cord. The canopy opened after a few tugs. Like Robinson, Carter had failed to tighten his harness and paid the price. Wanting no misunderstandings when he hit the ground, he tossed his pistol earthward. He intended to surrender, not fight, if enemy soldiers should find him.

Husky Joe Sedlak, who had played football for Oklahoma State before enlisting, left his perch in the top turret. With no time to retrieve his GI shoes from the rear of the plane, he followed Carter out the bomb bay doors headfirst and pulled the rip cord. His parachute exploded, and his loose-fitting, soft leather flight boots flew off into the Yugoslavian sky.[6]

■   ■   ■

Stewart and Boehme trimmed the ship and moved to bail out. But who should leave last—Stewart as pilot, or Boehme as the senior officer? Boehme won the argument. Stewart jumped.

Near the earth, a gale captured Stewart's parachute and swept him against a sharp mountain ridge. His canopy collapsed, and he dropped among snow-strewn rocks. A terrible crack broke the stillness. Sickening pain echoed from his thigh. He lay among the rocks, motionless but conscious. His right leg was broken above the knee, and his left ankle was sprained. He could not stand up.

Thunder boomed from the valley. Or was that artillery? Hard to tell.

Stewart needed food. He needed water. He needed a doctor. He needed the medical facilities of Harvard University. He needed a lot of things he would not get soon. Immediately, though, he needed shelter. Gray gloom descended. The wind whipped over the mountainside, and the temperature plunged. He crawled behind one of the larger rocks and covered himself with his still-fastened parachute. He could go no farther. Shock and fatigue overwhelmed him, and he passed out.

Stewart lay mostly unconscious all night and through the next day. Occasionally, muted thunder echoed from the valley below. It sounded like a small-scale battle. As darkness began to settle again, Stewart spotted a figure moving among the rocks. A peasant boy approached. "Americano!" called Stewart, beckoning the lad forward. The boy crept forward. "Americano!" repeated the pilot, pointing at the flag on his sleeve. Then Stewart aimed his finger at his leg to show it was injured. The youth surveyed Stewart remotely. Without a word, he turned and walked down the mountainside. Stewart's spirits fell. He would die of hunger and exposure if the boy did not return soon with help.[7]

■   ■   ■

Joe Sedlak landed on a slope and slid downward until he stopped next to a tree. He stood up clutching his abdomen in pain. Looking upward, he spotted Elmore suspended from a tree branch.

"John! Are you all right?" he called.

"I think I got a broken leg," moaned Elmore.

Sedlak looked closer. Elmore had lost his flight boots. His right leg was already swollen.

Harry Carter had landed nearby. He ran up and helped Sedlak recover Elmore from the tree. Together, they splinted Elmore's leg with branches and parachute shrouds.

A small group of Partisans soon arrived. Joe Sedlak's parents had emigrated from Czechoslovakia, and his Czech was close enough to Serbo-Croatian that he could make out some of their words. The Germans were nearby; they had to move. Someone brought up a horse. Sedlak and others helped Elmore onto the animal's bare back, but he fell off the other side screaming in pain. Hoisting him again, they traveled to a nearby house.

Within hours the whole crew had gathered, except for Stewart and Boehme. Unwilling to wait any longer, the Partisans ushered them off to the nearby town of Drvar.[8]

■   ■   ■

Drvar's name was derived from *drvo*, the Serbian word for wood. A remote town in western Bosnia, Drvar was surrounded by the forested Dinaric Alps and nurtured by a mountain stream called the Unac. In the 1890s, Austria-Hungary built a wood-processing factory and narrow-gauge railroads to transport the lumber. Drvar became a minor boomtown.

After the German conquest of Yugoslavia, Drvar had become part of the Independent State of Croatia (NDH). The ensuing Ustashe reign of terror provoked an uprising organized by the Partisans, who took control of the town on July 27, 1941. The date came to symbolize the start of the rebellion, rather like Lexington and Concord in American lore.

The town passed from Axis to Partisan control several times over the next three years. At last, in the spring of 1944, Marshal Tito came out of the hills and made Drvar his command center. Russian, American, and British liaisons—including Randolph Churchill—camped in a nearby plum orchard. Tito set up shop across the Unac in a wooden hut at the entrance to a large cave. Besides offering protection against

German air raids, the elevated site featured a commanding view of the surrounding valley.

On May 25, 1944, the Germans launched Operation Knight's Move, aimed at capturing or killing Tito. They struck as the Partisans prepared to celebrate Tito's birthday. First came a squadron of Stuka dive-bombers. Nine hundred crack paratroopers followed, some in gliders.

The attack was a complete surprise. At first, unaware of Tito's whereabouts, the Germans focused on capturing the town. Once they realized Tito was not inside Drvar, however, they noticed stiff resistance from a bluff across the Unac and attacked. Tito's bodyguards held the mouth of the ravine as the marshal and his staff lowered themselves down a crevice by rope. They fled eastward through the woods with the Germans in hot pursuit. Tito and his party climbed aboard a small train and steamed off as bullets whizzed past. They disembarked after a discreet distance and vanished into the dense woods. Hundreds of Allied air sorties covered their retreat.

Frustrated by their failure to take Tito, the Germans took merciless vengeance on the townspeople. Most of the populace, including women and children, were rounded up and shot. Eventually, the Germans withdrew, and the Partisans reclaimed what little remained of the town.[9]

■   ■   ■

Now, as Stewart's crew entered Drvar, the town lay in gaunt ruins. The crew lodged in a building on the main square, one of the few with a roof. An old woman showed them to an unheated room lit by a single candle. Wooden straw-covered slabs served as beds. Belatedly, they realized that their parachutes would have been useful as covers.

The next day the Partisans carried Elmore to Drvar's makeshift hospital, a ramshackle former schoolhouse. Joe Sedlak went along to see if he could be useful. Sedlak did his best to translate as an old doctor tended to Elmore's leg. After a few awkward phrases, the doctor turned and asked, "Are you trying to speak Czech?" He was a native

Czechoslovakian named Victor Vindakijevic. Now they communicated freely. The doctor applied a crude plaster cast to Elmore's leg, but he had no medicines for the pain.[10]

About 3:30 the next afternoon, as the crew visited Elmore's room in the infirmary's attic, an excited Partisan came running up the stairs. Another American was coming into town. Everyone but Elmore rushed out to the street. A half-conscious Scotty Stewart lay on a mule-drawn cart, half-buried in hay. He had been through hell.

Stewart had spent a second cold night on the mountain alone without food or water. At last, in the early hours of the morning, a figure nudged him awake. It was the boy he had seen the evening before, accompanied by men who might be the boy's father and uncles. One of them leaned over and said, "*Partizan! Partizan!*" Stewart managed a smile.

Evidently the boy had understood that Stewart was unable to walk. The group bore a decrepit old ladder to use as a stretcher. They placed Stewart on it, lifted him, and began carrying him down the mountainside. Stewart sensed them changing directions to avoid enemy patrols. At length they arrived at a one-room hut. After feeding him goat milk, cheese, and bread, they loaded him into the cart for the long, jostling ride to Drvar.

Doctor Vindakijevic was summoned to treat Stewart. Joe Sedlak translated again. His diagnosis was a comminuted fracture of the femur. The bone had broken in three places. All the doctor could do was set it in a heavy plaster cast.[11]

Now only their copilot for the day, Richard Boehme, remained missing. The crew would not learn of his fate until after the war. Boehme had been picked up by a band of collaborationist Chetniks who fought battles with the Partisans as the pilot journeyed with them. For two weeks, Boehme begged to be released. At last the Chetniks relented, and Boehme found his way to the Partisans. He returned to duty and rose to the rank of captain. He was killed in action on February 16, 1945, during a raid against the jet aircraft factory in Regensburg.[12]

■   ■   ■

The day after Stewart's arrival, November 20, another aircrew entered Drvar's town square. They were led by Lt. Robert A. Dean, a no-nonsense Texan with a mature, confident manner. His men called him "Pop," though he was younger than half of them.

On November 17, the day the Stewart crew had gone missing over Blechhammer, Dean's crew had failed to return from the same mission. His plane had developed engine trouble, and he was forced to try an emergency landing on the Island of Vis.

Vis, a craggy island with a fine natural harbor, lay thirty miles off the Dalmatian Coast. The British had built an airstrip on the Partisan-occupied island in May 1944 and still used it for fighter raids against the Germans. The field also acted as a haven for crippled American bombers.

No B-24 landing was easy. The plane's long snout obstructed the forward view, and its tricycle landing gear required pilots to touch ground nose-up. To compensate, pilots picked a reference point 100 feet short of the runway and lined it up with a rivet on the nose.

The Vis landing strip ran half the length of those designed for heavy bombers. Not only was it too short, but it ended at a hillside, making a second go-around impossible. One side of the field was packed with B-17 and B-24 wrecks. The other was crowded with aircraft in various states of repair. It looked like a junkyard for warplanes.

Dean dropped *Miss Liberty* to 50 feet of altitude—150 feet would be normal—and assumed a sharper angle of attack than usual. Just when it seemed he would land short, he boosted his thrust and reached the tip of the runway. The main wheels kissed hard. Dean pressed the nose down to reduce speed, but not so much that the forward wheel strut collapsed. He reduced power and touched the brakes just enough to slow the plane down without flipping it over.[13]

It was a masterful piece of flying, but another B-24 followed with an equally deft landing. Dean had met its pilot, Lt. David Blood, once before at Casper, Wyoming, during training. Although Blood had been a copilot then, he was already famous as a wild character. Big, bull-voiced, profane, and rowdy, Blood contributed to the stereotype of cowboy-like pilots. Dean cringed thinking of the bad name he gave to their fellow Texans.

The two crews found Vis crammed with supplies awaiting shipment to the Partisan army. Hurly-burly trucks and jeeps threw clouds of red dust as they sped about the island. Fighter-bombers buzzed away to attack enemy positions on the mainland.

While it was challenging to land a B-24 at Vis, it was even more difficult to lift off. The British staff stationed at Vis warned Blood and Dean that it was foolhardy, perhaps impossible, to take off again in a B-24. Bomber crews usually took their advice and departed in nimble C-47s.

Robert Dean and David Blood agreed on one thing: they could take off from that island in their B-24s. After overnight repairs, they filled their tanks with just enough gasoline to make it back to Italy. Dean felt confident enough to add weight by restocking with machine guns from the junked B-24s.

Blood's plane stood first in line. Gunning his engines while holding the brakes, he released them and tore down the runway. He achieved liftoff just as his plane ran out of airstrip. Dean pushed his engines past their recommended limits and followed. Both reached their bases without a hitch.[14]

■   ■   ■

Dean's men returned to action just two days after their adventure at Vis. Shrapnel knocked out two of their engines over Blechhammer, and they bailed out near Drvar.

It was good to see fellow Americans in such a forsaken place. Harry Carter recognized Dean's bombardier, Clarence Byers, from their stateside training days. Joe Sedlak met Dean's gentlemanly radioman, Emil Horak, whose parents had taught him to speak Slovak. Since Sedlak's

Czech and Horak's Slovak seemed equidistant from Serbo-Croatian, they decided to join forces in understanding the local lingo.

Dean's eleventh man, an aerial photographer, stuck out like a sore thumb. Private Clarence Martin appeared to be unencumbered by the slightest flicker of intelligence. The bucktoothed Arkansan closely resembled Mortimer Snerd, the goofball marionette created by the popular radio comedian Edgar Bergen. Profanity rolled off Martin's tongue like an Ozark folk song. He had once been a sergeant in the Eighth Air Force, but he had been busted for stealing English bicycles and exiled to Italy. Now Martin claimed he had crashed through the roof of a privy as he landed. The others conceded he smelled like it. If anyone could manage such a thing, it was a character like him.[15]

The next day was Thanksgiving, so the two crews decided to celebrate. They scoured the countryside for foodstuffs but managed only enough for one slice of dry turkey and a spoonful of potato per man. Still, all agreed it was the best meal they had ever eaten and gave sincere thanks.

■   ■   ■

For the next few days, the airmen arose from flea-infested straw bedding to drink sweet tea and eat dark bread at the tavern across the square. At lunch and supper, they ate cabbage soup, sometimes with mutton complete with eyeballs. Confronted with meals that stared back at him, Powell Robinson went hungry. The cook looked hurt and confused. Some of the airmen—usually those raised on farms—dug right into the greasy broth.

The water wells were all situated in barnyards. The airmen's escape kits held only so many halazone tablets, and they soon ran out. Within days, most of the airmen contracted diarrhea.

Stewart's men often visited Stewart and Elmore in the infirmary. Lice infested the skin underneath their casts, and the itching was maddening. Their friends cut willow switches so they could scratch beneath their casts.

With little else to do, the airmen strolled around town. On the opposite end of the square, two barefoot German soldiers huddled behind barbed wire. Every day, a guard escorted them around town to empty commodes into a bucket suspended on a pole between them. Several civilian collaborators shared their confinement.

Few houses remained standing in the town. All of them bore the marks of fire and explosions. The townspeople, however, seemed unbowed. The Muslims wore exotic fezzes. Everyone treated the Americans like kings. Few would take their money for food or services. They knew the role the AAF had played in saving Tito and liberating the area.

The Partisans offered the American officers a tour of Tito's famous cave. A group of them, including Harry Carter, crossed the Unac and climbed to the entrance. Communications wires still ran through the cave's mouth. Moss and ferns grew from the rock walls. A rushing waterfall at the rear of the cave provided water. The vista offered a clear view of the approaches from town. No wonder Tito had picked the spot as his headquarters.

On another stroll, Carter found a wrecked German glider. Nearby lay a decaying body wearing an American uniform. It was likely the remains of Lt. Robert W. Crawford, the only U.S. soldier killed during the raid.

Twice, the airmen heard the booms of distant battle, and word came that the Germans were approaching. The Partisans herded the airmen into the hills, but soon the danger passed, and everyone returned to town.

■   ■   ■

After a week, the commandant informed the airmen that they were to travel by train to Sanski Most, where an open field outside of town offered the possibility of evacuation by air. While the Americans would be moving away from the coast, Sanski Most had suffered less damage than Drvar and offered more resources. Stewart and Elmore would find better medical care there.

The next morning, the Americans walked through a light snow to the awaiting train and joined Partisan soldiers and civilians, including veiled Muslim women, in the crowded boxcars. The half-scale train reminded the airmen of the story of *The Little Engine That Could.* As the miniature wood-fired engine gathered steam and inched toward the rising mountains, each puff seemed to say, "I think I can, I think I can." The airmen doubted it. The locomotive belonged in a Buster Keaton movie. The few boxcars looked to be of pre–World War I vintage. Wind snapped through the bullet holes that perforated the flimsy wooden walls. They traveled the same route Tito had taken to safety six months before. The train was likely the same one that had carried him.

Comfort was not a consideration. Everyone but Stewart and Elmore stood through the journey. Tiny wood-burning stoves in the centers of the cars provided scant heat. The train climbed through the winding mountains and found a straighter path. After several hours, it crawled to a stop, and Partisans scrambled out to chop down trees and shovel snow into the boiler for steam.

The train chugged into Sanski Most on the morning of November 29. It had taken twenty hours to travel twenty-eight miles. The best the Americans could say about the long, cold ride was that it beat walking up and down the rugged mountainsides. Word came from Drvar that a German patrol had come looking for them just after they departed.

Three Americans, the survivors of a B-17 that had crash-landed near Sanski Most, welcomed them to town.[16]

CHAPTER 5

Bombs Bursting in Air

According to an old military saying, warfare consists of months of boredom punctuated by moments of stark terror. The adage was particularly fitting for World War II airmen.

Living conditions for flyboys far surpassed those for the infantry—a fact that irritated GIs to no end. No matter how harrowing the day's mission was, fliers returned to a secure airbase and slept in a decent shelter. They were better paid, they ate two hot meals a day, and their bases featured officers' and NCOs' clubs and movies.

Yet the GI had advantages over the flier. He always knew the security of the ground. A soldier could hollow out foxholes and "hit the dirt" during attacks. He could fire back at his enemies. His sense of danger was limited to his field of vision, usually measured in dozens of yards.

None of this held for bomber crews flying through a flak barrage. Their field of vision, of perceived peril, extended for miles. Once over a target, the aircraft waded through a multidimensional gauntlet of random explosions. At any instant, from any direction, razor-sharp, red-hot fragments might pierce the aircraft's hull and tear into a man's flesh.

There was no cover in the sky. There was no hiding place. There was no defense or return fire, at least against flak explosions. No defensive action could increase one's chances. There were no medics on hand. Injuries occurred hours from base. The high altitude exacerbated bleeding. The thin air, extreme cold, and heavy layers of clothing compounded the problem of applying first aid.

Fire was the airman's greatest fear, as burn wounds were the most painful, most disfiguring, and slowest-healing of all. Most fliers dreaded mutilation more than death.

The airman's next worst nightmare was being trapped inside a plummeting aircraft. Many airmen witnessed planes going down with few or no parachutes appearing. Some bomber crewmen could not wear chutes at their stations. In an emergency, an airman might have seconds to attach a parachute to his harness and escape the plane.

Once he bailed out, the airman might strike a propeller, wing, or tail. Even after he cleared the aircraft, he could not be sure his parachute would open. World War II airmen were not issued reserve chutes.

Overall, heavy bomber crews faced a uniquely stressful situation unprecedented in the long, cruel history of warfare. Only submariners faced similar three-dimensional dangers.[1]

■   ■   ■

Seymour Rosenthal played piano of the boogie-woogie stripe. The bombardier, whom everyone called "Larry" or "Rosy," could really play. No less a figure than the legendary trumpeter Bunny Berigan had said so when he sat in with Rosenthal's band during a memorable gig before the war.

Rosenthal's parents had emigrated from Hungary before the First World War—a lucky move since they were Jewish and Hungary joined Hitler's camp in November 1940. Young Larry grew up in Trenton, New Jersey, speaking Hungarian in his home.

Rosenthal had managed perfect scores on his Stanine classification tests at Nashville and had his pick of specialties. Rather than choosing to become a pilot or navigator, Larry decided to follow in the footsteps of his older brother David, a bombardier who loved the job.

Bombardier training was as arduous as that for any position on the aircraft. Besides learning his own business, the bombardier handled the plane during the bomb run and had to know something about flying. He served as the backup navigator and learned everything about navigation except celestial sighting. B-17 nose guns were manned by bombardiers, so Rosenthal spent six weeks at a flexible gunnery school.

Rosenthal often encountered anti-Semitism in the AAF, mostly of the unspoken "cold shoulder" variety. Fortunately, the AAF operated alphabetically. In training, Rosenthal usually found himself among Rosens, Rosenbergs, and other Jews. A flight officer named Stanley Schwartz became one of his best friends.

Upon graduation, Rosenthal was assigned to an aircrew led by Lt. Edward Fenfort. Rosenthal never hit it off with him. Soon he transferred to Lt. Robert J. Bartusch's crew.[2]

■   ■   ■

Bartusch looked and acted like a prototypical pilot. His compact five-foot-ten frame always seemed coiled for action. His tight lips, blue eyes, and cleft chin resonated self-discipline and serious purpose. His clipped manner of speech never wasted words.

Somehow the self-disciplined Bartusch clicked with the ebullient Rosenthal, who kidded Bartusch about his German extraction. "Hey Bart," Rosenthal would tease, "if we ever get shot down over Germany, I'm going to say, 'I'm with him!'"

Their copilot, Lt. Storey, proved to be a capable flier. While most pilots would have counted their blessings, Bartusch recommended Storey for a promotion to aircraft commander. Flight Officer Jene Hirschfield replaced him. A chain smoker, Hirschfield came across as introverted, nervous, and paunchy, particularly in contrast to his confident and tautly muscled pilot.

Perhaps Hirschfield's status as a flight officer accounted for his demeanor. A certain stigma shadowed the title. Neither commissioned officers nor enlisted men, flight officers inhabited the no-man's-land of military status. Lieutenants and flight officers both earned the same pay, $1,800 per year. Yet flight officers stood lower in the AAF pecking order. They were saluted by enlisted men but were addressed as "Mister," not "Sir." The rank humiliated those who held it, and the Air Force dropped it after the war.[3]

The crew trained in B-17s at MacDill Airfield near Tampa, Florida. Bartusch and Rosenthal spent much of their off-duty time at the officers' club. Bartusch would buy Rosenthal a double-bourbon and a cigar, plant him in front of a piano, and watch him set the place on fire.

A striking woman approached after one performance. Rosenthal recognized her as his commander's famously lovely wife, Margo Kurtz. "You play beautifully," she gushed. "Would you perform at my party Saturday night?" He complied gladly.

A few weeks later, Rosenthal was sitting at the piano again when someone came up from behind him and put her hands over his eyes. Rosenthal smelled perfume. It was the same lady. "I want you to meet somebody," she urged. "Come on!" She led him over to the bar and offered an introduction: "This is my husband, Colonel Frank Kurtz."

Kurtz was already famous as an Olympic diver, the holder of several aviation records, and as the much-decorated pilot of the *Swoose*, a B-17 salvaged from the initial Japanese attacks in the Pacific. Margo was pregnant with a child who would become the actress Swoosie Kurtz. The colonel shook Rosenthal's hand. "I want to thank you for being so nice to my wife," he said. "Now what the hell can I do for you?" Rosenthal asked for nothing, but Bartusch's crew soon found themselves reassigned to Langley Field, Virginia, flying new radar-equipped B-17G Pathfinders.

While Kurtz had intended to do Rosenthal and the rest of the crew a favor, he was also making them guinea pigs for a new technology. On one flight, they were assigned to discover whether the radar could detect thunderstorms. A general, supervising the project from the nose, ordered Bartusch to fly toward a predicted storm. When the B-17 began to bounce wildly, the general called the radar operator over the intercom. "Are you sure you can pick up thunderstorms on that goddamn scope?" Just as the radar man replied, "Yes, sir, I'm sure," the plane flipped backwards and headed straight toward the ocean. G-forces threw Rosenthal rearward to the bulkhead along with the general.

Bartusch wrestled with the controls. The plane's dive reached four hundred miles per hour, far above the prescribed maximum pull-out speed. The nose turret buckled. Bartusch managed to level the plane off just in time. "Land anywhere!" ordered the general. "I'll take responsibility. Just land it!" Ignoring all regulations, they touched down at the naval air station at Norfolk.

Boeing engineers examined the plane. They marveled that the wings had stayed attached.[4]

■   ■   ■

By the time the Bartusch crew returned to MacDill Field, Kurtz's 463rd Bomb Group had headed overseas. Bartusch and his crew were assigned to deliver a new B-17G Pathfinder to the 483rd Bomb Group in Italy.

Over the Atlantic, the Pathfinder's number two engine caught fire. With no place to land, Bartusch feathered the engine and tried to blow the fire out by hurling the airplane into a steep dive. Down and down they sped, accelerating toward the wide ocean. The altimeter dial spun from twenty thousand feet to fifteen thousand and then ten thousand. At last, as the water loomed alarmingly close, the flames petered out. It was the crew's second near-fatal episode in two months.

Ground crew at the Azores airfield replaced the engine. When the airplane was ready, Bartusch's men loaded it with beer and flew to Gioia, Italy. There the authorities took away their nice new B-17—along with the booze. It was difficult to say which loss they lamented more.[5]

Joining the 483rd, Bartusch broke in as a copilot with other aircrews for a few missions. Rosenthal flew with other crews as well. His first sortie was a milk run to northern Italy on October 4. It was the bomb group's hundredth mission, and the men threw a party that evening to celebrate. After the festivities, Rosenthal returned to his tent to find a letter from his father. His brother David had been killed while flying with the Eighth Air Force.

Four missions against heavily defended targets followed: Moosbier-baum, Regensburg, and two against the worst of them, Vienna.[6]

■   ■   ■

Bartusch's objective on November 22 was the marshaling yards at Munich. This was the same fubar raid during which Lt. Charles Stanley became separated from his formation and was tempted to bomb Ber-chtesgaden. A cloud bank swallowed the formation over the Alps. Half the planes diverted to Regensburg, but Bartusch's 483rd plugged on toward the primary target.

The broad-winged B-17s could fly higher than B-24s and had a better chance to climb above the cloud cover. Near the target, Bar-tusch's group reached the scheduled bombing altitude of 26,500 feet. The clouds were still too dense, so the flight leader ordered them to climb to 31,000 feet. Bartusch's far left propeller ran away as they ascended and would not feather. He pushed higher until the engine died completely and he had to drop behind the formation. Rosenthal released his bombs over the target, but three hung up in the racks, frozen by the extra altitude.

Bartusch headed for home but doubted he could make it across the Adriatic. Maybe he could reach Vis. After he descended to 26,000 feet, the windmilling propeller finally feathered, but the inboard engine on the same wing acted up. Bartusch turned on the autopilot, gave Hirschfield the yoke, and unstrapped himself to help flight engineer Carl Bush with the engines.

Minutes later the B-17 rose, lurched, and dropped its nose. The automatic pilot had somehow thrown the plane into a stall. Bartusch fought his way back to the cockpit, pushed the nose into the dive, overpowered it, and leveled out. The aircraft had dropped 6,000 feet in seconds.

Darkly mustachioed ball gunner Robert Steel scrambled out of the lower ball turret. Zack Johnson climbed out of the tail gun position. Neither spot was a good place to be just now.

Relieved, Bartusch turned off the autopilot. The plane stalled again and plunged into a second nosedive, this one worse than the first. Still unstrapped, Bartusch rose out of his pilot's chair, weightless. He pulled himself back into his seat, fastened his belts, and took the yoke. The B-17 accelerated. The out-of-control engine's cowling tore off. Down, down they dove. Doubt crept into Bartusch's mind. He could not pull her out. He pressed the bailout buzzer but heard no sound.[7]

Even without hearing the bailout signal, the men in the rear scrambled to jump out the side door. The unofficial leader of the enlisted men, Sgt. Cletus Kramer—the others called him "Colonel" as a token of their respect—made sure the guys in the waist got out. Zack Johnson, who had lost his oxygen mask, seemed disoriented and afraid. Kramer secured his parachute, made sure he was clear-headed enough to pull the rip cord, and pushed him out the opening. Once Johnson's silk popped, Kramer followed him into the free, cold air.

In the nose, Rosenthal watched flight engineer Carl Bush unseal the forward hatch and prepare to bail. Wind whooshed the navigational maps out of the compartment. "Wait!" yelled Rosenthal, grabbing at Bush. "Look at the altimeter." Bush wrenched free and jumped anyway. Rosenthal felt the plane's descent smooth out. Bartusch had regained control.

Rosenthal checked the plane and made his way to the pilots. "We're the only ones left," he reported. The rest had bailed out. Bartusch took the news in stride. They could not have known he would pull the plane out of the dive; he hadn't known it himself. Regardless, he faced other difficulties now. One propeller on the left wing was dead, and the other was acting up. He had no control over the ailerons. "Let's see how far we can go," he said evenly.

Rosenthal's maps were gone, so he could only give Bartusch an approximate heading for Vis. Then he reopened the bomb bay doors and dropped the three remaining bombs. At the lower altitude, they were no longer frozen to the racks.

A picturesque Alpine town appeared below. They had reached Klagenfurt, a small Austrian city near the Yugoslavian border. Before the pilots could make a turn, they were surrounded by bursting shells. Absent their maps, they had blundered over a flak battery. Shrapnel riddled their waist and tail. Maybe it was just as well no one remained back there.

The explosions dissipated. Rosenthal moved about the B-17 throwing out as much weight as possible. The ball turret would not jettison and a waist gun proved sticky, so he let them be. The crew's escape kits lay in a pile. Rosy hoped that, wherever they had landed, they would not need them.

Onward they flew. Yugoslavia was a mass of forested, snowy mountains. Bartusch guessed they had reached Chetnik-held territory, but he had been briefed that they would turn airmen over to the Germans. He wanted to go farther south, where he had a better chance of finding the Partisans.[8]

■   ■   ■

After forty-five minutes of ever-descending flight, the gauges showed they were low on gas. Bartusch suggested that the others bail out. Rosenthal moved to the nose hatch but had second thoughts. Returning to the cockpit, he yelled in Bartusch's ear, "Are you going to stay with this son of a bitch?"

"I'm riding her in," Bartusch replied. Rosenthal opted to stay. So did Hirschfield.

The problem was finding a flat stretch of earth. They were about to give up when Hirschfield spotted an open area next to a river bend. It was their only chance. Bartusch decided to go in wheels-up. He banked toward the narrow field and leveled before plopping down, sticking the ball turret into the muddy ground. The B-17 slapped past a grazing cow and scraped to a halt, sticking its nose out over the river's edge. The ball had anchored them just enough.

The stench of gas filled the air. Oxygen bottles hissed. The plane might blow up any moment. Bartusch pushed his pilot's window out, climbed through, and dropped to the ground. Rosenthal hurried out the nose hatch and met him. Both dashed outside and looked for Hirschfield. They found him wedged in the copilot's window. "Get me out of here!" he yelled. "I'm stuck!"

Bartusch and Rosenthal climbed onto the wing, grabbed Hirschfield's arms, and heaved him out. All three ran until they reached a safe distance. They looked back gasping for breath, expecting the B-17 to explode into a ball of fire. Yet there it sat. Could nothing destroy this plane?

The sound of horse hooves broke the silence. Several armed riders approached. Not knowing whether they were friend or foe, Bartusch pulled out his side arm and fired a few shots into the air. The horsemen veered off and disappeared into nearby woods.

Bartusch, Hirschfield, and Rosenthal looked at one another. More men would come, possibly enemy soldiers. Yet where could the three of them go? They did not even know where they were. Besides, the plane contained important supplies. They wondered if reentering it was worth the risk.

They had just decided to run for the hills when a roughly dressed boy of about ten approached. A large gathering of farm folk followed, some on horseback. The Americans held their breath. Their sidearms would be little help if these people were hostile. Rosenthal wondered what happened to Jewish fliers who fell into German hands.

"*Dobra Amerikanac,*" the youth yelled cheerfully. "*Dobra Amerikanac!*" His cap bore a red star. The Americans relaxed. Wherever they were, they had reached Partisan territory. Within moments the airmen were surrounded by smiling, curious folk. The cavalrymen rematerialized and joined them. All welcomed the Americans warmly.

As twilight deepened, the local Partisan commandant arrived to take charge. The small, dapper man reminded the Americans of the movie actor Adolphe Menjou. He introduced himself as Despot Dusan and greeted them warmly.

Bartusch and Rosenthal decided to chance returning to the B-17 for their gear. If the plane had not blown up by now, they reasoned, it never would. They entered, found the escape kits, and stuffed them into their pockets. They tossed other treasure to Hirschfield, including two A-2 leather jackets, several pairs of GI shoes, and three haversacks full of snacks and other survival gear.

Then the Americans climbed onto a cart drawn by a single horse. Their goods were loaded into another. Escorted by a band of Partisans, they arrived at Sanski Most after a two-hour journey. The commandant took them to his office and arranged a place for them to stay. When they returned to the carts, however, their goods had disappeared into the night. The Partisans seemed embarrassed but unable to do anything about it. They indicated a bad element was to blame.

Disappointed, the airmen moved on to their lodgings. Their host, Vlado Grozden, turned out to be a prominent businessman and community elder. He lived with his sister and a young Muslim servant girl named Mevlida. The three Americans would share a single bed in their attic.[9]

■   ■   ■

Although Bartusch did not blame the crewmen who had bailed out, all six paid a heavy price for their actions.

Even as Bartusch, Rosenthal, and Hirschfield bedded down for the night, five of the crew marched northward flanked by German soldiers. Clete Kramer had hurt his knee upon landing and did not get far before the Germans found him. He raised his arms in surrender, but one of them rammed him in the forehead with his rifle butt anyway. Soon crewmates

Carl Bush, Raymond Klapp, Robert Steele, and Paul Bergschneider joined him in captivity. A guard showed the airmen a bloodied life vest. It bore Zack Johnson's name and serial number.

Johnson had landed near the sleepy neighboring town of Oberndorf, Austria, world-famous as the birthplace of the Christmas carol "Silent Night." Several townspeople spotted his descent and went out to find him. An off-duty Waffen-SS officer joined the hunt.

The SS officer spied Johnson first. As the civilians arrived on the scene, they found him facing the airman, pistol in hand. Johnson stood upright, unhurt by the jump. The SS man shot Johnson in the head and his body went slack. He had been the victim of a capricious fate and the murderous Nazi contempt for human life.[10]

The five captured men from Bartusch's crew became interned in Stalag Luft IV, one of Germany's cruelest POW camps. Clete Kramer had grown up speaking German, a useful skill when dealing with the guards. His linguistics earned him no goodwill, however, after one of them overheard a crewmate addressing him as "Colonel." The Germans assumed he was a real colonel in disguise and began an exhaustive interrogation. It took some time for Kramer to convince them he was a mere enlisted man with no knowledge of Allied air operations.

Stalag Luft IV overflowed with prisoners relocated from other stalags in the face of Russian advances. Stories of their brutal journeys circulated around camp. Gossips wagged that their stalag would be evacuated next.

In late January, the rumors were confirmed. The *Kommandant* decreed that all POWs but the most severely wounded would walk. Most already suffered from malnutrition and dysentery. Some, like Kramer, had been injured upon landing. Since flight surgeons rarely flew combat missions, only five Allied doctors tended to over six thousand POWs.

The event that came to be called the Black March began on February 6 in sub-zero temperatures. The column stretched out three abreast to the horizon. The guards set a murderous pace and kept it up with threats and rifle butts. Civilians shouted *"Terrorflieger!"* as the POWs passed.

Five days passed without food. Even when food came, the daily ration was a mere quarter-loaf of black bread per man.

Opportunities for escape abounded, but few tried. Most did not have the energy. They were safer with the guards than with the civilians anyway.

After a 470-mile hike, they reached Stalag XI-B. No one knew how many had died on the march, but the airmen assumed the civilians had butchered any stragglers. POWs from all over Germany had been herded to the stalag—so many that it now held 100,000 wretched souls. Conditions in the complex were little better than they had been on the road. Rumors spread that Hitler had ordered all prisoners to be killed.

After just a week, Stalag XI-B was evacuated as well. The exhausted men retraced their steps back eastward, away from the Anglo-American lines. They staggered on for three more weeks, dragging their heels so the Allied armies could catch up. From the air, the mob looked little different from the ragged German army. Occasionally British planes strafed them. Dozens of POWs, some of whom had survived captivity since Dunkirk, were killed by friendly fire.

Near the end, the German command structure completely broke down, and the column disintegrated. Clete Kramer staggered onward despite frostbitten feet. Some of his guards wanted to shoot his whole group. Others argued against it. Kramer chimed in using his German. Perhaps his ability to use their language humanized him—whatever the reason, the sympathetic guards prevailed. "You're on your own," one of them said. "*Auf Wiedersehen.*"

Kramer's bunch turned west. On April 26, 1945, they encountered British troops. The six-month odyssey that began when he bailed out of Bartusch's plane was complete.[11]

CHAPTER 6

Stranded in Sanski Most

S anski Most rests on a plateau divided by the gentle curves of the river Sana. In heavy rains, its waters soak the surrounding flatland with fertile silt. The alluvial plain comprises one of the few level, non-forested areas in northwest Bosnia.

The name Sanski Most means Sana's Bridge in Serbo-Croatian. The town's main feature had been a concrete bridge supported by four broad piles. Now ruined, its spans undulated accordion-like into the Sana, but remained passible for those spry enough to scamper up and down its folds.

Most of the people who lived on the east side of the river were Serbs, but a few Croats resided there as well. Before the war, six Jewish families had lived in town. Now their whereabouts were unknown.

The west side of the river was inhabited mostly by Muslims. A majestic domed mosque rimmed with four minarets highlighted the Muslim quarter. Between the mosque and the bridge, on the edge of the river, stood a large three-story building that had once housed a court-room and related offices. A square dominated by several lofty trees fronted the courthouse. An old schoolhouse with an assembly hall rested on the opposite side of the approach to the bridge.

Every Monday, the town square filled with farmers selling their produce. In better times, the marketplace had bustled with lively cafes. Now only the Partisan kitchen offered prepared food, and all it served was a thin, tallowy soup.

The people of the region had suffered terribly during the war. Soon after Yugoslavia fell to the Germans, Bosnia became part of the puppet Croatian state, the NDH. Viktor Gutić, the local NDH commissioner, ordered all Serbs and Montenegrins to leave the area. Soon Ustashe oppression inspired a spontaneous Serbian rebellion considered to be the first act of resistance against the Axis occupation of Yugoslavia. A garrison of Germans ruthlessly crushed the Sanski Most Revolt (sometimes known as the Đurđevdan Uprising). They murdered twenty-seven male Serbian civilians and hung the bodies in Sanski Most's town square.

Unsatisfied, the Ustashe began a genocidal campaign against the Bosnian Serbs. Tito claimed that over a thousand men, women, and children were killed and buried in a mass grave near Sanski Most. The Chetniks blamed Croatians and Muslims for the crimes and retaliated. They struck a deal with the occupying Italians: the Italians would sanction and protect Chetnik raids against people from the two groups. In return, the Chetniks would not oppose the Italians or Germans and would fight against the Partisans on their behalf. For a time, the Chetniks thrived.

The collaboration ended when the Italians surrendered to the Allies in 1943. The Chetnik atrocities and their complicity with the invaders did not sit well with much of the Bosnian population, including many Serbs. General Mihailović did not directly command the Bosnian Chetniks, but his popularity waned as the Partisans gained ground.[1]

Sanski Most experienced Partisan/German battles in December 1942, during the summer and fall of 1943, and in May 1944 following the Knight's Move raid against Tito's headquarters in Drvar. When this last German offensive faltered, the town hosted the second session of the

ZAVNOBiH, the "Anti-Fascist Council for the People's Liberation of Bosnia and Herzegovina."

In effect, Sanski Most served as the Partisan capital of Bosnia pending the liberation of Sarajevo. The legislative session, held from June 30 to July 2, 1944, reaffirmed ZAVNOBiH as the "Highest Legislative and Executive Body of Bosnian Peoples" and promulgated a "Declaration of the Rights of the Citizens of Bosnia and Herzegovina." Rejecting both Croatian and Serbian claims to Bosnia, the assembly declared Bosnia and Herzegovina to be a federal unit equal to any other in a "Democratic Federative Yugoslavia." Later the Partisan national assembly, the AVNOJ, accepted the declaration of rights adopted at Sanski Most as policy for the nation.[2]

■   ■   ■

The first American airmen to seek sanctuary in Sanski Most arrived after two B-17s collided near the town in late March 1944. Seven survivors traveled to nearby Bosanski Petrovac, the rescue point in the area at the time. They were flown out on April 8.[3]

Several airmen passed through Sanski Most en route to the Bosanski Petrovac airstrip over the next six weeks. Late in May, however, the Germans captured the town as part of the Knight's Move offensive, and Sanski Most replaced it as the evacuation point for downed Allied fliers. Even when the Partisans retook Bosanski Petrovac, Sanski Most remained the main regional airstrip. More than eighty airmen were evacuated from there, and the Air Crew Rescue Unit made several airdrops at the field until it was closed for the winter on November 6.

Future evadees would hike south to Bugojno in central Bosnia, where a British mission headed by Captain John A. Tregidga was located. From there, the airmen would travel southward to Livno, Sinj, and the port of Split, where they could either catch a ship to Italy or be ferried to the Island of Vis for a flight back to Bari. Alternatively, airmen could take a western route to the port of Zadar—often known by its Italian name, Zara—for evacuation by sea.[4]

Six downed American airmen had passed through Sanski Most in late November and hiked to the coast via the southern route. Although their journey had been uneventful, the Partisans did not send Bartusch, Hirschfield, and Rosenthal along the same path. Even when the Stewart and Dean crews arrived from Drvar a week later, the Partisans made no effort to move them.

The reason was simple, though no one explained it to the airmen: the land routes had ceased to be safe. German Army Group "E" was withdrawing from Greece across central Yugoslavia to Zagreb. A collaborating Chetnik force commanded by Pavle Đurišić accompanied them. The western route to Zara was unsafe as well, as German forces were also retreating from Dalmatia. A battle raged near Knin, a strategic city at the junction of several roads to the coast.

The Americans were cut off from the sea. For the time being, absent a rescue by air, there was no place for them to go.[5]

■   ■   ■

For a week, Bartusch, Hirschfield, and Rosenthal enjoyed the hospitality of their host, Vlado Grozden. His teenaged Muslim servant, Mevlida, cleaned, cooked, and washed the airmen's clothes. Vlado offered bread and butter as well as ersatz tea, ersatz coffee, and ersatz cream—no doubt black-market goods. The airmen, in turn, contributed chicken, eggs, apples, and walnuts bought in the marketplace. They also offered candy Charms from their escape kits to sweeten the tea. Though limited by the language barrier, the family and the three airmen became fast friends.

When the Stewart and Dean crews arrived in Sanski Most, the Partisans lodged them in the unheated third-story attic of the courthouse on the town square. Straw and parachutes served as bedding. A twelve-year-old boy became their orderly. His neck bore a scar from a German bayonet.

The Partisans, like the Red Army, attached Communist commissars to military units to ensure political conformity. One such commissar objected to Bartusch's men living in nicer quarters than the newer arrivals. Marxist doctrine dictated all airmen should share equal accommodations, so Bartusch, Hirschfield, and Rosenthal were ousted from the Grozdens' home and moved in with the others.

Every airman became louse-ridden. The sole communal bathhouse was fired up just once a week. Occasionally, the airmen's clothes were steamed in a "Partisan barrel," but the lice never stayed away for long. The men became so overrun that they took turns picking bugs off one another like apes. Robert Dean's flight engineer, Red Fetter, had fair, almost translucent skin, and was particularly susceptible. The airmen bought lice powder from the local *apoteka*, but nothing helped.

The Partisans assigned a guard named Luka Atglivic to look after the airmen. Whether he was there to protect the Americans from harm or to keep them in line was unclear. Every night he entered the attic and slept next to Rosenthal, much to the amusement of the others. "Why me?" wondered Rosenthal. One night, he dismantled the guard's gun in revenge. In the morning, the guard woke up, uttered a Serbo-Croatian oath, and reassembled his rifle.[6]

The men shared an indoor outhouse on the second floor. Two side-by-side holes in the floor served as latrines. Everything was done standing up, by men and women alike. Americans never became accustomed to female Partisans entering the bathroom without knocking, giving them a cheerful "*Zdravo*," dropping their pants, and squatting next to them.

No toilet paper could be found. Brown globs streaked the latrine walls. The airmen improvised various solutions. Some enjoyed the irony of using their paybooks. Others resorted to the lower denominations of the local currency, Kuna, which were virtually worthless.

The Partisans' lone act of assiduous hygiene was shaving. Chetniks grew their beards long and bushy. A Partisan who came upon a bearded stranger was likely to shoot first and ask questions later. Robert Dean's navigator, Bernard Button, let his whiskers grow until he heard a child ask his mother if he was a Chetnik; he rectified the situation at the first opportunity.

The main barber at the Partisan canteen was a buxom young blonde woman with hindquarters like a linebacker. Emil Horak was taking a shave from her when she mentioned her parents had been killed in an American bombing raid. Horak winced as the razor scraped against his stubble, but her voice carried no rancor. Such things happened in wartime.[7]

■   ■   ■

Scotty Stewart and John Elmore were confined to the town's makeshift hospital due to their broken legs. It offered little more care than they had received in Drvar.

Few of the airmen paid attention to rank once they bailed out. Bartusch, as the first American pilot in town, acted as the de facto senior officer. When he learned of the two wounded men in the infirmary, he and Rosenthal visited to see if they could help. Conditions were appalling. Wounded Partisans oozed blood from half-treated bullet holes. Garbage cans filled with severed limbs littered the dingy hallways. A miasmic stench suffused the air. Only the cold suppressed the flies. Barefoot nurses scurried about. Rosenthal guessed most of them were illiterate. It appeared that the place's last cleaning had occurred during Archduke Ferdinand's time.

Bartusch and Rosenthal found Stewart and Elmore in great discomfort. Stewart had seen the amputated limbs and heard the screams as the doctor operated without anesthesia. "Don't let them take my leg off," he implored.

Rosenthal sought out a doctor named Pavel Martinac and asked if he spoke English. He did not. Rosenthal tested his other language: "Do you know Hungarian?"

"Don't speak that here!" the doctor protested. Hungary was a German ally. They moved outside to talk. The doctor promised to do his best to save Stewart's leg, but he lacked proper medicine and equipment.[8]

An idea struck Rosenthal. Every heavy bomber contained a rubber raft stocked with emergency supplies. Although the Partisans had stripped his B-17, they had likely not discovered the compartment where the dinghy was stowed. Besides, Rosenthal had neglected to destroy the plane's top-secret bombsight.

Bartusch, Rosenthal, and Hirschfield set out for their B-17 the next day. An elderly couple wearing Muslim clothes had moved in, although the plane still reeked of gasoline. Either they did not understand the danger or they were desperate enough not to care. A braying goat stood tethered outside. The three airmen tried to explain that they only wanted to take something from the plane, and that the couple could stay if they wanted. But the frightened couple unfastened the goat and hustled away.

Rosenthal disengaged the bombsight and tossed it into the river. Meanwhile, Bartusch and Hirschfield pulled the dinghy from its compartment in the wing. As expected, it contained a treasure trove of morphine syringes, antiseptics, sulfa, flare guns, chocolate bars, maps, and fishing gear. They stashed the goods in the pockets of their flight suits.

Rosenthal suggested they ride the dinghy down the Sana River to Sanski Most. Bartusch decided he would rather walk, so Rosenthal and Hirschfield set off downstream without him. They made good progress until darkness set in and the water turned to rapids. The raft spun uncontrollably. "Let's get to shore," cried Rosenthal, but Hirschfield lost their lone oar in the torrent. It took twenty minutes of paddling with their hands to bring the dinghy to shore.

Both men were soaked, cold, and unsure they could find their way back to town in the dark. Rosenthal spotted a light coming from a nearby farmhouse. They walked up to the door and knocked. No answer. After a few moments, they rapped again and stepped in. Huddled in a corner were a man, his wife, and two small children.

"We are Americans," Rosenthal assured them, "*Amerikanski! Dobra!* Good Americans!"

"*Amerikanac?*" they gasped.

By now the airmen were famished. Rosenthal pointed his finger to his mouth. "Hungry," he motioned. The woman nodded and prepared some warm milk and bread.

The two airmen heard a soft moan from the other room. A boy of nine or ten lay there with a badly cut leg. His head felt feverish. "We can fix that," promised Hirschfield. He injected a morphine syrette into the infected leg. When the youth fell asleep, the airman cleaned the wound with peroxide, sprinkled it with sulfa powder, and bandaged it.

In the morning, the grateful father hitched his horse to a wagon and gave the airmen a ride to town. Dr. Martinac accepted the medicines with tears of joy. They would save many lives.

A few days later Rosenthal and Hirschfield were summoned to Despot Dusan's spartan office. The commandant had heard of their good deed at the farmhouse. The town wanted to thank them for saving the boy's life. A celebration would be held in their honor that Saturday night.

A few days later, everyone in town gathered at the old schoolhouse, including airmen from other crews. An accordionist and a harmonica player provided lively folk tunes. The airmen danced with Partisan girls draped in gun belts and grenades. They all wanted a turn with the Americans.

After a time, the music stopped and the hall filled with chairs. Bartusch, Rosenthal, and Hirschfield sat in the front row with the commandant and his staff. The main event began, a play reenacting one of Marshal Tito's famous victories. "*Ovo je Tito! Drag Tito!*" the actors sang. "This is Tito! Dear Tito!" Everyone, including the Americans, sang along. Players shot live ammunition into the ceiling, and plaster dropped on the airmen's laps. After the performance, the commandant made a speech and presented the Americans to the audience amid wild applause.[9]

■   ■   ■

The airmen knew of the airstrip outside of town. Every day they scanned the skies for planes, but a low, perpetual cloud hung over the valley. Only Harry Carter dreaded their coming; by AAF rules, he would be sent home if he stayed missing in action for forty-two days. Nevertheless, Carter accompanied Bartusch and Rosenthal when they checked out the airstrip, a flat, grassy piece of land next to the river. The ground felt too soggy for a landing, even for the versatile C-47 transports used by the Air Crew Rescue Unit.

Three things would have to happen before they could be rescued. First, the airfield needed to solidify, which would not happen until cold weather froze it. Second, the transport pilots would need good weather, both in Italy and over Sanski Most. Finally, the stranded airmen had to contact headquarters to let them know their whereabouts. None of these were likely to occur soon.[10]

■   ■   ■

A Soviet captain served as a liaison with the Partisans. One day Bartusch, Rosenthal, and Hirschfield spotted him bathing in the icy Sana River. Amused, the Russian beckoned them to join him. *You Americans are spoiled sissies like the Germans*, he seemed to say. *You have everything. You think you are great, but you are not tough like us.*

Later the commandant invited the trio to dine with the Russian captain and his retinue. The meal was a chance for revenge, since the Americans did not speak Russian, and the Russians did not seem to understand English. Smiling broadly, the three Americans called the Russians every dirty epithet they could think of. The Soviets grinned back and responded in kind. Rosenthal guessed they were playing the same game.

The Soviets showed no other interest in the Americans. The Partisans were equally passive. Nobody seemed interested in arranging a rescue or even letting Bari know they were alive.[11]

■   ■   ■

One morning, word came that the Germans might attempt to capture the downed airmen in Sanski Most. The Partisans rounded up the Americans and rushed them into the hills. Even the crippled Scotty Stewart and John Elmore prepared to flee. By afternoon, however, a messenger told them to stand down. The airmen returned, grateful they did not have to spend a night in the wild.

The episode concerned the airmen. Maybe some retreating Germans had skirted the town. Maybe it had been a false alarm. Or maybe Sanski Most was not safe after all. They needed to reach out to the ACRU. By now their families had received those awful MIA telegrams. At the very least, the airmen wanted to let their families know they were alive.

Bartusch led a delegation of officers to the commandant's office. Sedlak and Horak interpreted. Dusan told them there was a British mission at Travnik, about eighty miles to the southeast. Bartusch wrote a letter stating that twenty-two airmen were sheltered in Sanski Most, including two who were badly wounded. The commandant promised to send it to Travnik right away.[12]

■   ■   ■

Charles Stanley's crew arrived in Sanski Most on Tuesday, December 5, raising the number of airmen in town to thirty-two. Their first stop was Commandant Dusan's office. Despite the language barrier, Stanley cautioned Albert Buchholz and Sam Spomer not to try their German. He did not want to raise any suspicion that his men were not Americans.

The commandant received them cordially, offered them tea, and assigned them to a home on the other side of the river. Seaver and Spomer, though injured, were not sent to the hospital. No one could help them there anyway.

The crew traversed the bridge, climbing up and down the steep fallen bridge spans and leaping between the gaps. Their quarters were a small second-story room accessed by an outdoor staircase in a house belonging to a heavily bearded railroad worker named Stojan Ubarić and his wife. The couple, both about forty years of age, welcomed them amiably.

The lodging was better than the courthouse attic, but it had its drawbacks. Anytime the crew wanted to eat at the Partisan kitchen or buy foodstuffs at the marketplace, they had to traverse the obstacle-course bridge. The crew had little desire to return to the canteen anyway. During their first meal there, Stanley found an eye in his soup. Cone discovered a cockroach and a jawbone with half-chewed grass stuck in its teeth. Due to their isolation, they also had little interaction with the other airmen.[13]

The afternoon after the Stanley crew arrived, a flight of heavy bombers returning from a mission flew overhead. A blast just outside of town sent people scurrying. The explosion frightened the townspeople and upset the Partisans. The airmen knew a bomber had let go of a hung-up bomb, but they could not convince them that it had been an accident.

Later that day, another, more distant eruption boomed. A P-51 Mustang crashed near town, evidently due to mechanical trouble. The pilot's parachute failed to open. A few airmen walked to the site. Someone had already stolen the man's boots and flight clothes. An imprint indicated he had bounced. No blood showed, but every bone in his body seemed broken. His dog tags identified him as Lt. C. G. Begg, a South African Air Force (SAAF) pilot.

Begg, a twenty-two-year-old married man from the Orange Free State, was remembered in the squadron records as an "exceptionally fearless type" who served as the unit's sports officer and played on its rugby team. He had been given credit for two aerial victories, the only flier in his squadron credited with such kills in a Mustang. Begg had been one of ten SAAF pilots sent out to patrol the area near Brod that morning. The formation broke up in heavy clouds, and most pilots could not find an opening to regain their bearings. Six of the ten failed to return to base that day. Only one of them eventually found his way back. Another became a POW, and the rest were killed.

The day after the tragedy, the airmen in Sanski Most attended the funeral, a dual service for the pilot and a Partisan soldier. Several Americans formed an honor guard for the procession. Emil Horak was put in charge to translate instructions from the Yugoslavs. On Horak's command, the airmen lined up in double file, shortest to tallest, one pace apart. The wooden caskets were placed on horse-drawn carts, and the funeral march began to the beat of a lone drum. The townspeople lined the streets dressed in their heavy woven clothes and soft goatskin shoes.

The cortege reached the grounds of a roofless Orthodox church. A bearded priest wearing ornate robes conducted the ceremony. When it was over, the coffins were lowered into the muddy churchyard. A pretty Partisan girl cried and tossed dirt on the graves. A wooden cross was placed over the South African. It read "C.G. Begg—1944."[14]

■　　■　　■

A few days later, the British agent in Travnik replied to Bartusch's letter. Major Toby Milbanke explained he needed to know the airmen's units and serial numbers before he could help them. No rescue would happen before he verified their identities.

The major did, however, alert Red Cross representatives of the airmen's presence. Soon they delivered Red Cross parcels filled with Nescafé coffee, dehydrated beef, rice, bouillon cubes, crackers, candy, chewing gum, sugar, salt, and tea. The packages also contained sundries such as razor blades, toothbrushes, toothpaste, soap, matches, and cigarettes.

Clarence Byers, the one man known to both the Stewart and the Dean crews, distributed the treasure.[15]

■   ■   ■

The airmen settled into daily routines. The main mark of time was the call of the Muslim faithful to prayer from the pinnacle of one of the mosque's minarets.

The commissary acted as a field mess and bar for the town. The menu consisted of soup and hard, flat cornbread mixed with sawdust. Everyone ate without charge.

A rotund, jovial woman named Rosita, Rosa for short, served as head cook and barmaid. In the afternoon, she served tea flavored with honey in small brass cups. In the evening, she sold *rakija*, the local moonshine. Once Emil Horak asked Rosa if the stuff had been aged. "Oh yes," she replied sincerely, "since Wednesday." Another time, he asked if she knew the difference between Catholic and Orthodox believers. Catholics prayed with their fingers pointed out, she motioned, while the Orthodox closed their hands in a dome. That was all she knew.

The airmen supplemented their diet with chicken and eggs purchased at the marketplace or from other vendors. Mutton and pork were rarer but available for a price. Money could be exchanged at the commandant's office at 4,000 Croatian Kuna to the dollar, but the merchants preferred dollars. Most of them were Muslims marked by distinctive garb and fezzes.

Bartusch, Rosenthal, and Hirschfield, armed with forty-eight dollars from each of the nine escape kits abandoned by their crew, were the wealthiest men in town. Two of the Dean crew's kits had been missing their money, so the men pooled their funds and made do. Each kit's forty-eight dollars included eight five-dollar bills and eight ones—very large denominations by local standards. Many shopkeepers lacked the cash to break an American five, and a four-pound leg of pork cost only one dollar.

Harry Carter and Joe Sedlak decided to supplement their diet by hunting for food. Not far from town, Carter spotted a rabbit. "I'll get it!" cried Sedlak, and he fired his .45. The rabbit blew into bloody smithereens. Hunting was not going to work. Eventually, they discovered an old woman who kept chickens beneath her stilted house, and they began paying her to prepare them meals. She doubtless needed the money. She was so poor she did not own a stick of furniture.

Carter spent most of his time visiting Scotty Stewart in the hospital. Whenever he could, Carter brought him meals, apples, and nuts. Often Carter helped Stewart scratch inside his lice-infested cast. Sometimes they played checkers using a silk escape kit map as a board and hard candy as pieces. Carter, who had once detested Stewart, become his main caregiver and companion. The rest of the crew could hardly believe his change in attitude.[16]

■   ■   ■

Dusk fell about 4:00 each afternoon. The only lights were candles and a few carbide lamps oozing a sallow glow and a distinctive stench. Curfew began at 9:00 p.m., but there was no entertainment anyway. Rosenthal tried to find a piano without success.

Most of the airmen could not socialize with the townspeople due to the language barrier. The airmen who spoke languages other than English were a little better off. Joe Sedlak made friends with a doctor named Vaslov Polikan, who often played violin for the Americans. Rosenthal's Hungarian was useful only with the other doctor in the hospital.

One did not have to speak the language, however, to participate in the townspeople's main pastime: chess. Everyone played, even the children. Whenever two old masters started a game, people gathered around to kibitz. Any match with an American drew a crowd, though few could hold their own against the locals.

Romance rarely entered the picture. Most airmen found the gun belt–clad women too sturdy and intimidating. In any event, the Partisan code forbade fraternization with their women. Most airmen assumed being caught with a Partisan female meant death, allies or not.

Marriage, at least with a civilian girl, was another matter. One day a small, mustached peasant brought his daughter into town and sought out the Americans. Joe Sedlak translated. The man wanted an airman to marry the girl and take her to America. The guys offered clean-cut Harry Hoogeveen, who fit the bill as both a bachelor and a farmer. Hoogeveen was about to protest when the girl offered her own ideas. She was in love with an airman who had passed through town before. She dictated a letter and Sedlak put it to paper. He promised to mail it as soon as he returned to America.

Sedlak had his own woman troubles. A sad old crone took to following him around town, cooing, "*Moya, moya, moya*" ("Mine, Mine, mine"). The poor woman had lost everything, including her son, whom Sedlak apparently resembled. Most of the guys found her amusing. Sedlak felt sorry for her but couldn't think of any way to ease her suffering.

The tedium, combined with the plethora of weapons, proved to be dangerous. One time, Emil Horak entered the hotel attic to find crewmate Ernest Peterson cracking walnuts with a Russian hand grenade. Fortunately, one had to unscrew the cap to arm the device.

On another occasion, Powell Robinson's .45 went off while he was cleaning it. The bullet whizzed past Harry Carter's ear and hit a knot hole in the wall. The noise brought their Partisan keeper into the room. "*Dobra!*" he exclaimed. "Good shot!"

A week passed without contact with the outside world. Heavy snow fell on December 13 and 14, further sinking the airmen's hopes for rescue. On December 16, airmen from two more crews arrived. The American population in Sanski Most was about to explode.[17]

CHAPTER 7

Herky's Boys Get Downed

When Pilot Herman Marrone—"Herky" to his friends and crew—rose early on the morning of December 11, 1944, he had no sense of impending doom. He felt no different even after he learned his destination for the day would be the synthetic fuel plant in Moosbierbaum, Austria, a key facility that was producing fuel for V-1 and V-2 rockets.

Just ten days before, he had flown his first combat mission over Vienna, a notoriously tough target. The flak had been heavy, but no planes went down. "Hell," Marrone remarked to his veteran copilot, "I've been more excited in a poker game."

Marrone flew his second mission on December 9, this time against Linz, Austria. Again, the planes from his bomb group escaped unscathed. The same day, sixteen airmen from Marrone's 449th Bomb Group who had completed their tours of duty died in a plane crash on the first leg of their journey home. The tragedy reminded everyone on base of the dangers they faced.

Marrone, however, remained unfazed as he rode out to the tarmac that morning. He had survived two other missions. He had flown through walls of flak. *What the hell*, he thought. *Why should this one be any different?*[1]

■   ■   ■

Marrone was as unlikely a heavy bomber pilot as one could find. For one thing, he was one of the AAF's few true volunteers. Most airmen enlisted because they knew they would soon be drafted. Marrone was exempt from the draft because he was his widowed mother's sole means of support. Nevertheless, he had signed up for the riskiest duty in the armed forces.

Marrone was Italian by heritage, another rarity for pilots. When he was growing up in the 1930s, Italian Americans were stereotyped as either psychopathic gangsters or comically inarticulate organ-grinders. Derogatory slurs like "wop" and "dago" filled everyday language. The world's most famous Italian, Benito Mussolini, was a strutting, second-rate enemy stooge.

In theory, the AAF afforded equal opportunity to all white male applicants. Despite its institutionalized racial discrimination, the Army claimed it could not afford to be prejudiced when the nation's survival was at stake. Nevertheless, the AAF's qualifying exams and weeding-out processes favored the sons of middle- and upper-middle-class families. These men were often better educated than the more recent waves of immigrants and scored better on standardized tests. Later in training, cadets faced elimination from instructors whose prejudices and anti-Semitism reflected antiquated ideas of how officers and gentlemen should appear and behave.

These factors produced pilots of predominately northern European stock. Few were Jewish or the sons of immigrants from southern or eastern Europe. The great fighter ace "Gabby" Gabreski was an exception. So was Herky Marrone.[2]

Marrone was also unusual in that he had not attended college. Originally, the AAF required all pilot candidates to have two years of higher education; it dropped the restriction when the talent pool proved too small. Nevertheless, most pilots had attended college at least briefly.

Marrone had been out of high school for six years when he entered pilot training. He spent the intervening years in the hardscrabble oil fields of western Pennsylvania. The strenuous outdoor labor suited him, but his lack of education handicapped him in flight school. The AAF's rigorous academic program daunted even those fresh from university campuses.

Nevertheless, Marrone discovered he could keep up with all but the most brilliant students. Eventually, he rose to be a second lieutenant and an aircraft commander. Many non-WASPs became copilots or were relegated to the rank of flight officer.

Outwardly, Marrone looked to be a tough, ruggedly handsome ladies' man who loved his whiskey and lived for the moment. He regularly corresponded with a girlfriend named Jane yet felt no compunction to be faithful to her. But Marrone's prowling eyes and cocksure manner masked a sensitive, reflective soul. He sent most of his paycheck home to his large family every month. He enjoyed an eclectic spectrum of music, from Mendelssohn to Hoagy Carmichael. A devout Catholic, he did his best to get to confession and Mass and to receive Communion whenever he could.[3]

■   ■   ■

Today, as Marrone approached *Silver Babe*, his plane for the day, he sported a tightly knotted necktie. On the odd chance he might be killed, he intended to go out in style.

The ground crew chief had run his checks, but Marrone's meticulous flight engineer, Al Topal, would have his say. "How does she look, Al?" asked Marrone. "She'll fly, Skipper," rejoined Topal. A veteran of sixty missions, *Babe* had been the group's first replacement B-24 and the first left unpainted to save the weight.

After Marrone and his copilot Jim King conducted their walk-around, they entered the cockpit and ran through their twenty-six-item preflight checklist. King looked serious. This would be his first combat mission. King had grown up in a wealthy section of Nashville, Tennessee, and was attending Vanderbilt University when he joined the AAF. Despite their contrasting backgrounds, he and Marrone had developed a comfortable comradery. King's brother, John, was serving in General George Patton's Third Army, so Jim kept a close watch on the war developments in France.

One by one the powerful Pratt and Whitney engines coughed and caught. Marrone saw the flare signaling the group to take off. The aircraft in front of him rolled. Thirty seconds later Marrone crossed himself, released the brakes, and pulled the throttles to full power. *Silver Babe* rumbled forward, gained speed, and nosed into the air. Olive trees at the runway's end swished under by mere feet.

The sky was clear for the first time in weeks. Near the Adriatic coast, P-51s manned by Tuskegee Airmen approached to protect against fighters. Al Goodling, the crew's baby-faced bombardier-navigator, admired the snow-covered Dinaric Alps. "That's where I'd like to spend my White Christmas," he remarked. Marrone wished he had not said it.[4]

At noon, 435 warbirds nosed into Austria. Soon their cruciforms cast shadows over the outskirts of Vienna. Some 100 Liberators, including *Silver Babe*, veered toward Moosbierbaum.

Marrone ordered Al Topal to check the fuel gauges. Twelve hundred gallons. Good. The cloudless sky advantaged the German anti-aircraft gunners. The expanse ahead filled with clusters of greasy splotches. *Silver Babe* bounced amid the concussions.

George Earll, the crew's radio operator, cast clusters of tinsel-like aluminum chaff out the rear hatch to confuse the enemy's radar. A tall, lean gentleman with an aquiline nose, Earll had met his beloved wife Patty in a college chemistry class. Patty had had difficulty putting a rubber stopper on a test tube, and George had rushed to her rescue. A bit too eager to impress her, he broke off the end of the test tube and gouged the palm of his hand. A romantic chemical reaction ensued. They married knowing George would soon have to go off to war. The AAF classified him as a pilot, and he did fine until his pitiful depth perception was discovered. He washed out and was sent to radio school.

Silver Babe bounced again. Earll's nervous knees buckled under the weight of his flak jacket and helmet. "The hell with this!" he ranted. Half-crazed with fear, it seemed to him that the sooner the chaff disappeared, the sooner he would be safe. He cast the entire box out.

Singing shards pierced *Babe*'s skin and pinged off the walls. A jagged piece deflected off Al Topal's flak jacket. Shrapnel cracked through Marrone's windshield but missed him. How, he wondered, had he not been afraid of flak before?

The barrage ceased after an eternal five minutes. Marrone took stock. *Babe*'s right wing rode low due to a damaged aileron, but all four engines purred. No crewmen were hurt. They had been lucky.[5] Marrone forced *Silver Babe* to fly straight and steady. His long years of physical labor helped. He and Jim King took turns wrestling with the yoke and pedals.

After an hour and a half, the group descended to twelve thousand feet. Marrone's crew took off their oxygen masks and relaxed. Some of them broke out K-rations for an afternoon snack.

Leveling the plane to check the fuel would cost Marrone some of the gas he was trying to save. Something told him he had better do it anyway. Al Topal checked the gauges and reported. "Skipper," he yelled over the roar of the engines, "we have 135 gallons."

That can't be right, thought Marrone. He had Topal double-check, but Al confirmed the reading. The shrapnel must have cut a gas line. Marrone ordered the men to lighten the plane.

The outboard engine on the right side cut out. A few minutes later, the engine next to it coughed. Marrone feathered it, dropped *Silver Babe* out of formation, and called the group leader to tell him they had to bail out. There was no time to worry about whether the enemy controlled the territory below.

Marrone pressed on his throat mic. "Put your parachutes on, guys."

Al Goodling emerged from the nose looking quizzical. A minute ago, they had it made. Now they had to bail out?

Everyone scrambled for their parachutes. Waist gunner Gregg Cloos grabbed the first one he saw. Earll had fastened GI boots to his chute and knew which was his. He seized Cloos and pointed. "Yours is over there!" Cloos let go and donned his own. Earll attached his chute to the rings of his harness. He and Ray Seery, the ball turret gunner, tightened each other's straps. "You know, Ray," Earll sighed, "I always wanted to make a jump. Now I'm not so damn sure." Both smiled. It all seemed so surreal.

Marrone rang the bailout bell and repeated the order over the interphone.[6]

■   ■   ■

A dreamy sense of calm overcame Earll as he dropped out of the rear hatch, feet first. He rolled on his back as he had been trained so his chest pack would open away from his face. He found the red D-ring and yanked. Nothing. A corner of silk protruded from the pack. The left snap on the flap remained fastened. He reached and pulled. The pilot chute exploded. Earll blacked out.

He came to in midair, and the only sound he heard was his own breathing. A few open parachutes spread above him. The snowy ground rose. Earll prepared to pull on the shroud lines to ease the impact, but before he could, he landed hard. The whiteness of the snow had confounded his poor depth perception.

Earll rolled in pain on the snowy slope, then rotated to a sitting position in a foot of snow. His right ankle hurt like hell. He released the parachute and tried to stand but failed. He sat down and hoped friendlies would find him before the Germans did.

A one-horse sleigh emerged over a hill crest. A rugged-looking older man with a bushy mustache held the reins. Two boys, maybe his grandsons, accompanied him. "Partizan!" they exclaimed. They gestured that they had seen his parachute.

The trio helped Earll into the sled and drove him to his lodgings for the night, a two-story farmhouse built into the side of a hill. Several generations lived there, men, women, and children. Some of the women tried to determine the problem with his foot, but their twisting hurt too much and Earll waved them off. They served him warm milk, black bread, ominous-looking soup, and a sip of moonshine.

A wrinkled crone sat by the wood-burning stove shaving a tightly rolled tobacco leaf with a knife. After her cigarette was fashioned, she reached into the stove with her ancient, calloused hand, pulled out a red-hot coal, and lifted it to her wooden face. The tip of the cigarette glowed. Earll gaped in amazement.

When it was time to sleep, the women helped Earll upstairs to bed. They tucked him under a thick down quilt, and he slept like the dead.

The next day, a horse-drawn cart carried Earll several miles to Bosanski Petrovac. Battle scars marred its once lovely façade. The town looked gaunt, plundered, and depopulated.

Soon young Al Goodling led the rest of the enlisted men into town. Gene Dennis, the last crewman to leave the aircraft, had landed in a tree. His leg was in about the same shape as Earll's ankle. The Partisans quartered them all in a cottage a block from Partisan headquarters.

The seven of them were together and in friendly hands. Just one question remained: Where were Herky Marrone and Jim King? No one had seen the two pilots bail out.[7]

CHAPTER 8

The Weakest Link Breaks

O fficial AAF policy held that the stress of combat would affect the bravest of men. Courage was like money—airmen spent some each mission, and no man had an unlimited supply.

AAF psychologists identified three stages of fear. At first, the danger of aerial combat seemed remote. Reality set in during the second stage. By the third, airmen understood they were fugitives from the law of averages; sooner or later, their luck would run out. At this stage, the tension became next to unbearable.

In battle, every soldier has his own motivation for standing and fighting when his instinct for self-preservation tells him to run away. Some do it for pride, some out of duty, and some believe in the righteousness of their cause. Others fear shame or punishment. Studies show repeatedly, however, that men stand and fight mostly because of the camaraderie they share with their fellow soldiers. They risk death to avoid letting down their comrades; they find courage in the company of their brothers-in-arms.

The pull of brotherhood was just as strong in the air as it was on the ground, perhaps more so. Bomber crews had trained together stateside, shared a long sea voyage or airplane flight overseas, and bunked together at their bases—officers with officers, enlisted men with enlisted men. Their shared experiences often alchemized into deep bonds that extended long past the war.

Most of all, a bomber crew was a team. The survival of all might depend on the actions of any single member. Morale depended upon every airman's confidence in his crewmates. For this reason, the AAF wanted crews to begin and end their tours of duty together.

Nevertheless, furloughs, promotions, and casualties inevitably forced substitutions. When members of a tight-knit crew were replaced by strangers, personality conflicts and distrust could erupt. The greater the number of replacements, the bigger the potential for problems. A crew was like a chain—a single weak link could break it.[1]

■   ■   ■

Hixon Eldridge and Archimedes Roper—nicknamed "Archy"—had been instructor pilots when they were reassigned for combat duty. Eldridge, a short, compact man, looked too small to fly the bulky B-24. Roper, four years older, a head taller, and several pounds heavier, appeared to be a more likely aircraft commander. Eldridge, however, had far more experience in B-24s and proved to be the tougher disciplinarian.

Roper got along fine with Eldridge. He felt the pilot appreciated the maturity and strength he brought to the cockpit, and he helped Eldridge keep the crew in line—no easy task.

The enlisted men in the front of the plane—thirty-one-year-old engineer Vic Melcher and nose gunner Richard "Red" Braun—were solid guys. So was Joe Colasante, who had finished a few years of college and had washed out as a navigator before becoming a gunner.

The same could not be said about the other guys in the rear. Radio operator Gus Perrone, a second-generation Italian from Philadelphia, spoke his parents' language more fluently than his heavily accented English. The pilots kept catching him listening to Axis Sally during missions, even though regulations strictly forbade it.

Tail gunner Eugene Quinn came by being a ne'er-do-well honestly. His father, a non-connected operator who took orders from nobody, had been a professional bookie in pre-war Baltimore. Quinn had inherited his father's independent streak. Two weeks after his promotion to corporal at Biggs Field, Quinn was granted a week's leave. He celebrated a few extra days and was demoted to private for being AWOL. Quinn's outfit shipped out without him. It seemed he would be relegated to ground duty, but he liked flying and asked to be reinstated. Quinn became available just as the new crews led by the former flight instructors were being assembled.

The Eldridge crew's first few missions with the 456th Bomb Group had not gone well. On their first, a ground crew member failed to secure the gas cap on a wing tank. The fuel siphoned out during takeoff and the plane filled with fumes. Gus Perrone dropped to his knees in prayer. Fortunately, Eldridge brought them back to base in one piece.

A few missions later, Don Womack, the crew's ball turret gunner, took a severe flak wound in his rear end. Eldridge raced back to base while the crew attended to him. An ambulance met them on the tarmac. It was a good thing—Womack had nearly bled to death.

Womack's injury was not the only close call. In November, flak damage forced Eldridge to land on one wheel. The plane spun into an olive grove, but everyone emerged safely. The nifty maneuver cemented Eldridge's reputation as a hot pilot.

Soon the crew was assigned greater responsibilities. Eldridge became a flight leader, and the other planes dropped their bombs on the lead of his bombardier, Bill Clark. Eldridge's original navigator, Robert Mann, was promoted to guide the squadron leader's plane and was replaced by Flight Officer Conrad Teague.

Teague did not match the crew's conception of officer material. In that homophobic time, when being gay was grounds for exclusion from the Army, it was whispered that he was a "momma's boy" and "marched to a different drummer." Although Teague was a capable navigator—he had been a top student at the University of California at Berkley when he joined the AAF—the crew was not as comfortable with him at the navigator's table as they had been with Bob Mann.[2]

Two other new crew members reported to Eldridge's plane in the early hours of December 11, 1944.

Boyish Olin B. Houghton replaced Don Womack in the lower ball. Houghton, who went by his middle name, Barker, was available because most of his crew had been lost on October 20 during an ill-fated raid against Munich. On the return flight, Houghton's plane lost one engine after another, forcing his pilot to make a powerless belly-flop landing on an island off the Italian coast. Stranded north of the Allied lines, the crew had split into three parties and fanned out. Houghton's quartet was rescued by the Italian underground and returned to base after a harrowing two-week odyssey. The other crewmen became POWs. Houghton returned to combat as a "bastard gunner," rotating among aircrews. During his third mission back, a piece of flak just missed him. He wondered when his luck would run out.

The final new member of the crew, aerial photographer Charles Fribley, would be flying his thirty-fifth and final sortie. In September, he had been credited with shooting down a German Me-109—a rare feat. Fribley's homely face reminded Houghton of Abraham Lincoln. The others noticed only his extreme jumpiness.

■   ■   ■

Their target would be the Vienna rail yards, the Germans' main supply point for the nearby Eastern Front. The site was so important that the Germans had stationed 315 flak guns to defend it.

Accordingly, as Eldridge's B-24J lifted off toward the most heavily defended target within reach, all five crewmen in the rear of the plane had good reason to be uncommonly nervous. Quinn, Perrone, and Colasante had recently tended to a critically wounded friend. Barker Houghton had survived a crash landing and another near-miss. And Charles Fribley's nerves felt raw as meat—the last mission was always the toughest.[3]

As the formation approached the target, Eldridge and Roper watched B-17s penetrate the dense field of flak ahead. Some were going down.

Hixon Eldridge led the second box of his formation. Clusters of shrapnel splattered the sky. A plane in the box ahead of his took a direct hit in the right wing. Parachutes spewed out as it spiraled down. More red and black bursts exploded. Concussions enfiladed Eldridge's plane. A grim-faced Roper could almost sense the shells hurtling skyward.

Bill Clark released their bombs. Another shell erupted off the plane's left rear, but the pilots felt no special impact. They cleared the inferno thinking they had escaped without damage.

Then Charles Fribley's nervous voice called from the left waist position. The number one engine was throwing oil and smoke. Eldridge feathered it. No need to worry, he thought. They could make it back to Italy on three engines.

Two minutes later, the other propeller on the left side ran away. Eldridge feathered that one, too, but decided to restart number one and run it until the oil was gone. Fribley called a second time, sounding even more panicky. Why was the engine smoking again? Moments later, Fribley repeated his question. Eldridge, too busy to respond, ignored him. After only fifteen minutes, low oil pressure forced him to feather number one again. He ordered the crew to lighten the plane.

Bill Clark crawled out of the nose and stood at the open bomb bay door. Other men formed a bucket brigade, passing along various articles to discard. Clark had just pitched out some ammunition belts when nose gunner Red Braun handed him something. Clark tossed it out. As soon as he let go, Clark felt a sick realization.

He had just thrown out his own parachute.

Clark's mind raced. Usually, the plane carried extra chutes in the waist in case others were damaged. Still, he hesitated. With the bomb bays open, the only way to get there was by tightrope-walking the foot-wide plank suspended between the two halves of the plane. Although he could grab the bomb racks for support, that first step would be a lulu if he slipped.

Archy Roper appeared. Shouting over the roar of the engines was pointless. He motioned with his hands that Clark should shut the bomb bay doors. Clark understood and nodded. They were causing drag; the plane would travel further if they were closed. Even better, shutting them would let him cross the bay in safety.

Clark reached for the hand cranks for the doors. Past them, on the other side of the bays, he spotted Charles Fribley clambering out of the waist and jumping into the open air. Gus Perrone followed. Three other parachutes opened below. Colasante, Houghton, and Quinn must have gone out the floor hatch. All five had abandoned ship without orders. The B-24 now had no rear gunners. If a German fighter happened on them, the plane was doomed. *My God!* thought Clark. *They must have taken Archy's motions as a signal to jump.*

Clark cranked the bomb bay doors shut and completed his trip to the waist. There he found a single remaining life-saving parachute. It was not a chest pack like the one he was used to, but a heavier rear pack—not that it mattered. He edged back across the narrow catwalk carrying his bulky prize.

Someone had to tell Eldridge the news that half the crew was missing. Clark passed the word to engineer Vic Melcher, who informed the pilot.

Eldridge's temper exploded. The bailout was a clear case of cowardice, insubordination, and dereliction of duty. It reflected badly on him as aircraft commander. Roper sat blinking, speechless. An airman abandoning his damaged plane without orders was no different than a soldier leaving his post under fire. It seemed that Fribley had panicked and jumped. The others, on edge themselves, had followed.

Minutes passed. The aircraft descended to seven thousand feet. Conrad Teague told the pilots they had reached Partisan territory. Everyone prepared to jump. Clark reopened the bomb bay. Roper and Eldridge each took a turn at the controls while the other removed his flying boots and replaced them with sturdy GI shoes. Farmhouses dotted the mountains below.

Suddenly, one of the two remaining engines burst into flames; the strain on them had been too much. Eldridge rang the bailout alarm.

The aircraft tipped. One of the pilots would have to hold her steady while the other jumped. Eldridge looked at Roper. "You go on down," he ordered.

Roper tumbled out the bomb bay, hit the slipstream, and spun wildly before he cleared the off-kilter tail and pulled the rip cord. Nothing happened. He yanked again. Then everything went blank.

Roper revived in perfect stillness, floating in midair. A nylon parasol hung overhead. His leather helmet was missing, and his head felt like someone had tried to rip it off. A parachute drifted serenely in the distance. *Good*, he thought. *Hixon got out.*

Roper was floating backward. Looking over his shoulder, Roper could see he was blowing toward a high stone wall. The ground rushed up, and he struck a clear spot, hard.

A uniformed teenager carrying a rifle ran up. His hat bore a red star. "Americano!" cried Roper. "Tito!" exclaimed the boy. A mother and daughter arrived, and then a larger boy. Laughing, they helped Roper to his feet and guided him to a nearby farmhouse.

Soon Partisans brought in Eldridge, Braun, Teague, and Melcher. Red Braun had landed awkwardly and broken his left wrist, and it ached. His friends fashioned a splint and sling as best as they could. The rest of the men were fine, but Eldridge was in a foul mood. A woman offered them some nasty-looking soup. "I'm not eating that slop!" he barked.

That night, gawking farm folk surrounded the airmen as the five of them bedded down on a single straw bed covered with heavy quilts. The Americans gave them a couple of their yellow Mae West inflatable life jackets, hoping they would go away. The peasants inspected them with fascination but showed no sign of leaving. The airmen gave up and slept. A woman kept the fire going as the onlookers stood vigil all night.

Bill Clark arrived the next morning. Around noon, the Partisans brought a cart for Braun. A few hours later, they reached Bosanski Petrovac and linked up with Marrone's men.[4]

■   ■   ■

The crews compared notes. Both had been shot down the same day, and both were missing crew members. Half of Eldridge's crew had bailed out prematurely and might be anywhere. More disquietingly for Marrone's men, Herky and Jim King were still missing. They should have arrived by now if the Partisans had found them.

The Partisans seemed unsure of what to do with the crews, so the airmen killed time by walking around town. Much of it had been razed by dive-bombing Stukas. After some time, an old man named Mr. Elye, called "Eli" by the Americans, appeared to serve as translator. He had lived in Minnesota for a time but returned to Bosnia before the First World War. Through Eli, the airmen came to grasp how much the town had suffered. Most people had lost a loved one to the war. The Germans had destroyed everything they could not carry.

The Partisans had repaid the Germans in kind. A group of them claimed to have just ambushed enemy tanks on a mountain road, thrown Molotov cocktails at them, and rolled them down the mountainside. If true, the victory was a major coup.

The Americans were sleeping peacefully when the women of the house rushed into their rooms in a panic. Eli explained. A strong German force with four tanks stood just twenty miles to the northwest in Bihać. The sounds of battle echoed in the distance. Perhaps the guerrilla raids had turned the Germans' attention their way.

The women took to the hills. The Americans evacuated to Sanski Most, journeying halfway in carts drawn by small, broken-down horses and the rest of the way by train. They arrived in Sanski Most after a twenty-four-hour sleepless journey.[5]

Herky Marrone and Jim King meandered in two days later, accompanied by a sinewy, English-speaking Partisan who called himself Lt. Michael. Their path had taken them through Drvar and Srnetica via rail. Along the way, the Partisans—with Lt. Michael translating—had told glowing tales of the comforts of Sanski Most: plentiful food, cantinas, women, comfortable beds…it sounded wonderful. Their arrival dashed all such hopes. The town appeared dark and dreary, and the food consisted of thin soup for breakfast, lunch, and dinner. George Earll and Gene Dennis had been confined to hospital—a loose term at best. Marrone had seen cleaner outhouses.

The crew gave the pilots the lowdown. About four dozen American fliers were sheltered in town. The Germans had retaken Bosanski Petrovac, the town they had passed through. They and Eldridge's men had gotten out just in time. More Germans occupied Banja Luka to the east and controlled the rail line to the north. They were surrounded.[6]

CHAPTER 9

Point of No Return

No heavy bomber could fly without extensive maintenance. The ground echelon comprised the largest component of any bomb group, with eight men serving on the ground for every airman. Wise pilots made friends with their planes' crew chiefs and treated them as partners in keeping them flying. By all accounts, AAF ground crews preformed with superb skill and dedication. Only the United States, the most motorized country in the world, possessed such a vast pool of top mechanics.

Nevertheless, mechanical failures were bound to occur. By the fall of 1944, many planes had become war-weary relics that belonged in the scrapyard. Aircrews far outnumbered the bombers. Every plane, no matter how tired and battered, flew to its limits.

As a result, mechanical failures caused most aircrews to abort at least one mission during their tours of duty. A squadron of twenty-five to thirty planes could expect two early returns per sortie. Usually, the pilots discovered the problems before the point of no return and made it back to their bases. Sometimes, however, bailing out was the only option.[1]

■   ■   ■

First Lt. Frank Macleod Dick of Brookline, Massachusetts, was studying electrical engineering at Northeastern University when he volunteered for the AAF. Classified as a pilot at Nashville, he passed through Maxwell Field at the same time as Cadet Charles Stanley with a 97 percent academic average. He washed out during pilot training but took the news in stride; he wanted to be a navigator anyway.

A scar on the right side of Dick's hangdog face, the result of a childhood fall, emblemized his difficult youth. His father had died when Frank was nine years old, so his mother worked as a secretary to support the family. Every month he sent her most of his AAF paycheck. His elder brother, Donald, mysteriously avoided the draft. Years later he divulged his secret: an MIT-trained engineer, Donald had worked on the Manhattan Project.

Dick's crew was assigned to the 461st Bomb Group in Italy. On their third mission, his pilot, Lt. Bernard J. Mohan, aborted an attack against Bucharest, Romania—unnecessarily so, in the eyes of the squadron leader. Mohan was relegated to copiloting duties. Four days later, Mohan was shot down and became a prisoner of war.

Now a man without a crew, Dick substituted with others and was soon promoted to lead navigator. Twenty-five tough sorties followed.

On October 4, 1944, the odds caught up with him. Dick's plane, piloted by Lt. Robert Chambers, took hits over Munich. Dick guided it to the nearest friendly territory, Slovenia, where the crew bailed out. Partisans collected them, but the Germans gave chase for a day and a half. At last, the airmen reached safety at a British mission. Eventually, a transport carried them to Italy.

After a week at Capri, Dick returned to action, well aware of how narrow his escape had been. He started flying again on November 11, rotating among the lead crews.[2]

Despite the status associated with being a lead navigator, Dick longed for the comfort of flying with men he knew. His original copilot, First

Lt. Clarence Marshall, had joined cavalry in 1937 but switched to the AAF early in the war. Dick had always thought Marshall would make a fine aircraft commander. Now, with their original pilot busted for the early return, Marshall was given the opportunity to form a new crew. Dick volunteered to join him.

Three other original crewmen signed on as well. Swedish-born ball turret gunner Gosta "Gus" Sundquist could have avoided military service because his job as a draftsman was deemed essential to the war effort, but he volunteered for the AAF anyway. Just as he was due to be sent overseas, a tornado wrecked his family's home. The Army offered him hardship leave, but he turned it down because he would be reassigned to another crew.

Swarthy Joseph DeRosa, the top turret gunner, possessed a firm cleft chin, mischievous brown eyes, and thick dark hair. Whenever he had the opportunity, Sgt. DeRosa regaled his comrades, and the occasional young lady, with songs from his guitar.

The radio operator, Gordon L. Commander, grew up in poverty in the Florida Panhandle. His parents still lived there in a ramshackle home. Tall, thin, and blue-eyed, he already lacked five teeth. As with many soldiers of his time, the Army had given him his first dental care.[3]

■   ■   ■

Six new crewmen joined them for Marshall's first mission as an aircraft commander on December 15, 1944. Their destination would be the Linz marshaling yards, a notorious target for the 461st. The bomb group had lost twelve planes there on July 25, the blackest day in its history. Marshall's plane for the day would be *Jake's Nabor*, a beat-up old B-24 that had joined the 461st on July 31 as a replacement for one of the planes lost over Linz. Few planes in the bomb group looked more haggard; Marshall and his hybrid crew would just have to take their chances with her.

Perhaps in recognition of Marshall's rookie status as an aircraft commander, the brass assigned Lt. Calvin Earl Jarnagin, a seasoned first pilot who had earned a Distinguished Flying Cross, as his copilot. Like Marshall, Jarnagin was a Texan who had started in the cavalry. He had applied for a transfer once he realized the Army treated horses better than its men.

Their bombardier for the day, Lt. LeRoy Nayes, had flown just two prior missions, but one had been with Marshall and the other with Jarnagin, so he knew both pilots.

The new enlisted men, however, were strangers to Marshall and to one another. As Nayes took his periodic oxygen checks, each responded with a distinct accent. Flight engineer Calvin Steinberg answered in Brooklynese. He served as their chief enlisted man even though he was just nineteen. Wiry tail gunner Sgt. Albert G. Hill replied with a soft Georgia drawl peppered with ungrammatical "ain'ts" that belied his detailed knowledge of every enlisted man's position on the plane. A devout born-again Christian, Hill believed the Lord would be with him, even if he were killed—a reassuring thought when one faced death every few days.[4]

Aerial cameraman James Martino's Italian accent reflected his upbringing with immigrant parents. He had volunteered for the duty thinking it was the quickest way to finish his tour, but most of his friends in the photographic section had disappeared over enemy territory. Martino himself had experienced several narrow escapes, including an emergency landing on Vis. Now, just three missions short of going home, it was odd that he had never run into any of the other crew members before.[5]

Jan Wroclawski's thick Polish accent stood out from the rest. The muscular nose turret gunner—the oldest of the crew at twenty-nine—had experienced more of life than the rest could imagine. He had been born in the United States, but his father returned the family to their native Poland when he was six years old.

An expert swimmer, glider pilot, and canoeist, Wroclawski had attended the Polish Olympic camp as a gymnast in 1935. The next year, however, when Hitler hosted the games in Berlin, Poland failed to send a male gymnastics team. Wroclawski's athletic career seemed to be over, so he became an apprentice watchmaker. He thought the Germans might leave him alone after they conquered Poland. After all, Jan spoke German, had married an ethnic German, and counted many ethnic Germans as his friends. Besides, he was an American citizen.

Things changed when Jan purchased his Jewish employer's shop to prevent it from being confiscated by the Nazis. The Gestapo took notice, and Jan's father-in-law, a police officer, warned him he was about to be arrested. The multilingual Wroclawski fled to Portugal and managed to save enough money for his passage to the United States. There he became eligible for the draft and joined the AAF. His wife in Poland died of tuberculosis while he trained as an aerial gunner.

Today's mission with Marshall would be Wroclawski's final combat flight—if he could only survive it.[6]

■   ■   ■

The 461st crossed the picturesque Austrian Alps and droned toward Linz. Everything seemed routine until Marshall's number one propeller started vibrating. Soon it spun uncontrollably and would not feather. The last thing Marshall wanted to do was abort his first mission as an aircraft commander, but he really had no choice. Reluctantly, he asked Jarnagin to call the flight leader to tell him they had to turn back.

Frank Dick gave Marshall a heading toward the safe zone in central Bosnia. Marshall ducked *Jake's Nabor* away from the formation and ordered the crew to jettison the bombs and all other excess weight, including the huge aerial camera.

Before long the number three and four propellers started choking as though starved of gas. Marshall ordered Calvin Steinberg to put them on a cross-feed from the other fuel tanks, but the engines failed to respond. The plane sank to nine thousand feet. Every minute cost five hundred more. Dick knew they had not reached Partisan territory, but *Jake's Nabor* would only carry them so far. Marshall told the crew to prepare to bail out.[7]

Sundquist, Commander, Martino, and Hill lined up at the camera hatch. Sunshine radiated from above. Below, bleak clouds pierced by the occasional mountaintop blanketed the earth. The bailout alarm rang. Sundquist left first, then Commander. Jim Martino followed, trying to look more confident than he felt. His parachute opened, and he floated amid the silent clouds.

Martino broke through the undercast to find a great body of water spread as far as the eye could see. Intermittent trees dotted the area, as though it had just recently flooded. Two parachutes floated on the surface with figures struggling beneath them, likely Sundquist and Commander. Martino's mind kicked into gear. If he did not do something fast, he would soon be in the same predicament.

Martino could not miss landing in the water. He might, however, avoid getting trapped under his parachute. He inflated his Mae West and released two of the three fasteners connecting his chute to his harness. He grabbed the straps with one hand and snapped the final clip open with the other. At the last moment, he let go and plunged deep into the frigid waters.

The Mae West buoyed him back to the surface. Martino gasped for air and looked around. His parachute settled to the side as he had hoped. His body, however, already felt numb with cold. He spotted a tiny island and swam toward it, his limbs growing weaker with every stroke. Blackness embraced him as he touched solid ground.[8]

■　　■　　■

Albert Hill followed Martino out of the plane and yanked his rip cord. He felt no jolt, so he looked up to see if his parachute had opened. A white canopy fluttered above. It had opened so smoothly he had not felt it.

The mists faded to reveal the water below. Hill had expected to see mountains, or at least land. *Am I over the ocean?* he wondered. Isolated trees spangled the seascape.

Somehow, in dozens of square miles of icy water, his parachute snagged onto a solitary, water-bound tree. So far, the Lord had taken care of Hill, but a watery wasteland still surrounded him. Providence would have to intervene again if he were to survive.[9]

■   ■   ■

LeRoy Nayes waited second in line to bail out from the front bomb bay. DeRosa stood before him. Behind were Wroclawski and Dick, with Steinberg watching to make sure they all left. DeRosa peered down at the undercast as if frozen by a premonition of doom. Nayes stepped around him. "Follow me!" he cried, and leapt.

Nayes counted to a quick ten and pulled the rip cord. Nothing happened. The plane moved out of view, and a knife seemed to pierce his ears. The pilot chute in his chest pack was wedged in the pin holders. His fingers found the pins and released them. He wrenched to a halt midair.

A deluge interspersed with lonely trees unfolded below. One spot might be a tiny island with a shack. The water rushed up and Nayes braced for a wet reception. Instead, his chute caught a stray tree branch and stuck. Like Hill, Nayes had hung up in one of the few trees in the floodplain.

Nayes remembered the island with the shack. He could not see it, but he thought he knew where it was. He felt exposed hanging there. The wrong people might have spotted him. If he had any chance of making it to the shelter, he should go soon, before dark, and before he grew weaker from hunger and exposure.

He decided to try it. Inflating his Mae West, he released himself from the parachute, dropped into the icy water, and paddled in the direction of the island. The trees thickened, and he lost his bearings. His water-logged clothing dragged. His limbs grew numb. He could not reach a tree, much less his elusive island. "Lord, this is as far as I can go on my own," he prayed. "My life is in your hands." His head bobbed up for a last gasp.

The next thing he knew, Nayes lay next to a fire in the dark wearing his long underwear and an overcoat. An old man mouthed a single word: "Partizan."

"American," breathed Nayes. As soon as he became partially dried and revived, his rescuer helped him into a small boat, and they set off into the mists. The man seemed to be in a hurry.[10]

■   ■   ■

Albert Hill hung from his tree like a forsaken marionette. He felt the urge to free himself but had nowhere to go. He grabbed the trunk, rested his feet on branches, and released the parachute. He emptied his escape kit into his pockets. Finally, he untied his GI boots from his harness and put them on. He was ready, though for what he did not know.

A flat-bottomed bateau glided out of the mists. A teenager no more than five feet tall beckoned him down. Hill plopped on, and the lad paddled off urgently, using a narrow ten-foot oar. Soon they found a tiny knoll protruding from the water. On it lay a blue-faced, semiconscious Jim Martino. Hill and the boy hauled him into the boat and pushed off.

Shots pierced the foggy air. The youngster darted his boat among the trees. Hill pried off some of Martino's soaked clothes and replaced them with his own. Their gondolier, wearing only a light jacket, seemed immune to the cold. He weaved through the labyrinth until they reached his destination, an island with a rickety shack sheltering an older man, perhaps his father.

The older man and Hill massaged Martino's face, arms, and legs and warmed him by a fire. He did not recognize Hill and could barely speak. Mercifully, he fell back into a deep slumber. Two hours later Martino opened his eyes. His ribcage and back hurt like hell. He had let go of his parachute a bit too high and cracked some ribs when he hit the water.

Soon Nayes and his rescuer joined them on the island. Fortunately, Nayes's Partisan spoke Italian. He told Martino they had to move on: enemy patrols still sought them.

After a small meal of bread and raw bacon, the group set off in the two boats. They had not traveled far when a German voice challenged them from a distant boat. Gunfire erupted. Bullets plinked into the water. Fighting was out of the question, as none of the airmen bore a sidearm, and the Partisans' lone gun was an antique flintlock without its flint. The airmen ducked while the Partisans worked the oars.

The Partisans rowed in and out of coves until their pursuers gave up the chase. Around dusk, they reached an island offering a small shed for shelter. They stayed the night, not daring to light a fire.

The group started off again in the morning. They paddled until late afternoon, when they came upon a larger, heavily wooded island sheltering eight refugees, an armed Partisan, and Jan Wroclawski.[11]

■   ■   ■

Like Martino, Wroclawski had loosened his parachute just above the water. Two German soldiers in a rowboat picked him up immediately. They continued their search, unaware that their captive was a world-class athlete who understood every word they spoke.

Wroclawski noted the Germans' heavy woolen overcoats and full backpacks. The expert canoeist waited for his chance. When they neared one of the barren islands, he leapt overboard, being sure to capsize the boat in the process. The Germans thrashed and sank. Wroclawski swam to the mound of dirt. Eventually, Partisans found him and brought him to this camp.

Wroclawski had dislocated his shoulder but felt okay. He had seen Joe DeRosa land in deep water. Wroclawski had spotted Frank Dick's chute, too, but lost track of him in the murky clouds.[12]

■   ■   ■

An elderly crone, two young Slavic women—one of them carrying a small child—and four men clung to their lives on the island. Martino and Wroclawski—who had picked up several languages in his travels—gleaned that they had fled from nearby Kutina when German and Ustashe terror squads began rounding up victims in retaliation for Partisan sabotage. They were trying to reach a Partisan refuge in the mountains.

The childless young woman told them an AAF officer had landed near a Ustashe-held village and was captured immediately. Two German SS men took charge, escorted him to *Jake's Nabor*'s wreckage, and asked him some questions. When the airman refused to answer, one of the SS men shot him down in cold blood. The woman could not say which officer had been killed.

She could, however, tell them they had bailed out over the Lonjsko Polje swamp at the confluence of the Ilova and Trebez rivers. Heavy rains had recently flooded the marsh beyond the limits shown on their maps. The infamous Jasenovac prison complex lay nearby. Tens of thousands of Serbs, Jews, and Partisan sympathizers had been exterminated there. Patrols from the compound often searched the swamps for escapees; the airmen and the refugees would have to be very lucky to evade capture.[13]

A steady drizzle fell through the night. Their flimsy lean-tos offered little shelter, and fires had to be kept low. Sleep eluded most.

They set out for a better refuge in the misty dawn, first by boat and then on foot. At midnight, a scout reported the path ahead was blocked by the enemy. They would have to retreat to the island and try another time. The group spent a dejected night retracing their steps.

After a day of rest, the Partisans decided to try something else: they would send the Americans to a village adjacent to a railroad line near Kutina. Intermittent German pillboxes guarded the tracks, but the airmen might find an opportunity to cross them. The plan would not work for a large group, however, so the civilians would have to follow in time.

The Americans took their leave and were escorted to their destination, a small collection of farmhouses offering barns as shelters. The

Germans patrolled regularly, so the airmen spread out among the struc-tures to avoid being captured as a group. They would meet at night to share news and decide next steps.

Several close calls over the next few days made the airmen nervous. Hill, Nayes, and Martino were each nearly caught by German search parties. Their luck could not hold out forever. The Americans asked the Partisans to escort them across the railroad tracks as soon as possible.

Soon the attempt was arranged. At the appointed time, the airmen met two boys who appeared to be no more than fourteen years of age. Their lives were in the hands of children.

Wroclawski translated as one of the boys gave instructions: "Watch your feet. Don't step on any branches. And whatever you do, don't touch the rails—vibrations carry."

Bunkers interspersed the tracks every two hundred yards. No section was beyond the sight of sentries. The group would have to cross at a midpoint. If they were discovered, machine guns would cut them down before they reached cover on the other side.

Upon reaching a promising spot, they crawled on their bellies as quickly as silence allowed. Near the tracks, the glow of a full moon peeked from behind the clouds and danced off newly fallen snow. Conspicuous shadows elongated their figures. Still, there was no turning back.

Flares shot into the sky from down the line. Gunfire and searchlights erupted. The airmen froze, eyes alert. Sensing the eyes of the enemy were diverted, the young guides motioned the airmen to stand up and run. They passed beyond the clearing and moved through the woods until their guides told them they could speak; the worst was over.

They reached the Partisan stronghold at Poljana three days later. Mice and rats infested the encampment. The ailing Martino was placed in a bed and covered in quilts. A Partisan warned Martino against molesting the female soldiers. "Touch them?" he protested. "I can barely move!"

Five days later, the Partisans sent the airmen on another long hike to a British mission at the Sixth Partisan Corps headquarters in Pakrac.

Along the way, their guide showed them the remains of a man who had been tortured to death by the Ustashe. Every bone in his body seemed broken.

They finally arrived on December 29. The well-supplied British offered luxuries such as powdered eggs and cigarettes. A generator provided lights during the evenings.

A British-manned Dakota transport picked them up three weeks later. Wroclawski stood between the pilots as the ship took off from the valley. Jan, who had braved so many dangers, blanched as the plane crept toward the mountain crest blocking their path. The Brits gazed at the approaching rock face with glacial equanimity. They scraped over with mere feet to spare. The pilot turned to the copilot. "What do you know," he deadpanned. "She's a bit too old for that."[14]

■   ■   ■

A few days after bailing out, Calvin Steinberg sat in an interrogation room in Zagreb. The Germans had captured him as soon as he touched down. Two SS officers sauntered in. Steinberg's name alone disclosed his Jewish origins. They might not respect his status as a prisoner of war.

We know about you and your crew, they bragged in perfect English. *You are from the 461st Bomb Group. You were on your way to Linz when you went down. We captured your crewmate, Lt. Frank Dick. We took him to your plane's wreckage the morning after you bailed out. We asked him about your crew. He refused to answer, so we shot him.*

Steinberg wondered what they were getting at. He was not privy to any secrets, and he knew nothing about where his crew was. As the SS men prattled on, probing him with their eyes, it dawned on him that this was not an interrogation. The sadists were seeking pleasure from telling him they had murdered his crewmate. Steinberg stared back impassively. He was not going to give these thugs the slightest iota of satisfaction.

Eventually, the Nazis ran out of blather. They departed, leaving the airman to his Luftwaffe captors.[15]

■   ■   ■

Marshall and Jarnagin had flown on for several minutes before bailing out. The extra time in the air served them well: both landed on solid ground. A farmer found them and contacted the Partisans. They reached Sanski Most three days later via Prijedor.

Four men from Marshall's crew had died: Gordon Commander, Joseph DeRosa, Gus Sundquist, and Frank Dick. Coincidentally, they were all members of his original crew. They had perished—and Calvin Steinberg was captured—purely due to mechanical failure. No other plane from the 461st Bomb Group was lost that day.[16]

CHAPTER 10

Flying on Borrowed Time

On December 16, 1944, the Fifteenth Air Force unleashed an "Oil Blitz" designed to cripple the enemy's fuel production once and for all. The same day, the Germans launched the massive ground offensive in the Ardennes Forest that came to be known as the Battle of the Bulge. The Eighth Air Force immediately stopped attacking strategic targets in favor of supporting the beleaguered Allied ground troops. Even so, poor flying weather severely hindered its operations.

The Fifteenth carried on against Germany's oil supply, attacking five major refineries on December 18: Odertal, Oświęcim, Blechhammer North and South, and Vienna/Floridsdorf. It lost twenty-seven aircraft that day, its highest toll since the Russians overran Ploesti in August. Five of those downed planes contributed twenty-three new airmen to Sanski Most's growing list of evadees.[1]

■　　■　　■

Harry Blank Jr. and his crew joined the 451st Bomb Group on December 2, 1944, just in time to join the maximum-effort raids of the Oil Blitz.

Blank's success in becoming a pilot testified to his fortitude and determination. His father had died in 1938 after a long bout with tuberculosis, and his mother supported their family by operating a tavern. Harry had wanted to join the service after the Japanese attack on Pearl Harbor but delayed for a year because his mother needed his help with the business.

His path to becoming a pilot had not been easy. During one training flight, Blank became lost and landed at a nearby airfield. His instructor told him he was "flying on borrowed time" and ordered him to write a thousand-word essay on the hazards of flight to be read aloud to his peers. Blank completed the assignment but finished each paragraph with the phrase "it is no fun flying on borrowed time." The fuming instructor ordered repeated flight checks for Blank, but he passed each one.[2]

Most of Blank's crew had also graduated from the school of hard knocks. They were quarrelsome and rambunctious, but they knew their business.

Radio operator Keith Owens was a regular guy who liked chasing girls, though he never caught any; gambling, though he always lost; and imbibing ten-cent beers, though he swore off drinking after every binge. He kept a daily diary but wrote to his mother so rarely she nearly gave him up for dead. Owens did not like authority or officers in general, but otherwise he found military life to be tolerable. He found its regular lectures on venereal disease to be downright fascinating. His radio courses were less interesting, but he passed them anyway.

Owens liked the other members of the crew except William Otway, the top turret gunner. Otway listed his civilian job as "professional hockey player" and claimed to have played for a minor-league team. He also professed to be an orphan. In truth, he was an illegal immigrant from Ontario whose true last name was Yurkoski. One of twelve children, he had run away from home at seventeen. Perhaps he had played pro hockey—he was good with his fists—but nobody knew for sure. He joined the American Army in 1937 at the age of twenty. A big-hearted, effusive man, he might hug you one moment and sock you in the jaw the next. No one messed with him.

Owens's best friend on the crew was nose gunner Richard "Dick" Kelly, a lanky, handsome man with a Roman nose. He and Owens sometimes hung out with their flight engineer, Tom Koballa, but Koballa was a lightweight drinker who could not keep up with them.

Tail gunner William Ceely mostly kept to himself. Ceely's mother had died when he was two years old, and his father had placed him with another family. A small man with pixie-like features, he carried himself with quiet, whimsical dignity. A cigarette dangled constantly from his lips. The hijinks shared by the other crew members were not for him.

Three last-minute crew changes occurred just before they shipped overseas. John Turk became Blank's copilot without any time for stateside flying. The AAF reassigned their bombardier to another crew, so their navigator, Flight Officer Robert Mitchell of Wausau, Wisconsin, became an instant navigator/bombardier.

The new ball turret gunner, William "Carey" Rainey of Brownsville, Texas, proved to be temperamental, cantankerous, and a heavy drinker. Within days of his joining the crew, their bomb group threw a party to celebrate—or mourn—being sent overseas. Rainey and Owens drank too much and fell into a fistfight. Neither was hurt and the incident was mostly forgotten.

Blank had lost three familiar men and gained two he did not know with no time to break them in. He hoped for a few practice flights in Italy before they went into combat.[3]

■   ■   ■

The day after Blank joined the 451st Bomb Group, his squadron commander took him on an orientation flight to test Blank's abilities. They formed a two-plane formation, with Blank flying tightly off the commander's right wing.

The commander called Blank over the radio. "Loosen up," he ordered. Blank's plane was too close for comfort. Usually, new arrivals flew too loosely. Blank replied, "No, sir. I fly like this all the time. It's easier this way." Blank never bragged, but he knew he was an excellent formation flier. He stayed with the commander on every turn.

Once they reached the ground, the commander approached Blank with wonder in his eyes. "That's the best formation flying I've ever seen," he gushed. "How did you do that?" Blank let him in on a technique he had invented. He let his copilot watch the instruments while Blank kept his eyes on the hands of the lead plane's pilot. That way he could tell how the plane would move without waiting for it to respond to the controls. The commander had never heard of anything like it. He predicted Blank would be promoted to flight leader before long.[4]

■   ■   ■

Blank's crew took only one practice flight before being scheduled for their first combat mission on December 16. Their target would be Brux, Czechoslovakia, the only enemy refinery comparable to the complexes at Blechhammer. A veteran first pilot took command, so Blank slid over to the copilot's chair. Turk was excused. Similarly, Mitchell was replaced by a combat-experienced navigator.

Their B-24 gave them problems on the hardstand, and they took off late. Unable to catch up to their squadron, they linked up with the Forty-Seventh Bomb Wing heading for Innsbruck, Austria, a shorter flight and a far easier target.

Everybody on board thanked their lucky stars until the number four engine started to smoke. The veteran flier feathered it and ordered flight engineer Tom Koballa to cut its fuel to prevent a fire. Koballa followed the order, but the substitute navigator panicked and mistakenly closed the gas valve for the engine next to it. Both engines on the right side stood idle as the plane dropped out of formation and headed for home.

Within minutes, tail gunner Bill Ceely yelled, "German fighters at six o'clock!" Owens, manning the right waist gun, spotted them too. A pair of Me-109s were charging straight at them. He turned to Otway at the other waist gun. "Look!" he cried. The fighters darted beneath their B-24 before either could shoot. The planes circled and charged from the rear. Tracers slid past Owens's window. Ceely returned fire, but the fighters turned for another attack.

A solo B-24 did not stand a chance against a pair of Me-109s, especially with two engines out. The pilot ducked into a cloud bank and announced he was making a run for Switzerland.

The number three engine kicked on again. Koballa had restored its gasoline feed. By the time the B-24 emerged from the clouds, the fighters were gone. Owens spent the ride home kicking himself for missing his chance to shoot at them.

Blank and his men became the talk of the camp. Few lone B-24s survived a fighter attack, much less a crew on their maiden flight. An airman buttonholed Owens in the mess hall. "I heard you got two enemy fighters on your first mission!" he exclaimed. Owens reluctantly set the man straight. Eventful as the mission had been, it was just one down with thirty-four more to go.[5]

The next day, copilot John Turk and navigator Bob Mitchell flew their first mission with another crew against the refinery at Odertal. The Germans, determined to defend their dwindling oil supplies, sent Fw 190 interceptors against their formation in force. Sixteen Liberators were lost. Now Turk and Mitchell were veterans, too.[6]

■   ■   ■

On December 18, the third day of the Oil Blitz, the Blank crew flew into combat as a unit for the first time. Their B-24, the *Little Butch II*, was an unpainted, six-month veteran of hard use. Nevertheless, the plane displayed no mechanical problems on the way to Blechhammer South.

The target was obscured by cloud cover, so the formation set up its Mickey radar for the bomb run. Just before bombs away, the gods of war frowned: the clouds parted, offering a clear view of the B-24s to the flak gunners below. All hell broke loose as the lead bombardiers made final adjustments on their instruments.

Owens's window offered an excellent view of the grim spectacle. Black fireworks exploded at eye level. A plane ahead took a direct hit in the nose. Its wheel doors blew open, but the shell failed to explode. A second punch to the belly followed. The aircraft turned east toward Russia. Another B-24 spouted smoke and dropped below. Other planes took hits but stayed in formation.

"Owens! Get me out of here! I'm hit!" cried Rainey from the ball. A Plexiglas panel had shattered. Owens moved to the lifting mechanism and began hoisting the turret into the plane. "Goddamn!" cursed Owens, "This thing is hard to pump up!" Something was wrong. Owens felt dizzy, and his vision blurred.

Owens awoke to find Ceely hunched over him pressing a portable oxygen bottle to his face. Now and then Ceely took a swig for himself. Owens had inadvertently disconnected himself from his oxygen hose. Ceely had emerged from the tail turret just in time.

Owens and Ceely lifted the ball into the waist, and Rainey climbed out. Despite his outcry, Rainey had suffered only a few cuts to his face. He set to work throwing ammunition boxes out of the bomb bay. Owens felt too weak to help. He rested against the bulkhead covered in his own vomit. Ceely sat beside him shaking uncontrollably. The engines did not sound right. The plane's broken bomb bay doors flapped in the wind—the bombs were gone.[7]

■   ■   ■

Blank coaxed the plane forward. The number one engine was dead, and the number four supercharger was misbehaving. Pilots were supposed to run their engines at maximum power for no more than five minutes, and by now he had run his good ones at that pace for over an hour.

Blank called the group leader to tell him he was low on gas. *Stay with the formation*, ordered the commander. Mindful of the fighter attack the day before, he wanted every B-24's guns at the ready for mutual protection.

The longer Blank stayed at full power, the less distance his plane would be able to travel. He ordered Koballa to transfer gas from the bad engines to the good. Koballa did as he was told and checked the gas gauges. The tanks for the good engines had lost, not gained, fuel. There must be a leak in the lines. Blank again asked for permission to drop out of formation.

"Permission denied," replied the commander. "Stay with the group."

Little Butch II was still over Hungary. Blank could obey orders and condemn his crew to bailing out over enemy territory, or he could risk a court-martial by disobeying a direct order. If he did, he might make it to Yugoslavia. He alone would be responsible for the consequences.

Blank did not hesitate. His first duty was to his men. "Goodbye!" he cried. "We'll see you later." If he ever met that commander again, the reunion would not be pleasant. He nosed his plane out of formation. Mitchell gave Blank a heading for the Partisan safe zone in Bosnia.

Owens had not recovered from his bout of anoxia, but he had the sense to plug himself back into the interphone system. Not much time had passed when he heard Blank's voice in his earphones. "Prepare to bail out. We're losing fuel rapidly. Koballa is watching the gauges. He'll let us know when we have ten minutes of gas."

A grisly thought entered Owens's mind as he tied his GI shoes to his harness. He had seen a training film in which a man had panicked after jumping and torn half of his stomach out trying to find his rip cord. Owens vowed he would not make the same mistake.

His parachute affixed, Owens edged out onto the catwalk spanning the open bomb bay. Maybe, he thought, he should send an SOS from his radio. He reached the other side and peered into the radio room. Frozen air whipped through a basketball-sized puncture next to his station. Good thing he hadn't been there during the bomb run. Otway, Koballa, and Mitchell huddled around the gas gauge. Mitchell spotted Owens. "Jump, Owens!" he yelled. He pointed downward. Owens aped his gesture quizzically. Mitchell repeated his motion. They must be on their last thimbleful of gas.

Owens did not need to be told a third time. He jumped.[8]

■   ■   ■

Blank spotted a clearing in the clouds and went for it. It was best to know what they would be jumping into. Mountains materialized below. The engines sputtered. Blank rang the bailout buzzer. As everyone scrambled out, he called the formation leader again to tell him they were gone. Maybe now the SOB would understand his decision to leave the formation.

Everyone else had jumped. Now it was the pilots' turn. Blank trimmed the plane and tried to slide his seat back. It was jammed. He was trapped between the steering column and the seat. Pushing the yoke forward would put the plane into a dive, and there were only a couple thousand feet between him and the mountains below. Still, it was the only way.[9]

■   ■   ■

Owens, mindful of the graphic training film, held the D-ring of his rip cord tight enough to crack it. One yank, and the chute exploded open, catching him meanly in the crotch. He worried the Germans might shoot at him in the air; that had been in the training film, too. Owens touched down, knees bent, hands catching the ground—a perfect four-point landing.

A crowd of men, women, and children gathered. An old bushy-haired farmer wearing a sheepskin coat cried "Partizan! Tito! Partizan!" Younger men with red stars on their caps arrived bearing rifles. A limping teenager tried a few words in English. Owens relaxed.

Folk gathered his parachute and escorted him to a nearby farmhouse. They sat Owens at a low table and poured clear liquid—*rakija*—into small glasses. Women stared in from a doorway. At a signal, they all took a swig. Owens gagged and coughed to the delight of everyone. Chunks of smoked meat, bread, and cheese appeared.

After several rounds from the bottle, the men shooed the women away. Owens inflated the Mae West and the men tried it on, along with his leather helmet and flight googles. One donned Owens's oxygen mask and spoke through its hose. Everyone laughed. As dusk gathered, Owens needed to relieve himself and asked for the facilities. One of his new friends pointed to a pigpen outside.

Owens was just finishing when he heard voices and the slow clatter of horse hooves. Figures emerged from the dark. Dick Kelly sat astride a horse led by a Partisan. His ankle had turned on landing. Bob Mitchell walked beside him. Owens threw his arms around him; he had never been so glad to see anyone. Mitchell was happy to be seen. He had free-fallen an uncomfortable stretch trying to get his chute open.

Kelly's ankle hurt, but it did not seem to be broken. Owens and Mitchell helped him into the house. The women cleared a room and threw straw on the floor with a few blankets. Owens slept soundly, comforted by his companions and the *rakija* in his belly.[10]

The next day, an elderly guide led Owens, Mitchell, and Kelly to Sanski Most. Owens could not believe his eyes when he spotted an American lieutenant strolling through town. After introductions, the man explained that some sixty Americans lived in Sanski Most, with more arriving all the time.

Carey Rainey and Bill Otway came in the next day. Bushy-bearded Chetniks had grabbed them first, but Partisans had scared them away. As with Mitchell, Rainey's parachute had not popped open when he pulled his rip cord. He had worked on it with the sincerest dedication he ever displayed in the Army.

The five men were assigned to a house with two other recent arrivals, Herky Marrone and Jim King. Their elderly host, "Pops," had learned English working in Duluth, Minnesota.

Eventually, Owens sorted out that his crew had jumped into the no-man's-land between Sanski Most and German-held Banja Luka. This was ominous news. The Germans stood far closer than he had supposed. The Partisans knew nothing of the whereabouts of Harry Blank, John Turk, Tom Koballa, and Bill Ceely. Word of their fate would not come until after the war.[11]

CHAPTER 11

The ICARUS Mission Arrives

Henry Wunderlich's maternal grandparents had been born in Germany. They often babysat, and young Henry picked up a good deal of their language as he grew up in Buffalo, New York. Eventually, Henry became aware that his grandfather, Andrew Ostermeier, held a stronger allegiance to the old country than his adopted one. In fact, the kindly old man regularly attended meetings held by the pro-Nazi German-American Bund.

Henry, as loyal an American as anyone, signed up for the Army at seventeen, but he had to wait until he was eighteen to serve. His father suggested he spend the time attending college, so Wunderlich enrolled at the University of Buffalo. There Henry discovered his poorly educated grandparents had taught him ungrammatical German. His professor lamented that he would have been better off learning the language from scratch.

The University of Buffalo's first College Training Detachment class—including a young private named Charles Stanley—arrived during Henry's second semester. Henry admired their sharp marching formations, smart uniforms, and rigorous curriculum. He volunteered for the AAF and passed the qualifying exams.

Wunderlich was awaiting flight school when his sergeant rounded the men up and announced that the Army already had enough officers in the pipeline. The recruits could either stay in the AAF and become gunners or transfer to the infantry. They had one hour to decide.

The cadets had not signed up to be gunners. Some bitterly opted for the infantry. Wunderlich decided to fly in whatever capacity he was given. Eventually, he became a tail gunner.

At first, he found the position to be disorienting. The B-24's turret extended far behind the aircraft, and the only parts of it he could see from there were twin tail rudders to his right and left. To enter the turret, Wunderlich had to grab the top handholds, swing his feet up, and slide in like a trapeze artist. To exit, he would chin himself, kick against the turret, and swing backwards into the waist. It would be a difficult maneuver in an emergency.

Worse, as with the ball turret gunner, Wunderlich suffered some danger of being trapped in the position. The tail turret needed to face directly rearward for him to exit. If the hydraulic system failed, his comrades in the waist would have to crank the turret manually to release him.[1]

■   ■   ■

At Casper, Wyoming, Wunderlich met the core of his crew: pilot Frederick Coe, copilot Kenneth "Dale" Hoffman, flight engineer John "Jack" Mulvaney, and radio operator Jules Levine.

The key to a good crew was a good pilot, and pipe-smoking Fred Coe proved to be exceptional. He was reflective, focused, and soft-spoken, and his warm blue eyes balanced his fierce cheekbones. The crew found him to be demanding yet fair. Coe's family owned a farm near Mt. Vernon, Ohio, and Coe hoped to settle into a quiet career in agriculture after the war.

Wunderlich thought the Army knew what it was doing when it assigned Flight Officer Dale Hoffman to be Coe's copilot. Coe flew so well that he needed little more than a sidekick to assist him. Hoffman was bigger than Coe, but younger and more approachable. His light touch provided a nice counterpoint to Coe's seriousness. He had likely been relegated to flight officer status because he was Jewish.

Jack Mulvaney, the oldest and most mature crewman, served as the flight engineer. A strongly built, black-haired man, he seldom spoke, but he had good reason when he did. Mulvaney had grown up in a Catholic family of eight children in the coalmining hills of Kentucky. He knew poverty and appreciated the opportunity the Army had given him to improve his lot in life.

If Mulvaney acted like the crew's big brother, Jules Levine took the part of the rascally younger one. A Jewish kid from Brooklyn, Levine was small and not particularly handsome, but he was loaded with chutzpah. The guys could not understand why the ladies found him so irresistible. A born tinkerer, he fit in naturally as the radio operator. Wunderlich enjoyed his company and nicknamed him "Smokey"—a reference to Levine's ever-present cigars.[2]

The crew joined the 459th Bomb Group in late October 1944. Over the next six weeks, Coe broke in with other crews while everyone else sat idle. At last, on December 18, they learned their maiden target would be the Oświęcim oil refinery. The core five—Coe, Hoffman, Mulvaney, Levine, and Wunderlich—would go. But since only Coe had seen combat, the rest of his men were replaced with veterans.

The 459th assigned its bombardiers from a pool. Coe drew Sylvester Brown Jr., a lean man with a pencil mustache who smoked heavily. He and the other bombardiers were cautioned to be especially careful with their aim on this mission. The Auschwitz III slave labor camp stood next to the Oświęcim plant, and no one wanted to hit it by mistake.

Navigator Ed Kutch had notched just three sorties but was already well regarded in the squadron. The top student of his navigation class, he remained modest and unassuming. He had learned that "a navigator is only as sharp at his pencil," and he always carried a healthy supply.

Top turret gunner Leo Wilensky, ball turret gunner Almondo Champi, and waist gunner/photographer Joe Foto would fill out the crew. All were well-annealed veterans from the same original crew. They had trained at Biggs Field in El Paso at the same time as Lt. Charles Stanley's men. On the night Stanley saw a B-24 slam into nearby Mount Franklin, they had been aboard the plane that barely avoided following it into the mountainside.

Joe Foto had grown up on colorful Bourbon Street in New Orleans and spoke with a gentle southern accent. In high school, Foto worked odd jobs for Gertrude Dix, a famous retired madam. Foto often washed her pink Cadillac convertible and drove it while running errands for her. As a reward, she loaned it to him for his senior prom, and he was the envy of the school. A natural athlete, Foto had boxed and played on a citywide championship basketball team.

Foto had recently mailed a letter to his brother Louis. "Someday," he wrote, "Mom may get a telegram which may be either 'missing in action' or well, you know. If I am ever missing the government will give all the details. What I am trying to get at is that [being] missing in action does not mean that I have been _____ , we may have bailed out over Germany and be prisoners or something.... Do you think I should try to explain it to her beforehand in case it ever happens?" Louis's reply had not yet arrived, so Joe had not written his mother to prepare her.[3]

■   ■   ■

Coe's men gathered at the *Eight Ball*, an old B-24J fitted with an aerial camera. As Joe Foto assumed his takeoff position in the waist, Jack Mulvaney stuck his head in and asked him whether he knew how to transfer fuel in this model B-24. Foto had never seen that kind of system either. Mulvaney muttered that he would figure it out and returned to his station.

Near the Yugoslavian coast, the formation encountered thick, billowing cumulous clouds. An eerie black fog swallowed them. Pilots could not see their own wingtips, much less the other planes. Everyone kept a sharp eye.

They broke out of the mire ten minutes later. No planes had collided, but a mosaic of bomb group tail markings bejeweled the air. The sky transformed into a hopeful blue, but the formation could not be reconstituted. Four extemporaneous groups formed. Two bunches headed toward alternate targets. Coe joined a pack led by his group leader, Lt. Colonel Harrison Christy, and resumed a course toward Oświęcim. A second cluster comprised mainly of B-24s from the 454th Bomb Group followed behind.

Coe's group crossed into Hungary forty minutes behind schedule. Time spent was gas spent. Christy's lead plane took a corrective turn. His navigator had missed some landmarks. More time and gas were lost.

Coe was wrestling with a finicky engine when top turret gunner Leo Wilensky failed to respond to an oxygen check. Coe called Joe Foto in the waist. "Come to the half deck," he ordered. "Leo needs help."

Foto grabbed two blue oxygen bottles, squeezed through the bomb bay, and found an unconscious Wilensky slumped in his turret. He pressed the oxygen mask over Wilensky's face and called Coe to report he was coming to. "Stay where you are," the pilot ordered. "We're near the target. Go back to the waist after bombs away."

Foto had not carried his parachute to the front of the plane. The flak would start soon, and he wanted it in case they took a hit. "I'm going back where my pack is," he replied. He hung up before Coe could respond and edged back over the catwalk as quickly as possible.

Henry Wunderlich sat in the tail preparing mentally for his first dose of flak. He could not wear his chest pack at his station, so his parachute lay in the waist on the other side of the turret doors. *I'm a fool*, he thought. *What if my turret gets blown off? What if the waist takes a hit and the parachute is torn apart? What if the parachute shifts and I can't find it? Next time, I'm going to bring a backpack parachute I can wear in here.*[4]

Just as Christy's men opened their bomb bays, the second echelon slanted across their path a thousand feet below. The navigational mistake had brought the two groups over the target simultaneously. Christy's bombardiers focused their instruments on the target. Their payloads stood armed and ready. Meanwhile, flak percussions from 150 defending guns jostled them about.

The pilots in the lower group looked up with horror. At any moment, hundreds of bombs would drop through their ranks. They veered sharply to the left as rivulets of 500-pounders slipped past. Disaster had been narrowly averted, but the evasive action disrupted their bombardiers' aim. The wiser ones held onto their eggs; others released theirs as best they could.

A later strike photo analysis indicated the raid had severely damaged the refinery. Likely, these hits came from Colonel Christy's force, which had a good visual fix on the target. Other bombs had destroyed barracks inside Auschwitz III bordering the plant. Slave laborers had no doubt been killed in the confusion.[5]

■   ■   ■

Vapor trails streamed from Coe's extreme left and right engines. The oil pressure in number one fell. Coe feathered the propeller and dropped back from the formation. As far as he could tell, the plane had not been hit; the issue was mechanical, but it was serious.

Jack Mulvaney pumped fuel to the reluctant engine. It restarted but died again ten minutes later, and the propeller refused to feather. Mulvaney reported the fuel gauges were "shocked" and could not be trusted to give a true reading. Lower ball turret gunner Almondo Champi delivered more bad news: a German airfield lined with forty fighters loomed below.

Coe wanted to dump weight to fly as far as possible. On the other hand, if the German fighters rose, the crew might need every gun belt.

Coe decided to make a run for it—they could not outduel fighters anyway. "Lighten the plane," he ordered. The giant aerial camera went first.

They passed into Yugoslavia losing altitude rapidly. Copilot Dale Hoffman's voice came over the interphone. "Get ready to jump," he ordered. "We'll ring the alarm when it's time."

Everyone reached for their parachutes. Wunderlich popped out of the tail turret, relieved to find his chute where he had left it. Foto grabbed his A-3 bag, a canvas valise. Inside were his escape kit and GI shoes. In the front of the plane, Mulvaney donned his GI shoes and secured his personal escape kit. No one bore a sidearm, as the 459th forbade them on missions.

The number two engine cut out, starved of gas. Number three coughed. Three short rings came from the alarm, alerting the crew to prepare to bail out. The warning was unnecessary; the engines said everything. Foto stood by the now-vacant camera hatch with his canvas bag in hand. *I look like a Fuller brush man*, he mused. He jumped when the third engine cut out without waiting for Coe's signal.

Wunderlich stepped up to take Foto's place at the hatch. The bailout alarm rang. Still, he hesitated. Champi rushed past him. "Bail out!" he yelled, and leapt. Wunderlich followed.[6]

■ ■ ■

Foto whooshed out of the plane's slipstream and pulled the rip cord. It came off into his hand with no corresponding pop. *Is this thing going to open?* he wondered.

As if in answer, the chest pack burst open like a jack-in-the-box. Foto found himself beneath the canopy with shrouds wrapped between his legs. His weight rested against his groin. He dropped his bag, lifted his body into the tangled lines, and adjusted himself. A church steeple rushed up. He heard voices and hit.

"I'm dead," said Foto aloud. *No*, he corrected himself, *I would not be in so much pain if it were true.* His hands and face were scratched and bloody and his ankle was turned. Sweaty chills sprouted as the adrenaline ebbed from his body.

A bunch of villagers approached as he collected himself. Two of them helped Foto to a nearby farmhouse. A man held up five fingers and pointed upward with his other hand. He must have seen five other airmen in parachutes. *Take me to them*, Foto signaled. Someone brought a donkey, and Foto mounted it. The two villagers escorted the airman through the fields to another house.

Wonder of wonders, a U.S. Army jeep sat parked in front of the building. An American must be inside. Feeling more like Sancho Panza than the Lone Ranger, Foto shouted a hearty "Hi-ho Silver!" Anybody from the United States would know the reference.

The man who emerged, however, was not an American. "Hello there," he intoned in a British accent. "How are you?" He seemed to have been expecting the airman to drop in, so to speak.

Foto had just met Major Toby Milbanke, one of some two hundred British Special Operations Executive (SOE) agents ensconced with Tito's Partisans. The major had been looking for Coe's crew since they had been spotted bailing out. He told Foto they were just a few miles from Sanski Most, a collection point for downed Allied fliers. Milbanke helped him into the jeep and drove him into town. All of Coe's men but the pilots gathered within hours.[7]

■   ■   ■

Milbanke knew Sanski Most well. His one-man mission—randomly codenamed ICARUS—had arranged for several previous evacuations from the airstrip outside of town. He had left for another Bosnian town, Travnik, when fall rains rendered the field inoperable.

In early December, the airmen stranded in Sanski Most had sent Milbanke a letter asking him to contact Bari on their behalf. After he verified their identities, he drove his jeep into town and took up residence in a secluded cottage. Soon another mission, codenamed BALLINCLAY, traveled from Bugojno to assist his efforts. Its two members were Captain John Tregidga, a South African from Cape Town, and Corporal John Davis, a thirty-year-old radioman from Liverpool.

The presence of the two teams indicated the high priority the SOE placed on the situation in Sanski Most. Together, the agents hoped to arrange air transport for the downed airmen, but the soggy landing field would have to dry or freeze to become operable again. The combined teams also intended to coordinate supply drops to the Partisans fighting in nearby Banja Luka. They carried "Eureka" short wave transponders with a range of thirty to fifty miles. Transports bearing "Rebecca" units would return the signals, ensuring accurate drops.

The three SOE agents had made their way around town meeting with the airmen. They counted forty-five Americans, including six confined to the hospital. Scotty Stewart's leg injury looked grave. Medical supplies were non-existent. The sooner a parachute drop could be arranged, the better.

The major cautioned Bob Bartusch and Larry Rosenthal not to trust the Partisans too much: "I'll bet these bastards haven't even told you that there's a two-way radio in that farmhouse across the river." Sure enough, a radio had lain inert there the whole time the airmen had been stranded.[8]

■   ■   ■

Fred Coe and Dale Hoffman escaped from the *Eight Ball* just before it crashed. They landed close to each other and quickly linked with a band of Partisans. Instead of heading toward Sanski Most like their crewmates, however, they were guided by Partisans southward to Livno.

There they joined up with Lt. Curtis Eatman and seven of his crew—Charles Haynes, William Evans, William McGee, Lamont Pakes, James Powell, Joe Dearman, and Edward Hahn. Eatman's men had been downed during a December 18 raid against Blechhammer. Eventually, the Partisans guided Coe, Hoffman, and Eatman's men onward to an American mission in Split, a harbor town on the Adriatic coast.

The other two members of Eatman's crew, gunners Andrew Jay and Harold Wamser, had been injured upon landing and had not been up to the journey. Instead, the Partisans sent them to the hospital in Sanski Most in the same antique train that had brought in so many others. For them and the other airmen trapped in the town, the quest to return home was just beginning.[9]

CHAPTER 12

A Conspiracy of Circumstances

Second Lieutenant Robert F. Kidder loved to fly. Even before he enlisted, Kidder had earned a flying license through the Civilian Pilot Training Program (CPTP), a government-sponsored course founded in 1939 to help the nation prepare for war. Like most of the four hundred thousand graduates of the CPTP—including several famous aces and future senators John Glenn and George McGovern—Kidder found his civilian training invaluable during flight school. He advanced through the various phases of training with ease and became a B-24 aircraft commander.

Kidder's copilot, Flight Officer Jerome "Jerry" Scherzer, also proved to be an excellent flier. Kidder wondered why such a good pilot had not been named a second lieutenant. He answered his own question when he noticed the letter "H" stamped on Scherzer's dog tags. Scherzer had been a victim of the AAF's quiet prejudice against the "Hebrew" religion. Kidder determined to get him a promotion as soon as possible.

The decision was typical of Kidder. Independent-minded and confident, he never accepted conventional Army wisdom at face value. He was particularly critical of his bomb group's policy regarding the breaking-in of pilots and copilots.

The AAF knew an airman's chance of survival increased if he managed to stay alive during his first combat experiences. To increase their odds, most bomb groups mixed neophyte crews with combat veterans for a few missions, but policies on phasing-in pilots and crews varied widely. The 485th Bomb Group threw Scotty Stewart's crew straight into combat. Charles Stanley, serving with the 464th, flew just one mission as an observer before his crew went up with him. In the 449th Bomb Group, a veteran pilot sat in the copilot's seat during Herky Marrone's first two sorties.

Kidder's 454th Bomb Group required every new first pilot to fly his initial five sorties as a copilot with veteran crews. On his sixth, an experienced copilot accompanied him and his neophyte crew. The original copilot did not rejoin them until the seventh sortie.

Kidder believed this extensive break-in period was blatantly unfair to the copilots. His own copilot, Jerry Scherzer, would not fly until the crew's seventh sortie. By then, Kidder would be considered a veteran and would mentor novice first pilots, leaving Scherzer on the ground once again. How was a copilot supposed to get broken in under this system? Moreover, how would he achieve the thirty-five sorties needed to go home? And how could Kidder justify giving Scherzer his much-deserved promotion to second lieutenant if he were not flying?

Another factor argued against the system: teamwork was critical to any crew's success and survival, and the copilot was the second most important member of the crew. An outsider in the copilot's seat increased the risk of confusion and error, because a stranger to the team, no matter how skilled at his craft, did not know the crew's routines, personalities, and idiosyncrasies.[1]

■   ■   ■

Kidder and his crew languished for a month without so much as a training flight as they waited for veteran crews to finish their tours. Meanwhile, Kidder kept his ears open. Many of the guys in camp, he discovered, had once been listed as missing in action. He learned not to worry when friends failed to return from missions—they often straggled in weeks after disappearing.

Kidder passed this information on to his parents. He also asked them for a Boy Scout knife. "They say they are very valuable if you have to walk back," Kidder wrote. "Guys do it all the time. You'd be surprised how many guys jump or crash land and then get back out."[2]

Kidder longed to get back into the air. At last, on December 15, he flew his first sortie, an innocuous trip to Linz, Austria—the same mission that ended so tragically for Clarence Marshall's crew.

Two days later Kidder took off as a copilot again, this time against the oil works at Odertal. His pilot was a tall, friendly redhead with a North Carolina accent named John Keyes Wolff.

Wolff exuded good cheer. At random intervals, he would burst into his favorite song. "You always hurt the one you love," he crooned, "the one you shouldn't hurt at all." Then he would repeat the lines. He couldn't carry a tune in a wheelbarrow, and Kidder doubted he knew the rest of the words.

Soon after takeoff, their aircraft displayed mechanical trouble. When it lost an engine over Hungary, Wolff was forced to feather the propeller, abort the mission, and turn back toward Italy. They reached their base and prepared to land. The tower instructed Wolff to get in line behind a flight of returning planes, but he was critically low on fuel and asked if he could be given priority. The tower denied his request.

Wolff would soon run out of gas. Against all procedures, he disobeyed the tower and followed another B-24 in. The prop wash nearly turned his aircraft sideways, but Wolff straightened it out and landed safely. Kidder breathed a sigh of relief as Wolff parked the aircraft on the hardstand. The guy was either a very hot pilot, a madman, or both.[3]

■   ■   ■

At three o'clock the next morning, a duty officer knocked on the wooden door to Wolff's tent. "Let's go, Wolff!" he hollered. The pilot moaned and rolled off his cot. Tom Stack, his navigator, stirred and rose. Their two tentmates ignored the noise, knowing they had the day off.

If Wolff was the head of the crew, Stack was its heart. His twinkling eyes and pleasant, oval face gave him the appearance of an Irish cop in a Dead End Kids movie. Stack worshipped his pilot and served as his confidant and chief morale officer.

Stack had overcome a childhood that was difficult even by Depression standards. His father died when Tom was young and his mother, Gertrude, sought help from the Catholic Church. Jesuit priests saw promise in Tom and educated him at a Catholic high school and the Jesuit-founded University of San Francisco. He was attending law school there when he volunteered for the AAF.

Stack sent most of his monthly paycheck to his mother and dutifully wrote her two or three times a week. His letters reassured her that he was going to confession and attending Mass regularly. Often, Wolff and fellow Catholics on the crew joined him at the service. Despite his close relationship with his mother, Stack failed to tell her that he had begun to fly combat missions, even after visits to Munich, Vienna, Graz, and Blechhammer. Hoping to spare her the worry, he continually fibbed that he was more likely to die of boredom than anything else.

Wolff's crew suited Stack's informal temperament. Distinctions between officers and enlisted men remained strictly pro forma. On Thanksgiving, the officers, plus Samuel Butler, the crew's diminutive tail gunner, engaged the enlisted men in a touch football game. Stack completed two long touchdown throws late in the contest, salvaging a face-saving tie for the officers.[4]

■   ■   ■

Now, however, as Wolff and Stack dressed quickly in the cold darkness, the pair meant business. Putting on their cumbersome outfits took a solid ten minutes.

"Ok, let's go," drawled Wolff. Stack felt too cold to respond. He grabbed a briefcase containing maps, his oxygen mask, and K-rations.

They gave their sleeping tentmates a goodbye pat and stepped out into the wintery pre-dawn light.

Bob Kidder, who would again serve as their copilot, met them in the assembly room. Soon the briefing officer revealed their target would be the Oświęcim oil refinery. When the groans subsided, the news got even worse. Their bomb group would fly in the Tail-End Charlie position. Everyone braced for a difficult ride.

Wolff's B-24H, the *Ancient and Honorable Artillery Company of Massachusetts*, awaited them at the hardstand. Named for the militia group that raised the bonds to pay for it, the aircraft had flown seventy-six missions, an odds-defying record that testified to its resilience.

It was, however, quite possibly the ugliest aircraft in the Fifteenth Air Force. The ground crew had repaired its many shrapnel wounds with bright orange patches. Against the worn olive green of its original paint, the stipples resembled a florescent case of the measles. In addition, the original bomb doors had been replaced with fresh aluminum ones, so its underbelly shone a bright, shiny silver. Overall, the plane resembled a psychedelic, spotted turtle.

Flight engineer Sig Piekarski, his crush hat tipped jauntily to one side, greeted the officers with his usual gripe. "Not again!" he moaned in his Chicago-Polish accent. "This bucket of bolts ain't gonna make it back some day. Why the hell do we have to get it so often?"

Tom Stack did not mind the old bucket so much. Its plainly labeled snout fit his sense of propriety better than the ribald nose-art decorating most other ships. Kidder, having flown her the day before, sided with Piekarski.[5]

■   ■   ■

Bob Kidder assessed Wolff's crew with an outsider's eye. They seemed like good guys, but Kidder missed his own men. He had trained them and knew their capabilities.

The most noteworthy thing about Wolff's boys was their extreme youthfulness. Most crews featured an "old man" over twenty-five, but this bunch had none. Even Wolff, whom they called "Pop," was only twenty-one. Their bombardier for the day, Flight Officer William Lane, appeared young even for a twenty-year-old. Ball turret gunner Herbert Eldridge barely needed to shave. Tail gunner Sam Butler—two weeks shy of his nineteenth birthday—had the squinty-eyed, curly-haired look of a miniature Joseph Cotton. Tom Stack called him "Hungry" because of his adolescent metabolism.

Nose gunner Willis Hodgeman—just twenty-two years old—was one of the few men in the AAF with real parachute training. He had made a dozen jumps as a paratrooper but had injured an ankle on a landing and been excused to join the AAF. Now he sincerely hoped he would never have to jump from an airplane again.

The crew's muscular waist gunner, Andrew Wozar, had been raised by parents born in Czechoslovakia. His elderly father had died the year before he enlisted. Two of his brothers had also entered the service, leaving their mother, Anna, in an empty nest to await their return.[6]

■   ■   ■

Radio operator Henry Rinna, twenty-one, hailed from Detroit. His parents, both born in Italy, operated a grocery store where they proudly displayed a group picture of their three serviceman sons. A pretty young lady from the neighborhood, Dorothy Dalton, admired one of them in particular.

One day Henry returned home on leave, and Dorothy and her sister June spotted him walking with a buddy. Dorothy had just come off shift from her defense plant job and did not want to meet her crush looking like Rosie the Riveter. She tried to avoid him, but the boys hopped in the buddy's convertible and followed the girls down the street. "Come on," beckoned Henry, "we'll give you a ride." Dorothy insisted she didn't get in cars with strangers. "But our families know each other," implored the handsome man-in-uniform. June, less shy than her sister, climbed in front with the driver. Dorothy reluctantly joined Henry in the back.

Henry sauntered into his parents' home that evening and whirled his cap across the living room. "I've just met the girl I'm going to marry," he announced. They wed while Henry was on his final leave before going overseas.

Initially, Henry's father, Rocco, opposed the hasty marriage. Too many unscrupulous women married servicemen for the money. Some were "Allotment Annies" who married one or more men for the spousal check of $50 per month. Others wed soldiers for their $10,000 life insurance policies and divorced them if they returned alive. AAF men were particularly attractive in this racket because of their high mortality rate. Dorothy won Rocco over by telling him he could keep the insurance money if the worst came to pass. From then on, he treated her as part of the family.[7]

■   ■   ■

Wolff lifted off and circled the *Ancient and Honorable* to the group's rendezvous point. Great lumbering machines multiplied until they filled the sky. Tom Stack's heart swelled with awe and hope amid his jitters.

A thick band of black clouds interrupted Stack's reverie near the Yugoslavian coast. Hopelessly blinded by the fog, every man on Wolff's crew kept a sharp lookout for a possible collision. They emerged ten minutes later to find a mass confusion of planes scattered ahead of them. Soon most of the planes reorganized into two groups. Wolff joined the rearward bunch and pressed on toward Oświęcim.

As they passed over the Austrian Alps and entered Hungary, Wolff's number two engine hiccupped once, twice, and again. Then it stuttered and stalled. Wolff got on his throat mic. "We've got trouble, Sig. Make sure the fuel lines are set for transfer. Tom, keep me posted on our heading. We'll stay as tight as we can for as long as we can."

Wolff had aborted a mission the day before. He would not quit this one easily. He revved the working engines to keep up with the formation, burning gasoline ferociously. After a while, he realized he could not keep up and let the plane drop back. He would finish the mission alone.

Wolff reached the Initial Point of the bomb run and turned toward the target. Dead ahead, the two extemporaneous formations reached the target simultaneously. The lower echelon veered left just in time to avoid being hit by the bombs dropped by the upper one. Dense clusters of black explosions buffeted both groups until they passed beyond the flak zone. Wolff followed minutes later, the only target now for the flak gunners below. Concussions shook the *Ancient and Honorable* as though it were gripped by a great, trembling fist.

William Lane fiddled with his bombsight knobs. Most bombardiers dropped their payload on the mark of the lead plane. This might be his only chance to aim on his own, and he wanted to get it right. Lights to the left of the bombsight indicated the bomb bay doors were open. Lane made his final corrections. The bursts closed in. Lane flipped his switch and yelled, "Bombs away!" The *Ancient and Honorable*, thrilled with the release of its burden, bounded upward. Wolff swooped left as sharply as he dared. Stack gave him a heading toward Italy.

They lost sight of the formation near Lake Balaton in Hungary. Wolff asked Piekarski for a fuel check. They were down to six hundred gallons—not enough to make it back to base. Kidder radioed for Little Friends—fighter escorts—but none were in the neighborhood. A thick undercast gathered.

After some time, Stack guessed they had reached Yugoslavia. That was progress, but then the plane dipped into clouds. Frozen moisture choked the engines' carburetors. Wolff tried to blow the ice out by blasting away at the throttle, but it was no use.

Stack and Wolff discussed their options over the interphone. Neither liked the idea of trying for the airstrip on the Island of Vis. Wolff, as hot a pilot as any, was daunted by its short runway. Stack's concern was finding it, as the dense fog hid all landmarks. If he missed it, ditching in the cold Adriatic would be close to suicide.

The plane sank to twelve thousand feet. Vis ceased to be an option. At least they were beyond the German fighter bases. Wolff ordered the crew to throw out all excess weight. The hydraulics were disabled, so Piekarski cranked the bomb bay doors partway open manually. The crew disgorged everything that was not nailed down. Wolff looked at Bob Kidder. "Go help," he said. "I'll fly the plane." Kidder left his seat to pitch in with the work in the half deck.

In the rear, Wozar, Butler, and Eldridge hustled to dispose of their flak jackets, ammunition, and guns. Dislodging the huge .50 caliber machine guns took time. Disposing of the massive boxes containing twenty-seven-foot-long belts of ammunition—the "whole nine yards"— was even harder. The plane was now low enough that they could breathe without oxygen, so the trio removed their masks, electric heating cords, and interphone connections to move about more freely.

Meanwhile, in the nose section, Stack stood with his head in the Plexiglas dome navigators used for celestial readings. He could see Wolff's furrowed face as they spoke. It was decision time. The number four engine had grown worse, and Wolff had given it a few more bursts of power, but to no avail. "Are you sure," Wolff asked Stack, "we are not over the Adriatic?"

"Either I'm the worst navigator in the Air Force," replied Stack, "or we are at least forty miles from the sea."

"We can't clear the mountains," said Wolff. "Give me a heading east. There's a better chance of finding a valley in that direction."

Stack did not have to consult his maps for that bit of navigation. East was ninety degrees. Wolff knew that. Maybe he was more disturbed than he let on.

"Ninety degrees," snapped Stack.

"Ninety degrees. Roger and out," replied Wolff.

Wolff banked hard left and straightened her out. The *Ancient and Honorable* cut through the fog while the crew worked like demons to lighten her.

Wolff pressed the button on his throat mic again. "I can't hold her. I'm losing…"

Wolff's voice trailed as the number one engine cut out. Ice, no doubt. Numbers two and four sputtered. One good propeller would not keep the plane aloft for long.

Stack watched the anxiety mount in Wolff's steel-blue eyes.

"Bail out!" erupted Wolff. "For God's sake, bail! Everybody bail out! Confirm waist! Confirm nose! Confirm waist!" He looked straight at Stack's face. "Clear the nose!" he ordered.

Stack stepped down from the bubble and turned to Willis Hodgeman. "Get the hell out! Bail out right now!" he yelled. Hodgeman clipped on his parachute while Stack disconnected from the interphone, stuffed some K-rations in his pockets, and yanked open the nose wheel door.

"Dammit, Tom," the ex-paratrooper protested, "this is my thirteenth jump! I don't want to go!"

"Get the hell out!" Stack repeated. "We haven't any time!"

Hodgeman sat down on the ledge of the hatch and rolled outward, but his lower harness belt caught on rivets lining the doors. He dangled face down, flailing his arms and legs, trying to free himself. Stack said a quick prayer and gave him a good kick. Hodgeman dropped into the mists and vanished.

Stack plugged in his interphone again and stuck his head back into the Plexiglas dome. His eyes met Wolff's. "Clear the nose right now!" Wolff insisted.

"Roger and out," responded Stack.

"Waist confirm, for God's sake. Confirm!" repeated Wolff as Stack disconnected.

Stack stepped toward the nose doors and glanced at the .45 pistol holster hanging beside his fold-down table. "What the hell," he thought, "I can't shoot anyway." He left it. The roaring engines filled his ears. Wolff was gunning them, desperately trying to hold the plane steady long enough for the others to get out.

Stack sat at the nose wheel ledge and bowled out, careful not to catch his harness on the hooks like Hodgeman had. He pulled the rip cord, and the parachute bellowed. A memory dawned, one he had not recalled in months. While training in Wyoming, Wolff had scared the men speechless by diving at mountainsides, slowing down as if to land, and passing over the rocky crests with little room to spare. When asked what he was doing, the pilot said he was practicing in case he ever needed to make an emergency landing. A sick feeling crept into Stack's stomach.[8]

■   ■   ■

Kidder, Lane, Piekarski, and Rinna hustled around the half deck, casting equipment out the bomb bay. Kidder, the one closest to the cockpit, heard Wolff's bailout order and passed the word.

Piekarski finished cranking the bomb bay doors open while Lane and Rinna strapped on their chutes. Rinna crept onto the catwalk and tumbled out. Piekarski jumped next, then Lane. Satisfied that they were gone, Kidder returned to the cockpit to see what he could do. He was climbing into the copilot's seat when Wolff stopped him. "Go ahead and bail out," he ordered.

Kidder paused. "You coming?"

"Yeah," replied the pilot without returning his gaze.

Kidder attached his backpack-style parachute to his harness and glanced at Wolff one last time. The pilot's harness remained unbuckled. Kidder retreated to the bomb bay and leapt.[9]

His canopy snapped open. Below, a small settlement emerged. One of the crew had landed. A group of women swarmed, yanking at the figure's parachute. The hillside seemed to accelerate toward him. Kidder's body swung wildly and hit hard. Before he could gather his wits, a short, bow-legged old peasant pulled at Kidder's parachute. Kidder dug into his jacket for his pistol.

"*Ne, ne!*" cried the man. "Tito!"

"Okay, Tito," replied Kidder. He withdrew his hand from his jacket. Apparently, the codger only wanted his parachute material.

A teenage boy guided Kidder to a cottage, where he found young William Lane and a pair of Partisans. *Follow us*, they beckoned. *Hurry!*

Kidder and Lane trailed them up the mountainside. At dusk, they reached a farmhouse, slid past the livestock lolling about the first floor, and climbed a ladder to the living quarters. There they found Stack, Piekarski, Rinna, and Hodgeman huddled around a fire burning on a stone base in the middle of the room.

Willis Hodgeman was bent over in pain. Something in his abdomen had ruptured when his parachute opened. The Germans had perforated his parachute with bullet holes, and he had aggravated his old ankle injury on landing. Sig Piekarski was limping badly. Henry Rinna had barely escaped a troop of SS soldiers. They had passed so close to his hiding spot that he could see the fresh shine of their boots.

Four crewmen remained missing. It made sense that Wolff would have jumped last and landed beyond the rest. Yet where were Eldridge, Wozar, and Butler? No one had seen them jump. Moreover, Stack knew they had not responded to Wolff's calls to the waist.

Their host, an old man named Ilija Brdar, had worked in America and spoke to them with the help of a worn English-Serbo-Croatian dictionary. The Germans, he explained, had retaken Bosanski Petrovac, about ten kilometers to the southwest. But don't worry, he reassured them, they didn't come out at night. The airmen were safe for now. He fed everyone stew and passed around a jug of white lightning. Soon even the wounded were feeling no pain.

The Polish-speaking Piekarski struck up a conversation with a female Partisan. Her tired smile betrayed no emotion as Sig prattled on. After a time, she shook her head and gave a wooden reply. Piekarski looked discouraged.

Someone asked what she had said. Sig quoted her exactly: "You Americans have done too much for us already."

The airmen cracked up. They needed a good laugh. Still, when it came time to sleep, Tom Stack made sure Sig bedded down well clear of the soldier girl.[10]

In the morning, someone found a horse for Piekarski, and guides led the airmen eastward through the icy snow. Traveling off-road to avoid patrols, they reached the railway stop at Sanica after a two-day hike.

A miniature train arrived in the middle of their second night of waiting. A dim sliver of light emanated through the slats of one of the freight cars, the first sign of electricity the crew had seen since bailing out. Inside, a man wearing a British army uniform introduced himself as Corporal John Davis. He served as radio man for an SOE team stationed in Sanski Most, the area's gathering place for evadees. Major Toby Milbanke and Captain John Tregidga had sent Davis down the line to Drvar to pick up batteries for their radio. These now served as the power source for his lightbulb, a tiny but welcome beacon of hope to the weary airmen. Maybe Davis's batteries would allow the British agents to contact Italy and arrange for a rescue.[11]

■   ■   ■

The train reached Sanski Most the next morning. Davis escorted the six Americans to the British outpost outside town and presented them to Major Milbanke. "One of your men is here," the major announced. "He's in the hospital. I'll let him tell you his story."

Davis guided Kidder, Stack, and the rest of the men to the squalid Partisan infirmary. There, propped up on a bed, lay a banged-up Herbert Eldridge.

"Pop, Andy, and Hungry are dead," Eldridge told them. "Pop saved my life by crash-landing the plane. The others didn't make it."

Eldridge had spotted the parachutes of the guys who had bailed out, but the *Ancient and Honorable* had gone into a dive before he, Wozar, and Butler could strap on their own chutes. By the time Wolff leveled her off, the plane was too low for them to jump. The three assumed their crash positions—Eldridge against the bulkhead of the bomb bay, Wozar and Butler against the hull. Wolff lowered the landing flaps but left the wheels up. The propellers shaved through fir trees until the great bird scrunched against timber and rock with a metallic wail.

Eldridge found his feet, surprised to be alive. Fire blazed all about. Wozar lay dead, his head tilted as if his neck had broken. Butler had died as well. There was nothing Eldridge could do for them. He climbed through a jagged hole blown through the ship's skin by an exploding oxygen bottle. Soon the whole wreck erupted in flame.

Outside lay the mangled body of John Keyes Wolff. The pilot had been cast through the windshield on impact. Death must have been instantaneous. Eldridge's busted watch showed the time of the crash as 2:40 p.m.

Three Yugoslavian civilians arrived an hour later with some Partisans and an oxcart. They hid Eldridge underneath its straw and started off. After a long, bumpy ride, they reached the town of Lusci Palanka. An English-speaking man named Marko Zeric took Eldridge into his home and tended to his wounds. He assured the airman that his friends would be given heroes' burials.

The funeral was held the next day in the local Orthodox churchyard. Major Milbanke received word and drove his jeep to the site to attend. The Partisans draped the dead in parachute fabric and placed them in wooden coffins. Wozar and Butler, they told Eldridge, were burned beyond recognition. It was impossible to tell them apart. The coffins were placed in a single grave and covered with dirt. Partisans hammered three unmarked pine crosses into the ground.

Afterward, Milbanke drove Eldridge into Sanski Most with armed Partisans mounted on either fender of his jeep. The airman had been confined to the hospital ever since.

Stack and his crewmates wept as Eldridge completed his story. "Hungry" Butler would never reach his nineteenth birthday. Andy Wozar's widowed mother would receive a telegram notifying her that her son would never return home. John Wolff had sacrificed himself trying to save them. Eldridge owed his life to him. He was a hero worthy of his nation's highest honors.

"Let's find a priest," suggested Rinna. "We should say some prayers."[12]

■   ■   ■

Bob Kidder was not about to speak ill of the dead. Wolff had met his last full measure of duty with great courage. Still, as an outsider, an

Charles Stanley Sr., B-24 pilot.
Courtesy of the author

The Stanley crew enlisted men. Top row: Albert Buchholz, Forrest Smalley. Bottom row: Claude Tweedale, Darrell Kiger, Peter Homol. *Courtesy of the author*

Mary Alice Schmitz in May 1943. *Courtesy of the author*

The Fertile Turtle, a.k.a. *Yellow Victor*, in flight with *Yellow How*. *Courtesy of the author*

Stanley crew in Romania. Standing: Claude Tweedale, Herr Schmidt (local man), Peter Homol, Sam Spomer, George Jeaflea (host), Al Buchholz, Darrell Kiger, local man, Forrest Smalley, local man. Bottom row: Ed Seaver, Bob Plaisance, Leo Cone, Charles Stanley Sr. *Courtesy of the author*

Lt. Harry Carter, navigator-bombardier, Stewart crew. *Courtesy of Harry Carter*

Lt. Scotty Stewart as a cadet. *Courtesy of Caroline and Charlie Stewart*

Sgt. Joe Sedlak, gunner, Stewart crew. *Courtesy of Terry Sedlak*

B-24 from the 485th Bomb Group illustrating closeness of planes in formation. *Courtesy of Lt. Seymour Weinstein, 485th Bomb Group*

Lts. Bernard Button, Clarence Byers, and Robert Dean on leave in Rome. *Courtesy of Bernard Button*

Sgt. Emil Horak, radio operator, Dean crew. *Courtesy of Emil Horak*

Sgt. Harry Hoogeveen, ball turret gunner, Dean crew. *Courtesy of Harry Hoogeveen*

Steinbeisbahn narrow-
gauge locomotive.
Courtesy of the author

Lt. Seymour "Larry"
Rosenthal, navigator-
bombardier, Bartusch crew.
Courtesy of Larry Rosenthal

Lt. Bernard Button and Sgt. Ernest Peterson with
Partisans, one of whom is named Huharem Galesic.
Commandant Despot Dusan on far right. *Courtesy of
Bernard Button*

Postcard of prewar
Sanski Most.
Several airmen
were housed in
the attic of the
building behind
the bridge. The
minaret called the
Muslim faithful to
prayer. *Courtesy of
the author*

Marrone crew. Standing: Raymond Seery, James Stevenson, Albert Topal, Gene Dennis, George Earll. Sitting: Allen Goodling, James King, Herman Marrone. *Courtesy of George Earll*

Sgt. George Earll, radio operator, Marrone crew. *Courtesy of George Earll*

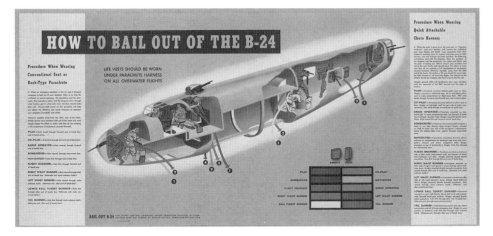

B-24 cutaway showing bailout patterns. *Courtesy of the U.S. Air Force*

Eldridge crew. Standing: Robert Mann, Archy Roper, Hixon Eldridge, William Clark. Crouching: Don Womak, Joseph Colasante, Eugene Quinn, Richard "Red" Braun, Vic Melcher, Gus Perrone. *Courtesy of the author*

Lt. Conrad Teague, navigator, Eldridge crew. *Courtesy of Archy Roper*

Sgt. Olin "Baker" Houghton, ball turret gunner, Eldridge crew. *Courtesy of Julie Houghton*

Lt. Frank Dick, navigator, Marshall crew. *Courtesy of Gordon Dick*

Lt. Leroy Nayes, bombardier, Marshall crew. *Courtesy of Leroy Nayes*

Cpl. James Martino, Sgt. Jan Wroclawski, and Sgt. Albert Hill after bailout. *Courtesy of the author*

Lt. Harry Blank, B-24 pilot. *Courtesy of Harry Blank Jr.*

Sgt. Keith Owens, radio operator, Blank crew. *Courtesy of Keith Owens*

Sgt. William Ceely, tail gunner, Blank crew. *Courtesy of Tom Ceely*

A tail gunner's view of B-24s from the 451st Bomb Group. *Courtesy of the U.S. Air Force*

Lt. Frederick Coe, B-24 pilot. *Courtesy of Jay Frederick Coe*

Lt. Edward Kutch, navigator, Coe crew. *Courtesy of Barry Kutch*

Cpl. John Mulvaney (center), flight engineer, Coe crew, with family. *Courtesy of John and Sherry Mulvaney*

Sgt. Joseph Foto, gunner/ aerial photographer, Coe crew. *Courtesy of Joseph Foto*

The original Wolff crew. Top row: Sig Piekarski, Henry Rinna, Herbert Eldridge, Andrew Wozar, Will Hodgeman, Samuel Butler. Bottom row: Jim Morris, Tom Stack, John Wolff, Dick Fedderson. *Courtesy of Tom Stack Jr.*

Lt. Robert Kidder, copilot, Wolff crew. *Courtesy of Robert Kidder*

Lt. Thomas Stack, navigator, Wolff crew. *Courtesy of Tom Stack Jr.*

The Rinna brothers photograph displayed in their parents' shop. From left, Herman, Tony, and Henry. *Courtesy of Ron and Henry Rinna Jr.*

Lt. Ted Keiser, B-17 pilot. *Courtesy of Sharon Wheeler*

Lt. Robert Griffith, copilot, Keiser crew.
Courtesy of Robert Griffith

Lt. Ken Wheeler, navigator, Keiser crew.
Courtesy of Sharon Wheeler

Members of the Keiser crew after bailing out. Top row: Paul Hoffmann, Wesley Chester, James Martin, Ken Wheeler. Bottom row: Edmund Charlesworth, Woodrow "Tex" Riley, Mario Spaltro. *Courtesy of Wesley Chester*

Lt. David Blood, B-24 pilot. *Courtesy of the author*

Lt. Lewis Baker, copilot, Blood crew. *Courtesy of the 485th Bomb Group Association*

Lt. Blood at flight briefing (behind projector). *Courtesy of the 485th Bomb Group Association*

Lts. Baker and Blood (center, rear row) at Christmas dinner 1944, the day before they were shot down. *Courtesy of the 485th Bomb Group Association*

Sgt. Fred Sherer, flight engineer, Blood crew. *Courtesy of Fred Sherer*

Sgt. Thomas Tamraz, gunner, Blood crew, on B-24 wing. *Courtesy of Thomas Tamraz*

Cpt. James Johnson, flight surgeon, poses in *Hell's Angel* before its final flight. *Courtesy of the 485th Bomb Group Association*

Sgt. Michael Yaworsky (second from left) and FO Eugene Cogburn (middle, supported by women, with Yugoslav family and Partisan [with rifle]).
Courtesy of the 485th Bomb Group Association

Lt. Scotty Stewart recovering in stateside hospital after rescue.
Courtesy of Caroline and Charlie Stewart

Postcard of Potoci train station before the war.
Courtesy of the author

Prewar postcard of the harbor at Split. *Courtesy of Joseph Foto*

Lt. (j.g.) Timothy Pfeiffer, the OSS agent who helped airmen in Split. *Courtesy of Tim and Sophie Pfeiffer*

Col. Hubert Zemke, Allied commander, Stalag Luft I. *Courtesy of the author*

Sgt. Eugene Quinn as a
POW. *Courtesy of Eugene Quinn*

Lt. Lawrence Zellman, P-38 pilot, the final
airman harbored by the Chetniks to be
repatriated. *Courtesy of Bonnie Yates*

Lt. Charles Stanley
Sr., fiancée Mary
Alice Schmitz, and the
parachute wedding dress.
Courtesy of the author

aircraft commander, and the last man to see the pilot alive, Kidder second-guessed many of Wolff's decisions.

He thought Wolff should have trained his men to stay on interphone while lightening the plane. If just one of the men in the rear had heard the bailout order, the tragedy would have been averted. In addition, Wolff had apparently not designated anyone the duty of making sure that everyone bailed out. Once the pilot realized they were not responding to his order to jump, he should have sent someone to pass the word.

Finally, Wolff should not have ordered Kidder to help lighten the plane. If the copilot had stayed in the cockpit where he belonged, he would have known the men in the waist had not acknowledged the bailout order. He could have delegated someone to tell them to jump, or he could have done it himself. Instead, Kidder had had no idea they were still aboard when Wolff ordered him to bail out.

Kidder, the last person to see Wolff alive, had witnessed the hell-bent determination on the pilot's face. He had made no preparations to jump; it seemed he never intended to do so. Kidder felt some pilots harbored a secret desire to try a forced landing—the ultimate test of a pilot's skills—just to see if they could do it. Stack had told him that Wolff had made practice landing runs over the Wyoming mountains. Kidder suspected that Wolff had believed he could land his B-24 on a forested mountainside and survive. To Kidder, attempting the impossible was not heroism; it was hubris.

Still, Wolff's sacrifice had not been in vain. Against all odds, Herbert Eldridge had survived. Maybe Wolff had achieved the impossible after all.[13]

Catastrophe is often the result of a conspiracy of circumstances. Several problems doomed the *Ancient and Honorable*, beginning with Wolff's aborted mission the day before. If not for the pressure to avoid a second scrub, he might have headed back to base when his engines first acted up. Moreover, the elements clogged his carburetors with ice, an issue that could not have been predicted or avoided.

The plane was likely struck by flak over the target, although no one reported any impact. Presumably, the bailout alarm malfunctioned or was knocked out. Wolff must have tried to ring it when the crisis came, and the tragedy would have been averted if it had worked.

Most importantly, neither Wolff nor Stack had been briefed on the availability of a flat, unobstructed stretch of land outside of Sanski Most, less than fifteen miles northeast of the crash site. Although the airstrip was closed to transports in November, it could still have been used for emergency landings.

An intelligence officer in Bari had researched such a contingency. On November 23, 1944, Lt. Colonel Ernest L. Walters wrote to General Nathan Twining's office to ask for aerial photos of possible emergency landing sites in Yugoslavia to be disseminated during mission briefings. Walters received a reply that no Yugoslavian airstrips were available at that time because of "serviceability or special operational consider-ations." Accordingly, an escape bulletin disseminated to bomb groups on November 30, 1944, stated, "At the present time there are no approved crash strips in Yugoslavia.... All known crash strips are either unservice-able or cannot be used for other reasons."

This assessment was only half accurate. The airfields could not be used for evacuations, but crash landings were possible. Someone had blurred the distinction.

If he had been better informed, Wolff would have headed straight for Sanski Most, saving precious minutes of air travel. He would have reached it in time for an emergency landing attempt on a stretch of flat, clear earth. While success would not have been assured, he would have stood a much better chance than on a forested mountainside. Instead, the young lives of John Wolff, Andrew Wozar, and Samuel Butler were cut short during Wolff's brave, desperate attempt to save his men from the machinations of fate.[14]

CHAPTER 13

The Flying Shithouse and the Ghost Ship

U niversal male conscription, known commonly as "the draft," was a central fact of American life during World War II. The draft touched everyone, from the 50 million men who registered with the Selective Service to their families, friends, sweethearts, and employers.

Ted Keiser's father was a prominent attorney who served on the Lansing, Michigan, draft board. When Ted enlisted, his father saw to it that he received a plum stateside job as a clerk. Keiser could have spent the war living comfortably with his wife, Ann. Instead, he volunteered for the AAF. Keiser, a broad-shouldered, six-foot-one specimen, met the physical and mental requirements with ease. He graduated flight school and was soon flying B-17s.

Keiser's crew joined the 301st Bomb Group just in time to take part in one of the last great raids against the Ploesti oil fields on August 18, 1944. Ten days later, they flew against another dangerous target, the Moosbierbaum synthetic fuel plant in Austria.

Keiser lost an engine over the target, and the radio room caught fire. Another B-17 took even worse hits and dropped back. Keiser left the safety of the formation to escort it home, despite the damage to his own plane. He and his copilot, Russell Rose, received the Distinguished Flying Cross for their bravery and initiative, cementing their reputation as the best pilot duo on base.

On September 10, Keiser and Rose flew their thirteenth mission, a raid against Vienna. Just after bombs away, a hunk of shrapnel hit Keiser just below the left shoulder where his flak vest offered no protection. His jacket and gloves filled with blood, so Rose took over and flew the plane safely back to base.

For a time, it looked like Keiser had received a "million-dollar wound" that would send him home. After a month, however, the shoulder healed, and he returned to active duty.[1]

Keiser's oldest crewman, Edmund "Charlie" Charlesworth, was drafted in 1940 even though he had been in the National Guard for a decade. After two years in the infantry, he asked for a transfer to the AAF. He passed the qualifying exams but could not become a pilot because he was over the maximum age of twenty-seven and a half. The Army assigned him to aerial gunnery school instead.

After Keiser's men arrived in Italy, their flight engineer, Mario Spaltro—an Italian-speaker from Portland, Maine—decided he no longer wanted the responsibility. Keiser wanted his most mature crewman in the position and assigned Charlesworth to take over the job. Spaltro moved to the waist gun.[2]

Ball turret gunner James Martin and his younger brother Paul were raised by missionary parents in the interior of Brazil. When the boys became draft eligible, Jim volunteered for the AAF. Paul became a conscientious objector, a rare and unpopular choice at the time.

"Class IV-E" objectors like Paul—those whose beliefs precluded them from any type of military duty, even as medics, quartermasters, or signalmen—were confined to Civilian Public Service (CPS) camps performing forestry, conservation, and farm work. They received no pay because Congress refused to pass appropriations to support them. In contrast, German POWs earned eighty cents a day for their labor.

As a result, Paul dug ditches as a near slave while Jim flew combat missions over Europe. The brothers honored each other's choices and remained on the best of terms. Their father accepted both decisions. Jim, he declared, was fighting to preserve Paul's right to religious liberty.

Jim Martin learned the horrors of war first-hand. He watched several B-17s go down or explode midair. He also witnessed airmen bailing out of their blazing planes only to fall helplessly to earth after their parachutes caught fire.

Martin coped through prayer. He asked God for protection before missions and thanked him after each safe return. Martin became so familiar with God in his prayers that he dropped the formal "Thou" in favor of the more familiar "You." His renewed religiosity, however, did not turn him into a pacifist like his brother. Martin celebrated as much as anyone when he spotted bombs hitting their targets.[3]

■   ■   ■

Keiser's men flew with other crews while he recovered from his injury. Russell Rose was promoted to first pilot. Their bombardier, Michael Mavroidis, suffered a severe leg wound. With two of his officers gone, Keiser moved into a new tent upon returning from the hospital.

One of his new roommates was Richard "Ken" Wheeler, who had aspired to be a pilot since he was a child. A friend of the family had owned a 65-horsepower puddle-jumper, and Wheeler learned to fly as a teenager. Eventually, he enrolled at the University of Washington to study aeronautical engineering. His studies helped him post perfect "nine" stanine scores on the AAF classification exams, and he could have opted to become a pilot. Instead, he listed "navigator" as his specialty of choice because he was also an avid sailor and hoped to sail around the world after the war.

Wheeler had been assigned to the tent because both of his original pilots were dead. His pilot, Al Luster, was killed in a midair collision on

November 18. A week later, his copilot, Bill Moffett, disappeared without a trace while flying a lone-wolf night mission.

Wheeler, Keiser, and their tentmates called themselves the "Rinky Dinks." Though they were not necessarily crewmates, Wheeler designed a patch for them featuring a winged outhouse, which they called the "Flying Shithouse," bestowing dubious 500-pound droplets on hapless targets. No plane in the group carried the name, but somehow the moniker seemed appropriate for every B-17 they were assigned to fly.[4]

■   ■   ■

On the evening of December 17, Keiser checked the squadron roster to see who would fly with him the next day. Charlie Charlesworth, Jim Martin, and Mario Spaltro were listed, along with two other original crewmen, radio operator Paul Hoffman and diminutive tail gunner Woodrow "Tex" Riley. Tentmate Ken Wheeler would serve as his navigator for the first time. Joining them would be three new faces: copilot Robert Griffith, bombardier Stanley Schwartz, and waist gunner Calvin Chester.

Keiser felt lucky to draw the experienced Bob Griffith, who had rung up even more missions than Ted and had already earned his own Distinguished Flying Cross. Lean and dark with expressive brown eyes, Griffith remained as unstressed by combat as a sane man could be. Boredom, not anxiety, was his main concern. Between missions, he fought the tedium by studying algebra and Italian.

Keiser knew nothing about Stanley Schwartz except he was a heavy smoker, sounded like a New Yorker, and carried two sets of dog tags in case the Nazis captured him—one showing his true Hebrew religion, and the other claiming he was Christian.

Schwartz had grown up in Brooklyn speaking Yiddish as his first language. With his blue eyes and blond hair, he resembled the rising comic actor Danny Kaye, who also descended from Jewish-Slavic stock. As with many Jewish recruits, the AAF made Schwartz a bombardier rather than a pilot and ranked him as a flight officer rather than a second lieutenant. He had been a close friend of Larry Rosenthal of the Bartusch crew when they attended bombardier school together in Texas.

Waist gunner Calvin Chester, who used his middle name, Wesley, was a native of Georgia who regularly slipped "you alls" into his speech. He was tall with sloped shoulders, and his full lips broke into a good-natured smile at the slightest provocation.

Chester had earned thirty-five mission credits, many of them over dangerous targets such as Vienna, Munich, and Blechhammer. He had seen several planes go down and was as aware as anyone of the hazards of aerial combat. He had happened to be aboard the same plane as Michael Mavroidis when the bombardier nearly lost his leg to shrapnel. Nevertheless, Chester's deep Christian faith allowed him to face the danger with equanimity. After missions, when others lined up for their salubrious shots of whiskey, Chester gave his ration away to someone who needed it.[5]

■   ■   ■

Keiser's ship for the day did not have an official nickname, but if any B-17G deserved to be called "The Flying Shithouse," this was it. As they prepared to take off that morning, the ground chief told Charlesworth that three of its four engines were due for replacement. Charlie, inured to dealing with war-wearies, did not bother to mention the tidbit to his pilot.

Soon after Keiser took off toward Odertal, his number three engine began to act up. Ignorant of the wretched state of the other engines, Keiser urged the ship forward. He dropped four bombs into the Adriatic, hoping to deliver the other six, but fell behind the formation over Hungary. The target seemed within reach when number two began to smoke. Keiser feathered the propeller and grumbled into his throat mic, "Boys, we're going home."

Ken Wheeler knew the crew would not get mission credit unless they dropped their bombs. He called Keiser and suggested a railroad bridge near Gyor. The pilot agreed and diverted to the target, but Stanley Schwartz missed the mark. Jim Martin wished they had just dumped the bombs to save the gas.

Twenty minutes later, Keiser was forced to feather the number one engine. Now only the right-side engines operated. Keiser ran them at full emergency power, hoping to reach Vis. Martin climbed out of the ball turret and helped the others jettison weight.

A damaged B-24 closed in from behind. The Liberator, operating on three engines, could fly faster than Keiser's B-17, but its pilot cut power to create a two-plane formation. None of Keiser's men recognized the tail markings, and the plane could not, or would not, respond to their radio calls. Machine guns bristled from every opening. Shouldn't the waist guns have been tossed out to lighten the plane? Wheeler wondered if the ghost ship was one of the AAF planes salvaged by the Germans to serve as flying Trojan horses.

Minutes passed, but the B-24 made no hostile move. Copilot Bob Griffith called out for Little Friends, and a pair of P-38s joined them. No German fighters would bother them now.

Wheeler announced they were approaching Zagreb. His maps showed heavy flak defenses. Keiser steered a safe distance around.

Inexplicably, the B-24 failed to follow and instead flew straight into the flak zone. Dozens of 88 mm bursts surrounded it. Somehow, they all missed. The Liberator rejoined Keiser's B-17 on the other side, suffering no ill effects. Soon, however, Keiser lost the B-24 and the fighters in a thick fog. Fuel was low. His hope of reaching Vis evaporated in the mist.

Keiser dipped below the clouds to look for a landing spot, but a wet snowfall obscured his view. Craggy peaks jutted below. He was more likely to smack into a mountain than to find open ground. Keiser's altimeter indicated eight thousand feet. The mountains accounted for half of that.

Number four belched and blew a cylinder. Flame and smoke erupted from its exhaust. Charlesworth stood between the pilots. "I think we'd better get out of here," he urged.

"I think we'd better too," replied Keiser.

"I'll take care of the guys in the back," volunteered the engineer.

Keiser pressed his throat mic. "Let's get the hell out of here, boys!"

Woodrow Riley's high-pitched Texas twang replied from the tail: "Can you repeat that, please?"

A smile played at Keiser's mouth, but he tried to sound stern. "Get the hell out!" he insisted.

Riley did not need to be told a third time. He emerged from the tail and pulled the red handle on the side door, jettisoning it into the air. "Now I'm ready," he said to no one. He sat on the jamb and was gone. Hoffman, Mario Spaltro, and Wesley Chester trailed behind.

Charlesworth crossed the bomb bay and peered into the waist. Only Jim Martin remained. Charlesworth followed him to the opening. "You first, Charlie," offered Martin.

Charlesworth smiled. "No, after you." Martin decided the Alphonse and Gaston routine had gone on long enough and toppled out. Charlesworth followed, somersaulting headlong into the foggy void.

Ken Wheeler heard Keiser's order from his position in the nose. He released the nose hatch door and kicked it open. Clouds loomed above and below. "Oh God," he prayed, "tell my family I'll be safe." He jumped. Schwartz tumbled out as well.

Keiser told Griffith to go, and he obeyed. Now alone in the cockpit, Keiser assumed Charlesworth would report back to him before leaving the plane. Minutes passed. Visibility dropped to near zero. Checking the altimeter, Keiser realized he was perhaps two hundred feet above the peaks. The crew must be gone. He bolted to the hatch and dove, yanking the rip cord as he leapt.[6]

■   ■   ■

Six thousand miles away, in a small house in Midland, Washington, Wheeler's wife Lorraine woke up screaming. She had seen a vision of Ken suspended from a parachute. It was December 18, 1944, 4:00 a.m. Pacific War Time.

At the same moment, Keiser's mother awoke in Ludington, Michigan. Her husband was missing from their bed. Their bedroom clock showed it was 2:00 a.m., Central War Time. A light shone from downstairs. Puzzled, she descended the stairway. Ted's father sat in his living room chair, staring into space. "What's the matter?" she asked.

His reply was barely audible: "Ted's in trouble, and I can't help him."

In Yugoslavia, the time was 1:00 p.m. The Keiser crew had just bailed out.[7]

■   ■   ■

Ken Wheeler dangled from his parachute amid swirling snowflakes. The D-ring of the rip cord remained in his hand. It was worth a drink at the officers' club if he ever returned to base.

The wind pitched him about. Yanking the shroud lines on the proper side should stop the swinging. He reached upward, found a group of cords, and tugged. The canopy collapsed into a narrow stream. Wheeler plunged earthward like an anvil was strapped to his feet.

The rushing air caught the parachute and forced it open. Wheeler's D-ring jolted off into space. A coniferous mountainside jutted skyward. Wheeler braced for impact, but silver fir branches snagged his chute and gave way tenderly. He nestled to a halt thirty feet above the ground, as if the gentle hand of God had set him down.

The crack of small arms fire shattered his reverie. He must have landed near a skirmish. He had to get down, but he was suspended too high to release his harness. His best bet was to climb down a nearby tree. Maybe he could cut a shroud, lasso a branch, and pull himself toward it. A short-blade bayonet lay hidden beneath his harness. Maddeningly, he could not reach it.

An indistinct shape materialized from the mist-filled woods. Nerves taut, Wheeler watched the figure move closer until it was below him. It stopped and looked about.

It was Charlesworth. Wheeler had to get his attention without giving away their position. He cupped his hands and whispered a shout. "Help!"

Charlesworth shot his head upward. Wheeler mouthed in another stage whisper, "Throw me your knife." Nodding, the engineer tossed it high. Wheeler fumbled it and the blade tumbled back and was buried deep in a foot of snow. Charlesworth retrieved it and lobbed the knife upward again.

This time Wheeler caught it. He cut a few shroud lines, tied them together, and fixed a loop. Snaring a broken branch cowboy-style, he pulled himself to the trunk and released his harness buckle. The chute rebounded high into the branches above. It would surely betray his landing spot.

Wheeler climbed down and padded away from the fading gunfire with Charlesworth. After a few minutes they found a trail of footprints marring the virgin snow. They decided to follow it.[8]

■   ■   ■

Jim Martin lay on his back half-buried in snow. Gunfire echoed in the distance. He sat up, drew out his pistol, cocked it, and returned it to his holster. This was no time for pacifism.

He buried his parachute in snow and moved south. A valley stretched to his right, and he veered downhill. Then a thought struck him like a thunderbolt: his yellow Mae West highlighted his chest like a target. Martin stripped it off and hid it under the nearest log. Pleased with himself, he sat down and lit a cigarette. Smoke eddied upward.

A voice called. Was it English? A response came. Martin followed the snow-dampened sounds. Before long, he joined Wesley Chester, Ken Wheeler, and Charlie Charlesworth. They decided to proceed farther southward, the most likely direction to find their crewmates.

At nightfall they hid under the snow-weighted branches of a fir tree, rested their backs against the trunk, and shared Charlesworth's salvaged parachute for warmth. Their escape kits offered a few chocolate bars for sustenance.

Black enveloped them. Unless their footprints betrayed them, they were safe for now.[9]

■   ■   ■

Copilot Bob Griffith found himself facedown on a pile of rocks, a mountainous slope surrounding him. He had no memory of striking the ground. The taste of blood prompted him to probe his mouth. Four front upper teeth were missing. He rolled over and pain shot from his ribs and back. The boom of artillery resonated in the distance. He needed to get away. He hid his chute and dragged himself down the slope, each step an echo of agony.

Halfway down, Griffith stopped dead in his tracks. Before him, among the trees, was a man training a rifle on him. He was not a German soldier, nor did he wear the red star of the Partisans. His most distinguishing feature was a long, bushy beard. Recognition flashed in the man's eyes. He lowered his rifle and beckoned Griffith to follow.

Soon they joined another bearded man at a small lean-to. This one spoke some Italian and identified himself and his comrade as Chetniks. Darkness fell, but they lit no fire.

Griffith awoke the next morning with even stiffer ribs. After a meager breakfast, the Chetniks led him through the forest as briskly as his pain allowed. At dusk, they arrived at a vacant farmhouse. Griffith's guides saw him to the structure, motioned that he should stay, and vanished. Hours later, six Partisans ambled through the door. The Chetniks must have reached out to them through intermediaries.

Eventually Griffith caught a wagon caravan to the port of Zadar. On New Year's Eve, a British crash coat—a high-speed armed launch—carried him to safety in Italy.[10]

■   ■   ■

Wheeler, Martin, Chester, and Charlesworth emerged from their snowy pine boughs at dawn and set off southward again. Toward afternoon, the trees gave way to a clearing that must have been a farm in better times. A ramshackle two-story home sat at the dell's edge. Thin smoke wafted from the chimney. The airmen sought cover and watched.

Near dark, they decided Wheeler, Martin, and Chester would scout the building. Chester, the largest, would knock on the door if all seemed safe. Charlesworth, the best shot due to his experience in the National Guard, would cover them from the woods with a .45.

Wheeler led them toward the barn. He was about to peer into a window when a woman wearing a long skirt and a worn coat turned the corner. A babushka concealed her hair, and she seemed neither old nor young. Her eyes showed no fear as she folded her hands across her bosom.

Wheeler threw out a word he hoped she would recognize: "*Ameri-kanski.*" The woman nodded and pointed up a dirt path. "*Tedeschi,*" she advised, the Italian word for Germans. Even without knowing the language, her warning rang true. She beckoned the airmen to enter her home. Charlesworth put away his gun and joined them.

Inside was a girl of about three. The woman conveyed that she would find her husband and departed, leaving her daughter behind. She clearly trusted the airmen. Before long she returned with a man of about thirty-five, wearing homespun knickers, high socks, and a horsehair jacket. He motioned to the Americans to follow him into the woods.

Deep in the labyrinth they found a clearing. A stout old codger wearing a rumpled black business suit stood there as if he expected them. "I am Miller," he said in accented English. "Who are you?"

"Americans," they replied, pointing to the flags on their shoulders.

Suspicion reigned in the man's eyes. "Where are you from?" he asked. The airmen hailed from Washington State, Ohio, Georgia, and Pennsylvania. How, they rejoined, did a Yugoslavian learn to speak English? Miller had worked in Detroit before the Great War. He had many fond memories of America, particularly the ample paychecks. A daughter still lived in Montana.

After some discussion, the old-timer seemed satisfied. "You must be hungry," he offered as he signaled to the trees. Two teenage girls, perhaps his granddaughters, emerged carrying bowls of sliced ham, hard-boiled eggs, and brown bread. Miller broke a loaf open. The middle remained unbaked. "There is no yeast to bake bread properly," he apologized.

The famished Americans cared little about the loaf's raw center. They polished off the meal in seconds. Later, they realized the family had likely gone hungry for days afterward.

Miller grew serious again. "Who do you want to see?" he asked. Wheeler understood his meaning: Chetniks or Partisans? A wrong answer might still mean disaster. Wheeler pulled a word out of the air. "Partisans!" he blurted. Miller nodded. Wheeler had given the response he sought.

One of the girls suffered from impetigo, a skin rash with blisters. Wheeler applied an antibiotic salve. Charlesworth, observing that the girls coveted his parachute, gave it to them along with needles and thread from his escape kit. They gushed in thanks.

"We'd better move on," offered the old man.

The party moved single file deeper into the woods. After a time, a pair of doubtful-looking sentries bearing German rifles and red-starred caps leveled their aim at them. "Tito! Tito!" Miller reassured them. Appeased, the guards let them pass.[11]

■   ■   ■

After several more hours of hiking, the group climbed a steep thousand-foot slope to their destination, a small plateau named Frkašić. A company of Partisans occupied the natural fortress. Captain H. B. Plowman, an American OSS officer dressed as a civilian, introduced himself. He had long been attached to the Partisan Fifth Corps and had helped dozens of airmen escape.

Mario Spaltro, Paul Hoffman, and Tex Riley had already arrived. Keiser, Griffith, and Schwartz remained missing. The Partisans had informed Plowman that one of them was in German hands, but they did not know which one. Nothing had been heard of the other two.

Miller offered the hirsute Charlesworth some friendly advice as they walked through the camp: "You had better get rid of that beard." Being mistaken for a Chetnik could prove fatal. Charlesworth split off to find a place to shave.

Wheeler noticed a Partisan girl of no more than fourteen carrying a Thompson machine gun. Miller pointed to the sixteen notches on its stock, one for each German she had killed. The Germans had murdered her family, he explained. She would slay as many of them as she could.

A large log barn stood at the center of the camp. Inside, Partisan soldiers hugged the walls, many of them wounded. A small fire on the dirt floor supplied paltry heat. A Partisan steered Wheeler to a small antechamber illuminated by an oil lantern. A woman of about twenty-five lay on the straw-strewn floor next to a bed. She had just given birth. Her newborn child slept in a wooden box under some covers. The Partisan motioned that the airman should take the bed. Wheeler shook his head and pointed at the young mother. She looked up, mustered a weary smile, and declined. Too tired to argue, Wheeler plopped down.

Before long, screaming artillery shells interrupted Wheeler's slumber. Thunderous explosions shook the building. Plowman appeared. "We've got to get out of here," he urged.

The bombardment ceased as the Americans ventured outside. Craters pocketed the ground. A Partisan had been killed, but none of the airmen were hurt.

Small arms fire broke out next. A guide showed the airmen the way down the slope opposite to the attack. Plowman buried his radio in a pile of manure and caught up with them at the bottom.

They arrived at another Partisan stronghold the following evening. Word came that Frkašić had fallen, but no one knew the fates of Miller, the young mother, or her newborn child. After a night of rest, Plowman sent the airmen onward, escorted by a Partisan guide.

Four days later, on Christmas morning, the airmen arrived at the port of Split. There they met Lt. (j.g.) Timothy A. Pfeiffer, a naval officer detached to the OSS. Pfeiffer, a Princeton graduate, had been part of a

U.S. diplomatic team that met with Tito in Vis in August. His translator, Vedran Jihovy, remained constantly by his side.

Pfeiffer fed the airmen "C" rations and made them as comfortable as possible. They pooled a few dollars from their escape kits, and Pfeiffer bought them a turkey for Christmas dinner.

Five fellow Americans soon arrived. They belonged to the strangely silent B-24 that had accompanied them over Croatia, wandered over the flak at Zagreb, and disappeared in the fog. The B-24 crewmen explained the mystery: Their radio had malfunctioned upon takeoff. They had lost an engine over the target, and their navigator set a heading for Vis, but his oxygen mask failed near Zagreb and he passed out. Absent his guidance, pilot Lt. Walter Holland had flown over the city, and they had nearly been shot out of the sky. Eventually, they were forced to bail out over the rocky island of Korčula. Six crewmen, including Holland, were injured on landing and stayed behind at a Partisan hospital.

Two days later, Frederick Coe, Dale Hoffman, and the eight members of Curtis Eatman's crew joined Keiser and Holland's men in Split. Soon they all hopped aboard a British crash boat and sped to the Island of Vis, where they boarded a C-47 transport for Bari.

Bob Griffith reached Italy on New Year's Eve. Now everyone on Keiser's crew but the pilot and Stanley Schwartz were accounted for. One was known to have been captured.[12]

■   ■   ■

Ted Keiser had heard gunfire as soon as he hit the ground. He had barely sat up when a boy of perhaps ten appeared and beckoned Keiser forward. The pilot rose gingerly, released his chute, and followed his young guide.

The kid set a rapid pace. The shooting faded as they hiked uphill among the trees. At the crest, they came upon a farmhouse. A man wearing a red star on his cap, likely the boy's father, greeted them. He introduced himself as Elya Santviac and showed Keiser his shelter for the night—the loft of a smelly hen house. Possibly, he wanted to be able to deny knowing the airman had taken refuge there. Keiser was just grateful for a bit of food and the dry shelter.

The next morning, a rail-thin Partisan named Nikola, who looked to be seventy years old, arrived to serve as his guide. They spent days passing through Partisan waystations. Keiser's crewmen had ventured southwest toward the Adriatic. Nikola guided Keiser the opposite way, perhaps because he knew of the fighting the others had dodged. Fourteen hours later, after midnight on Christmas Day, the pair arrived in Sanski Most.

Despite the hour, Keiser and his guide reported to Captain John Tregidga, the South African SOE officer stationed in town. Tregidga offered them a drink of *slivovitz*. The old-timer pointed at Keiser. "Good walker," he declared in English. The old man looked fresh as ever.

Ted Keiser became the seventy-first downed American airman delivered to the already-crowded town. He was now trapped 120 miles from the coast. No one seemed to have a plan to get him and the other stranded Americans back to Italy.[13]

■   ■   ■

It was Keiser's Jewish bombardier, Stanley Schwartz, who had been taken prisoner. Fortunately, his ruse of wearing false dog tags labeling him as a Christian paid off. Blond-haired and blue-eyed, he resembled the Nazi ideal more than many Germans. His interrogators assumed that "Schwartz"—a common German surname—indicated Aryan ancestry. They even suggested he ought to defect. When he insisted that he was an American by birth, they accepted his response and passed him on to Stalag Luft I. He was liberated on May 2, 1945.[14]

CHAPTER 14

An Unmerry Christmas

Forty airmen poured into Sanski Most between December 16 and 26, 1944, more than doubling the number of evadees being harbored there. The retreating Germans still blocked the path to the Adriatic coast, and the airstrip outside of town remained too waterlogged to be serviceable.

Meanwhile, the 51st Troop Carrier Squadron, the air transport unit now serving the Balkans, delivered supplies to British forces fighting Greek Communists near Athens. The effort alarmed Tito. If the Allies would fight the Communists in Greece, they might turn on him as well.

For years, the British had pressed Tito and King Peter's government-in-exile to present a common front against the enemy. General Fitzroy Maclean told Tito that Britain would consider granting him official recognition if he formed a joint government with King Peter. On December 2, 1944, Churchill reminded Tito that the arrangement must be predicated upon post-war elections. Tito promised such elections on December 21, but King Peter remained unconvinced.

Tito and the British also reached an impasse over the terms of a proposed humanitarian program. The British wanted to monitor the distribution of foodstuffs and other goods, fearing Tito would use it to set up a Communist regime. Tito argued that any such restriction would violate Yugoslav sovereignty and accused the British of letting Yugoslavs starve over technicalities.

Meanwhile, the Americans tried to send representatives to the Yugo-slavian capital of Belgrade on December 16, but Tito refused permission.

So it was that high-level relations between the Western Allies and Tito grew ever more strained while scores of airmen languished in remote Sanski Most with no end in sight.[1]

■   ■   ■

Sanski Most's central kitchen continued to be the airmen's main source of nutrition. So many airmen ate there that the Partisans felt crowded out of their own commissary.

The newer arrivals soon realized that other, tastier food could be found for a price. On Mondays, the marketplace featured goods often sold by the kilo using scales and counterweights. The Americans learned the Serbo-Croatian words for the staples: walnuts, apples, eggs, chickens, and tea. They used their fingers for numbers.

The airmen's high-altitude flight suits served well for the tempera-ture, which hovered around thirty degrees during daylight. Several of them, however, had lost their flying shoes with the snap of their para-chutes, a growing problem as the snow accumulated. The wisest had donned GI shoes before bailing out.

About half the Americans lived in the attic of the courthouse adjacent to the main square. The luckier ones stayed in houses scattered around town. Crews grew tribal, rarely talking to others. Whenever a group found a good thing, such as girls or food, they kept it to themselves.

The town lacked proper sanitation. Like their predecessors, the new arrivals found the toilet facilities to be appalling. Their escape kits con-tained halazone tablets for water purification, but they soon ran out. Most airmen contracted dysentery. Only those with iron stomachs, including Rosenthal, Stanley, Hoogeveen, Kidder, Robinson, Wunderlich, and Roper, dodged it.

No one escaped the lice. Nevertheless, few dared the Wednesday public showers more than once. There seemed little point. No real soap or towels were available. All attempts to rid their clothes of vermin failed. The fastidious Herky Marrone took to breaking the thin ice atop the river to wash his face and hands. A few of the men had packed flea powder, but it disappeared quickly. Only a handful carried toothbrushes. If a man owned one, his whole crew shared it.

The sole amenity besides the bathhouse was the barber shop. The blond Partisan with the generous bosom and linebacker's legs continued her robust business. Marrone discovered her and enjoyed a shave and a haircut. At least he felt clean from the neck up.[2]

■   ■   ■

Eight airmen convalesced in the wretched Partisan hospital: Scotty Stewart, John Elmore, Red Braun, Gene Dennis, George Earll, Willis Hodgeman, Herbert Eldridge, and an RAF or South African Air Force flier nobody knew anything about. Hodgeman had contracted pneumonia in addition to the stomach rupture he suffered during his jump.

The day after George Earll arrived, a matronly, English-speaking nurse examined his swollen ankle. She had trained at Birmingham-Southern College in Alabama and her accented English sounded both Slavic and southern. She taught basic sanitation to the junior nurses, who were mostly barefoot, illiterate volunteers. It was an uphill battle.

The nurse apologized that the X-ray machine—the "Roentgen," she called it—did not work, but she guessed Earll's ankle was not broken. It would probably be fine if he let it heal.

Earll's ward remained cold and drafty despite a pot-bellied woodstove burning in the corner. Each of the dozen lice-ridden beds held a sick or wounded man, several of whom were amputees. Less fortunate patients lay on the floor. Earll offered his bed to them, but they refused. "These are proud men," the senior nurse explained. Her reassurances did not ease Earll's conscience.

Broken shutters tapped against broken windows that failed to ventilate the stench of gangrenous flesh. When nature called, Earll grabbed a crude crutch and hobbled to a narrow hallway leading to a windowless latrine. A hole in the floor served as the commode. No toilet paper existed. There was no place to bathe or even wash one's hands for either the patients or the nurses.

One day, the attendants surprised Earll by stripping and washing the patients' clothing and beds with soap made of lye and ashes. He caught his nurse friend and asked why. "Typhus," she murmured. The airman shuddered and wondered if he would be better off somewhere else.

The mysterious British-accented airman complained constantly about the conditions. *So much for the famous stiff upper lip,* thought Earll. He did not blame the man, but he was not pleasant company.

Earll worried his wife Patty must have received a missing-in-action telegram by now. He spent much of his day sending her telepathic messages telling her that he was all right. The rest of the time he played cards with Gene Dennis, who lay in the bed next to his with a broken leg.[3]

■　　■　　■

On December 21, a pair of C-47 transports dipped below the overcast to drop supplies just outside of town. Dozens of parachutes filled the sky. Partisans rushed to collect the goods, intended to support the fighting near Bosanski Petrovac to the southwest and Banja Luka to the east.

Two days later, the Allies bombed Banja Luka. Reports came that over four hundred Germans were killed, but so were two hundred civilians. Many of the refugees in Sanski Most had relatives there. Some began to give the Americans the evil eye. Even the battle-hardened Partisans seemed unhappy.[4]

The next day, Christmas Eve, the British agents sent the Americans flight lunches and C-rations from the supply drop. Hixon Eldridge's men tore at their packages like children opening gifts from Santa. They celebrated by drinking honey-sweetened tea and singing Christmas songs.

Melancholy reigned in "Pop's" house, where Herky Marrone, Jim King, and five of Harry Blank's crew—Keith Owens, Bob Mitchell, Richard Kelly, Bill Otway, and Carey Rainey—resided. Their spirits failed to lighten even when Marrone brought in box lunches courtesy of the British. They, too, sang carols, but the mood seemed forced, and their voices petered out. Nobody bothered with a Christmas tree despite the plethora of firs growing in the surrounding countryside.

Charles Stanley had asked for a Catholic church shortly after he arrived in town. He had been directed to a bombed-out structure near Sasina, a village five miles away. It lacked a roof and looked abandoned. Stanley, fearing booby traps, dared not venture inside.

Giving up on finding a Catholic Mass for Christmas, Stanley and crewmate Darrell Kiger attended a midnight service at an Orthodox church in town. Joe Sedlak, Richard Heim, and Joe Foto appeared too, as did Larry Rosenthal and Bob Bartusch. "Are they going to let me in?" joked the Jewish Rosenthal. They admired the candlelit iconography as the priest conducted his rites.

The Americans could not understand a word. They left without realizing they had witnessed a regular Midnight Office, not a Christmas midnight Mass. Orthodox Christians celebrate Christmas on January 7, not December 25.[5]

If any of the airmen had wished for a white Christmas in line with the recent Bing Crosby hit, they got one. They awoke that morning to three fresh inches of snow.

Stanley had not realized he posed a politically charged question when he asked for a Catholic house of worship. Catholic Croatians formed the backbone of the hated Ustashe. Whoever sent him out into the countryside had played a cruel joke on him. A Catholic church stood at the north end of town, the Church of the Assumption of Mary.

Herky Marrone, Richard Kelly, Jack Mulvaney, Tom Stack, and Henry Rinna attended Mass there Christmas morning. Since the priest preformed the service in Latin, the Americans followed the rites easily. Marrone found the church to be lovely in its simplicity.

Later Marrone visited George Earll and Gene Dennis at the hospital. "Hubba, hubba, hubba!" he greeted the nurses. "Hubba, hubba, hubba," they replied with their Slavic accents. A wounded female soldier had been admitted to their ward. She endured her suffering without a whimper, despite being shot through the hip. Marrone gave her hard candies as a token of his respect.

December 25 fell on a Monday, and the marketplace bustled with vendors as usual. Several Americans went shopping. Keith Owens bought a large bone-handled knife, five kilos of honey, and a colorful sweater. The merchant threw in a red-starred garrison cap. Owens tried it on, convinced he could pass for a Partisan. Archy Roper marveled at the sheepskin coats and red fezzes worn by the Muslim men. Most women hid behind veils. He imagined they appeared much as their ancestors did a hundred years before.

Even though the Partisans were officially atheists, the commandant made a holiday feast available at the commissary for a nominal fee. Most of the airmen attended. The cooks served turkey or chicken, potatoes, squash, bread, and fig preserves, with cakes, apples, and cookies for dessert. They also delivered dinners to the airmen confined to the hospital.

Stanley's crew ordered chicken. Darrell Kiger preferred Spam and opened a can. Just as the processed stuff emerged, a lump of plaster from the ceiling dropped into it. The gods seemed to be punishing him for his affront to the holiday.

The commandant brought out wine, *rakija*, and cigarettes. Stanley and Tom Stack declined. Owens and a few others responded with toasts. "To Tito!" they cried.

The British agents brought their battery-powered radio to commissary and tuned it to the BBC. A German offensive in the Ardennes Forest had formed a huge bulge in the Allied lines, surrounding an American division in Bastogne. When the Germans demanded their surrender, General Anthony McAuliffe had responded with a succinct "Nuts!" The outcome remained in doubt. Jim King wondered if his brother John, serving with Patton's Third Army, would enter the fray.

A drunken English-speaking Yugoslav understood the news. "You're losing," he taunted. "You'll be chased off the continent!" The airmen told him to shut up but were not sure he was wrong.

They could not know the German offensive was already beginning to grind to a halt. Due to Allied air raids, the Germans had stockpiled only a five-day supply of gasoline for the attack. Hundreds of Wehrmacht tanks and trucks had already run dry.

Most of the airmen sitting around the radio in godforsaken Sanski Most had participated in the Oil Blitz. By starving the Nazi war machine of critical fuel supplies, they had made a significant contribution to the decisive victory soon to be won in distant Belgium.[6]

■   ■   ■

Marrone filled in a diary entry as he bedded down for the night. "Most of the boys are quiet today," he recorded. "Guess they are thinking of home and the inevitable telegram their families must have received from the War Department."

He read Tom Stack's mind. Stack hoped the MIA telegram had not yet reached his mother. He had been wrong, he knew, not to have told her he was flying combat missions. The missing-in-action notice would seem all the more shocking because he had failed to prepare her.[7]

Telegrams had indeed been sent to the homes of the first wave of arrivals. The families of the Eldridge and Marrone crews, shot down on December 11, received MIA notices just in time to ruin their Christmases.

Stanley's mother received her last letter from Charles on December 14. Days passed without another, but she was not overly concerned. Her son did not write daily, and a freak two-foot snowfall had interrupted mail service.

Word finally reached her on December 19. She took the news better this time. Charles had returned from being MIA very quickly in October. She decided to withhold the information from Mary Alice until after Christmas. Maybe good news would arrive by then.

The snow had hit Buffalo, too. No mail was delivered to the Schmitz household on the 14th or 15th. When it finally arrived on the 16th, it included Charles's Christmas presents for Mary Alice—a pearl necklace and matching earrings from Capri. That seemed a hopeful sign.

A week passed without further news. On the 23rd, another Christmas present, six red roses and six carnations, were delivered. This again seemed promising. Mary Alice did not know Mrs. Stanley had purchased them at Charles's prior request. Still, there was no letter.

Mary Alice feared Charles must be missing again. On Christmas Day, Mary Alice distracted herself by going to the movies. The main feature was *The Very Thought of You*, the story of a soldier who goes missing but returns to his sweetheart after an extended absence.

This sounded very much like her own situation to Mary Alice. Her story would surely have a happy ending too. A light snowfall greeted her as she left the theater. Crystalline mounds formed on the elms lining the streets. Wedges of sunshine pierced the clouds. A wave of euphoria swept over her. Everything was all right—she just knew it.

That night Charles's mother sat down to write to Mary Alice. She could not delay any longer. "It's happened again," Mrs. Stanley began. "Charles has been missing in action over Yugoslavia since Dec 2.... We can only wait, hope and pray, then pray some more. I'll let you know as soon as any more news comes through."[8]

■   ■   ■

The morning after Christmas dawned like any other in Sanski Most.

Tom Stack went to the Catholic church to pray for a quick evacuation so he could tell his mother he was safe. Archy Roper ate a soup breakfast at the commissary, supplemented by a pair of boiled eggs. Afterward the blond barber gave him a shave, and he returned to his house to play cards with the guys.

Midway through a hand of Hearts, electrifying news arrived. Planes would arrive at dusk. The airfield outside town had solidified, and the British agents had finally arranged for an evacuation.

Everyone scurried to pack. Tom Stack took the news as the answer to his prayers. A few airmen bought parting souvenirs with the last of their cash. Bill Otway splurged and spent twenty-five dollars on a colorful rug. *What the hell*, he thought. He did not need the money anymore.

At 3:00 p.m., the ICARUS team received confirmation that five planes were on their way—ETA 5:00 p.m. Everyone agreed the wounded should board first. The rest would go in order of arrival.

The airmen said goodbye to their hosts. Many gave away their food supplies in thanks. The heavily whiskered Stojan Ubarić kissed Stanley and his crew on both cheeks in farewell. The injured and sick were helped to the airfield.

All was in readiness at 1700 hours. Airmen helped the Partisans tramp down the snow. Dusk had fallen, so they lined the runway with kerosene-burning ash cans. Major Milbanke drove out in his jeep and turned on his headlights and the Eureka shortwave radio.

Minutes ticked by. The planes were late. Everyone searched the low clouds. Pilots wondered if the C-47s would dare to land considering the darkness, the overcast, and the surrounding mountains. At last, the drone of airplane engines emerged from the distance. The airmen's hearts soared. A cheer rose. Partisans fired green flares, the all-clear signal.

The murmur from the skies circled, then faded. Smiles withered as the airmen realized the rescue attempt had been abandoned. Crestfallen, they trudged back toward town. Rumors flew. Bob Kidder heard the batteries powering the Eureka device had failed. Larry Rosenthal, Joe Sedlak, and Tom Stack had seen a red flare among the green ones, a mistaken danger signal. Or maybe the ceiling had just been too low for a safe landing.

The soup kitchen had closed for the night. Roper and his roommates fixed some dehydrated beef from the flight lunches. The stuff tasted like bitter sawdust.[9]

■   ■   ■

The Partisans must have felt equally disappointed at the failed rescue attempt. The situation was getting out of hand. Refugees continued to stream into town, and food was growing scarce.

The main problem, however, was inflation. The Croatian puppet government had raised the money supply from the 8 million Kuna in circulation in 1941 to 149 million. Everyone knew Kuna would be worthless after the war. Vendors preferred the gold-backed dollars from the airmen's escape kits. They reserved their goods for the Americans, leaving the general populace to grumble. Moreover, many airmen failed to understand the going prices and overpaid, at least at first. Soon after he arrived, Henry Wunderlich bought a kilo of apples for a dollar. Later he learned that 100 Kuna, about two cents, would have been plenty.

Prices rose as supply failed to meet demand. Eggs, once 50 Kuna, now sold for 100. Chickens, once pegged at 1,000 Kuna, were up to 1,500—if they could be found at all. The airmen also bought tchotchkes and other non-perishable goods such as knives, guns, clothing, and carpets.

Commandant Despot Dusan exchanged Kuna for dollars in his office. Early on, a dollar converted to 1,000 Kuna. After the December 18 influx of Americans flooded the market, the dollar leapt to 4,000 Kuna. After Christmas, it rose to 5,000 Kuna. At $48 per escape kit, the airmen had carried about $3,400 into Sanski Most. This translated to 17 million Kuna—over one tenth of all the money in Croatia, more than enough to destabilize the local economy.

In addition, the airmen's conspicuous consumption violated Communist principles. A visiting commissar had already ousted Bartusch, Rosenthal, and Hirschfield from their comfortable lodging with the

Grozdens. One never knew when he might reappear. Commandant Dusan might suffer severe consequences if he failed to enforce Marxist doctrine.

A few days after Christmas, the commandant called Bob Bartusch, Larry Rosenthal, Hixon Eldridge, and Archy Roper into his office. Joe Sedlak and Emil Horak translated. Dusan told them all Americans must henceforth use Kuna in the marketplace and shops. They must also rein in their spending habits. It was not a request. Partisan "keepers"— enforcers—would make sure they complied.

Roper agreed to spend no more than 70 Kuna per egg. Bartusch and Rosenthal concurred, but kept mum about their huge stash of money. They had entered Sanski Most with nine escape kits containing $432, now valued at 2,160,000 Kuna. One rescue attempt had failed already. There was no telling how high prices might rise, or how long their dollars must last.

The airmen still roamed the town freely, but always with red star-capped shadows in their wake. The keepers meant business. One time, Henry Wunderlich had to relieve himself after curfew. He stepped outside and headed to the nearest tree. A sharp order came from behind: "*Stoj!*" Wunderlich knew it meant "halt" and froze. The keeper came over and sneered. "*Amerikanac!*" he bellowed, pointing toward the door. The airman reentered without accomplishing his mission.[10]

Money was not the only source of friction with the Partisans. While most Americans behaved well, others violated the Partisan code, if mostly in venial ways.

The Partisan code was more than a set of ethics; it was a way of life. Each Partisan had sworn to display bravery, stoicism, self-discipline, and sexual abstinence unless married. Women comprised one-eighth of the fighting force. The Army could not lose them to pregnancies.

The Americans knew fraternization was strictly forbidden, and most of them did not find the sturdier Slavic women to be attractive anyway. Many civilian girls wore forbidding veils. Female soldiers carried intimidating guns and grenades. There was also a language barrier to conquer.

Nevertheless, most of the airmen were young, single, and bored. Some yielded to temptation. Many women found the rich and exotic Americans to be fascinating, a situation bound to arouse suspicion and jealousy in the local males.

On one occasion, Joe Foto and a few crewmates happened upon a group of pretty, olive-complexioned girls, a rare find. Foto and the gang chatted them up. "*Ne Dobro! Ne Dobro!*" their keeper interrupted. "No good, no good." They were Dalmatians who had fraternized with the Germans. Foto got the picture and left them alone.

The incorrigible Herky Marrone spent Christmas afternoon drinking *rakija* with a Partisan girl named Darinka. Using a mixture of Italian, Serbo-Croatian, and broken English, she explained she would soon die of a heart condition. The next day, they met at her house. She wanted to take him to bed, but Marrone demurred. He worried a jealous Partisan might slit his throat.

The next evening, the scorned woman grabbed Marrone's knife and would have stabbed him if his roommates had not intervened. "Boy! Whatta woman!" observed Marrone in his diary. Undeterred by a trifle like attempted murder, he continued to see her over the next couple of days.

Owens and his group had their own supply of girls, four teenage sisters. Owens made time with Hedy, the eldest, and thought he could have gone "all the way" if he wanted to. Like Marrone, however, he stopped short. Too risky.

The Partisans also frowned upon excessive drinking. While they regularly imbibed, they were expected to hold their liquor and never displayed public drunkenness.

Clarence Martin, the goofball from Bob Dean's crew, had found a stash of moonshine out in the countryside. One night he wobbled back into town well after the nine o'clock curfew. "*Stoj!*" shouted a sentry. "*Zdravo!*" Martin slurred and kept coming. A more trigger-happy guard might have shot him. His crewmates marveled at his chutzpah and luck.

Perhaps the worst incident occurred when Herman Marrone discovered that one of his men, Gregg Cloos, had stolen some Partisan supplies. Marrone regarded the crime as especially heinous considering the debt the airmen owed the Partisans. Nevertheless, Marrone thought he had better not turn Cloos in, as they might shoot him. Instead, Marrone warned his crew to keep an eye on him.[11]

■   ■   ■

The day after the first rescue attempt failed, word spread that two transports would try again at noon. There would not be enough room for everyone, but at least the wounded could be evacuated. Once again, Stojan Ubarić smacked the Stanley crew on both cheeks. The hospitalized men dragged themselves from their beds. The airmen gathered at the field and helped tramp down the snow. Again, the engine noises circled, but the planes dared not descend through the low clouds. The airmen's hopes sank a second time. Strike two.

The next day repeated the previous two. This time, five transports were in the air. The airmen trudged out to the field feeling like victims of the boy who cried wolf. No one felt surprised when the planes failed to touch down. Strike three.[12]

CHAPTER 15

The Tourist Takes Charge

Captain James Bashford Johnson—pediatrician Dr. Johnson in the States—awoke at 5:30 a.m. full of nervous anticipation. He had decided to fly a combat mission that morning, as he had once per month since May. It was December 26, and if he did not get into the air soon, his next paycheck would not include flight pay. Most of his sorties had been easy runs to northern Italy, but a few had been chancy raids deep into the heart of the Third Reich. Since targets were never disclosed prior to the pre-mission briefings, today's risk would be strictly luck-of-the-draw.

Although Johnson's monthly flights increased his base salary by a hefty 50 percent, he had convinced himself that they served another, higher purpose. As a flight surgeon, he had the power to excuse airmen from missions with a diagnosis of combat fatigue. This he rarely did. Always on the lookout for malingerers, he often threatened recalcitrant fliers with court-martials. Disturbed by the griping of the jittery airmen he ordered into the air, Johnson told himself they would accept his decisions better if he could tell them he had shared their dangers and understood their anxieties.

One of Johnson's more infamous cases involved Pvt. Bob Hickman, a tail gunner whose straggling B-24 had been jumped by a host of German fighters. His crew persevered by shooting down six of their attackers. Each crewman won a Silver Star—a rare feat—but nine were injured in the melee. A cannon shell fractured Hickman's skull, and he spent months in the hospital. Hickman recovered physically but suffered from recurring nightmares. Dr. Johnson sent Hickman back into combat anyway. Hickman survived his thirty-five-sortie tour, but his copilot, Lt. Matt Hall, was killed eleven days after receiving his medal.

Today Johnson stashed a compass, matches, and some candy bars in his pockets. He also tucked away a Red Cross/Geneva Convention pass labeling him as a non-combatant, as well as a multi-language card asking to be guided to the nearest U.S. authority. Ready for anything, he hung his Brownie camera around his neck to record the day's adventure.[1]

■   ■   ■

Sunlight pierced the dreamy, dull gray of morning. After breakfast, Johnson joined the airmen scrambling aboard the open beds of olive-green trucks. Solemnity stilled everyone as they trundled off toward the briefing building. All shared the same unspoken question: Would today bring a milk run, or a dangerous mission against a heavily defended target?

The hush continued as the men filed into the briefing hut. In front stood the large curtain-covered map that would reveal today's target. Johnson searched the sea of faces for Lt. David Blood. The doctor wanted to talk to him, and it was not because of the man's wit and charm.

Blood was a hulking Texan who always needed a shave, the kind of pilot who contributed to the stereotype of hard-drinking, yahoo aviators. His upper lip sported a Robert Taylor pencil mustache, a look he did not quite carry off. His high-heeled cowboy boots did not help.

Before the war, Blood had earned his living with back-breaking labor in an iron foundry. The AAF could make him an officer, but not a gentleman. His belligerent bull voice dominated every conversation. He knew everything and shouted down anyone who disagreed with him, especially when he did not know what he was talking about. His overbearing manner embarrassed even his friends.

Physically, Blood was everything that Johnson was not—masculine, broad-shouldered, and imposing—but if the flight surgeon felt jealous, it was only because he coveted Blood's copious share of the great adventure. The bullying Blood was the most hated man on base, but Johnson liked him. The amateur psychologist felt that Blood, even at his most bellicose, was essentially harmless. No doubt, his cocksure bluster disguised some deep-rooted insecurity.

Johnson knew that Blood's weight far exceeded the 200-pound limit for pilots, but he could not bring himself to ground him. Blood was no angel, but he was a hot pilot—maybe too hot. He was rumored to have performed a low-level buzzing of the Leaning Tower of Pisa, a major infraction.

Blood's risky takeoff from the emergency airstrip on the Island of Vis—along with fellow Texan and now Sanski Most resident Robert Dean—had only enhanced his legend. Dean had sensibly headed straight for Italy. Blood circled back and buzzed the airfield just to show those limeys how wrong they had been to tell him the runway was too short for a B-24 takeoff. In the process, he just barely missed the mountain at the end of the runway. One unnerved crewman vowed he would never fly with Blood again and transferred out.

"Stick with me, boys, and I'll have you home by Christmas," Blood promised his men. He urged them to volunteer for dangerous night missions to pile up mission credits, but they declined.

Maybe Blood was just too dumb to be scared, but Johnson reasoned that one had to take the bad with the good when it came to hotshot fliers.[2]

■   ■   ■

Johnson had no trouble finding Blood in the briefing room. The man was slightly smaller than a Sherman tank. Johnson weaved his way through the stools—really the packing boxes for bomb fins—and peered up into the big Texan's face. Would Blood mind if he tagged along today?

Blood glowered incredulously. What did this little guy with the milquetoast voice and the absurd camera think he was doing? Hadn't he heard the rumors that this would be a rough mission?

Before Blood could respond, an adjutant called the meeting to attention. "Seats!" he cried. Everyone found one.

The commander unveiled the giant map in the front of the room. A red cellophane strip stretched all the way to Blechhammer South. Johnson had picked a hell of a day for a joyride.

Staff briefed the pilots, navigators, bombardiers, and radio operators in accordance with their specialties. After the normal pep talk from the group leader, a chaplain closed with a prayer. Everyone spilled outside roused, anxious, and alert. They threw their gear onto open truck beds and boarded them for the mile-long ride to their awaiting planes.

Johnson's truck lumbered off into the apricot dawn. The rumbling tires jostled the men into one another, eliciting uncharitable curses. Johnson inwardly chastised them for always lowering their gaze toward the muddy ground. Instead, they ought to raise their eyes toward distant Mount Vulture—"Old Sawtooth" to them—and admire the extinct volcano's jagged beauty.[3]

■   ■   ■

The flight line hummed with activity as ground crews topped off the planes' gas tanks. Each B-24 would carry an extra three hundred gallons for maximum range.

Johnson had selected Blood partially due to the reliability of his aircraft, *Hell's Angel*. Today, however, she looked tired. Spots of aluminum peeked through her eroded olive-green paint. Blood's navigator for the day, Flight Officer George Benedict, noted the prayer offered by the ground chief at a neighboring hardstand. Legend had it that he had never lost a B-24. Too bad *Hell's Angel* was not one of his planes.

Sandy-haired bombardier Eugene Cogburn boarded *Hell's Angel* with a look of disgust. He had witnessed Blood's antics around the base and had managed to avoid him until now. *What luck,* he thought. *Of all the pilots in the squadron, I had to draw this buffoon for my first mission.*

Copilot Lewis Baker and ball turret gunner Wilmot "Gibby" Gibson appeared disgruntled too, but not because of Blood. Baker had flown with the boisterous Texan before—including during the audacious takeoff from Vis—and appreciated the heft he brought to the cockpit. Standing only five-foot-four and weighing just 130 pounds, the curly-haired Baker needed a strong presence in the commander's chair.

This had been even more the case since June, when Baker's right shoulder and back were hit by shrapnel over Munich. Three surgeries followed. The shoulder remained weak, but not enough to send him home. A visit to a fighter base gave him an idea: since flying heavy bombers was too difficult, perhaps he should try fighters. Baker's commanding officer agreed and told him he would recommend a transfer. The deal seemed done until Dr. Johnson stepped in and nixed it, claiming Baker ought to be able to fly B-24s. "He's crazy!" grumbled Baker in his diary.

Gibby Gibson looked even smaller than Lewis Baker. He had started flying in May and would have long since rotated out if not for a remarkable string of bad luck. A roommate cleaning his sidearm had accidentally shot him in the abdomen. While convalescing, Gibson contracted malaria and infectious hepatitis. Still not entirely recuperated, Gibson was one of the several unfortunates whom Dr. Johnson had forced back into combat.

And here, boarding *Hell's Angel*, was the meddling flight surgeon who had committed disservices against both Baker and Gibson. Neither was overjoyed to see him.[4]

■   ■   ■

Johnson, for his part, had formed strong opinions about many members of Blood's crew. He regarded his flight engineer, Fred Sherer, to be quite capable despite his youth. A blond, good-natured Alabaman, Sherer was the only member of Blood's original crew still flying with him. He and Blood had struck up an officer–enlisted friendship rare even for the informal AAF. A football lineman in high school, Sherer indulged Blood in impromptu boxing bouts whenever the pilot felt the urge.

Johnson cast a suspicious eye at waist gunner Sgt. Thomas Tamraz, who fainted whenever the doctor gave him an injection or drew blood. The flight surgeon suspected he was bucking for a Section Eight by feigning mental instability. In truth, except for his phobia of needles, Tamraz had guts to spare. He had flown several dangerous missions with the Eighth Air Force, including some against Berlin. Later he transferred to the Fifteenth and joined Blood's crew. Blood's buzzing of the Leaning Tower of Pisa and the Vis airstrip had not fazed him a bit.

Johnson also suspected the swarthy Tamraz of being a Turk, somehow a bad thing in the doctor's estimation. In truth, Tamraz's family were Assyrian, Eastern Rite Christians who barely escaped the Assyrian genocide committed by the Ottomans and the Kurds during and after the First World War. Tom's father, Yohannon, never forgot his first sight of the Statue of Liberty—a symbol of the freedom and opportunity he sought for his family. Tom grew up speaking English, Turkish, and Assyrian, a rare neo-Aramaic language related to the tongue spoken by Jesus Christ.

Johnson barely noticed Tamraz's nondescript pal, tail gunner Warren LaFrance. He and Tamraz had shared many misadventures since they met stateside. On the night before they shipped overseas, they went AWOL to keep dates with twin sisters. Both reasoned the Army would rather send them into combat than court-martial them after eighteen months of training. Upon their return, the tipsy pair walked straight up to the MP at the gate and admitted their guilt. "Have a good time in Europe," chortled the MP as he waved them past.[5]

■   ■   ■

Blood finished his checklist and woke up his engines. A deafening chorus from two dozen other B-24s joined in. The air filled with acrid blue-gray exhaust. Blood taxied the beast off the hardstand, its struts squealing under their obese burden.

The steel mesh runway lay on a slight grade. Unless a strong wind blew to the contrary, planes took off downhill and landed uphill. Today they would use the downward angle as usual. Nevertheless, when Blood's turn came, *Hell's Angel* could not muster enough speed for takeoff. Blood decelerated, rolled out of the way of the other planes, and called for a gas truck to top off the tank. Not wanting to fall too far behind, he decided against taxiing the mile back to the high end of the runway. Instead, after the rest of the planes had passed, Blood prepared to execute a power takeoff much as he had at Vis.

The crew shot each other incredulous looks. Taking off in a ground-loving, overloaded B-24 was always a nerve-wracking feat. To do so uphill against the wind was madness.

Blood revved the engines, released the brakes, and pulled the throttles all the way back with his right hand. Baker placed his left hand on top of Blood's and called out the air speed indicator numbers. At the critical mark, they heaved back on their control wheels. The nose gear teased off the ground, bounced, and rebounded. Blood willed *Hell's Angel* into the air.

One of Gene Cogburn's duties as bombardier was to open the bomb bay doors to release any water that might have splashed in during takeoff. If he waited too long, the water would freeze and jam the doors. The right doors opened, but the left refused. He hailed Blood and reported the malfunction. Normal procedure was to abort the mission. *Forget it*, snapped Blood. *I have never aborted a mission and I never will. Drop the bombs through the doors if you have to.*

Meanwhile, flight engineer Fred Sherer discovered that one of the gasoline tanks had lost fuel. The gas caps topped the wings at their highest point so they could be filled to the brim. This spot also produced the most lift, and thus the most suction, and gas tended to siphon from the caps during climbs. Between this and Blood's power takeoff, *Hell's Angel* had lost two hundred gallons, nearly the whole reserve supply.

Blood went to full throttle, caught up with the formation, and settled into the Tail-End Charlie position. Silver B-24s filled the sky ahead.

Over Yugoslavia, a riot of twin-tailed P-38s joined the formation. Soon, however, Blood's number two engine began to vibrate badly. The drive shaft sounded defective. Five planes turned back with mechanical problems. Blood flew on.

The formation approached the target at noon. Cloud-free skies presented an excellent opportunity for visual bombing, but equally clear shooting for the flak gunners below. A volley of shells rocketed skyward. Explosions spewed metal shards. *Hell's Angel* shook. Baker shut his eyes, but Blood stared the barrage down, nervous as a glacier. Time slowed.

The port bomb bay doors still refused to open. As Cogburn prepared to knock his bombs through, orders came over the radio: slower B-17s were crossing below. The B-24s would have to go around again. This was bad. Passing over Blechhammer once was brutal—twice was suicidal.

Blood's formation circled back. As they penetrated the target zone again, the flak seemed fiercer than before. Another eternity passed. The lead bombardier dropped his bombs. Cogburn followed suit. The left-side bombs clanged through the doors.

A flash erupted from in front as Lt. Arthur Lindell's B-24 took a direct hit in the midsection and split in two. Both halves spun earthward. No parachutes emerged.

More explosions lacerated Blood's right wing and tail. The cranky number two engine conked out. Fuel billowed. Blood feathered the smoking engine to prevent an explosion. Wind blasted through the dangling bomb bay doors, dragging at the plane and frosting its windows. Blood had always said that "flying a B-24 is like wrestling a bear." Now it was especially so.[6]

A half hour later, Blood dropped *Hell's Angel* out of formation to save gas. Everyone scanned the sky for fighters. Flight engineer Fred Scherer was busy helping the pilots, so Tom Tamraz took his post in the top turret. Famished from the long flight, he wolfed down a Hershey bar from his pocket. Soon the chocolate and the monotonous engines lulled him into a deep sleep.

George Benedict gave Blood a heading for Vis. They passed over Hungary, losing altitude every minute. Tamraz awoke with a start. An eerie silence had replaced the drone of the engines. Something felt terribly wrong. He looked down from his perch in the turret and saw Sherer tap the three-foot-long fuel gauge. "We're out of gas!" he yelled.

Sherer did not wait for orders. A B-24 glided like a rock. He grabbed the nearest parachute, strapped it to his harness, and jumped out the yawning bomb bay feet-first.

That's my chute! thought Tamraz. Before he could react, Captain Johnson fixed his Brownie camera to his harness and followed Sherer out. Tamraz snapped to. He had heard no bailout signal, but it was time to move. It was every man for himself.

Tamraz reached under his seat, pulled the release cord, and tumbled down from the turret in a tangle of wires and oxygen tubes. He landed astraddle George Benedict, who had just emerged from the nose. A free chute lay nearby. It must belong to radio operator Michael Yaworsky, who was in the rear manning a waist gun. He could grab one of the spare parachutes stashed back there. Tamraz released Benedict and hooked the pack to his harness. Yaworsky's GI boots were attached. Tamraz hoped they would fit.

Benedict had disappeared. Tamraz raced to the bomb bay and dove out headfirst. Remembering his training, he coolly rolled onto his back. Three open canopies floated above. His free fall had taken him far from the others. He pulled the rip cord and settled into a nice, quiet ride.[7]

■   ■   ■

Fred Sherer's parachute snagged on a tree, suspending him fifteen feet above the snowy ground. A scream for help came from the distance. There was only one way to get down: Sherer hit his harness release and hit the earth hard. He was still checking whether he was in one piece when a peasant approached pointing frantically at the other side of a ravine.

Gene Cogburn lay there screaming. Sherer rushed over to discover that the bombardier's left leg had caught in a crevice and snapped like a dry branch. Bones protruded from his shin. It was the ugliest thing Sherer had ever seen.

Dr. Johnson stumbled upon the scene still carrying his camera. If only he had packed a medical bag instead. At least his escape kit contained a syrette of morphine. Johnson stuck it in Cogburn's leg and had Scherer help him splint it with branches and parachute shrouds.

The peasant took Cogburn's gun, fired it into the air, and gave it back. Soon another man arrived leading a horse. They gingerly mounted Cogburn on its back. Johnson and Sherer trailed them to a nearby farmhouse overlooking a steep mountainside.[8]

■   ■   ■

Soon Michael Yaworsky, Warren LaFrance, Wilmot Gibson, and nose gunner Bob Kolvet, a 200-pounder with a glorious handlebar mustache, straggled in. None were hurt, though Gibson and LaFrance were shoeless. A Partisan had taken Gibson's GI shoes. LaFrance had lost his flight boots to the snap of his parachute. The hapless LaFrance had been smart enough to pack a canvas bag full of emergency supplies, yet foolish enough to cast it out of the camera hatch thinking he would find it on the ground. Of course, he never did.

The next day, Partisans brought an oxcart for Cogburn and led the airmen toward Drvar, a two-hour hike. As they departed, Captain Johnson effusively bestowed the entire forty-eight dollars from his escape kit to his hostess. The other airmen shook their heads. No one knew how long they would be missing or what conditions lay ahead.

Blood, Baker, and Benedict awaited them in Drvar. The three of them had found one another soon after reaching the ground. Blood was limping. Too heavy for his parachute, he had sprained both knees upon landing. The AAF set weight limits for airmen for a reason.

Blood counted noses. Only Tom Tamraz remained unaccounted for.[9]

■   ■   ■

Tamraz's parachute broke through the clouds. Below, pine-filled, craggy mountains probed the sky. A convoy of troops loitered in a nearby clearing. Tracer bullets flew in his direction. *It's just like the Fourth of July,* mused Tamraz. *No,* he reminded himself, *that's machine-gun fire, and those men are trying to kill me.*

The languid swirl of his descent transformed into a backward rush. Before he could right himself, his parachute caught on the high branches of an evergreen tree. Tamraz unfastened his harness, shimmied down the trunk, and moved away as stealthily as he could.

Before long, Tamraz heard tramping feet and froze. Several German soldiers accompanied by four bearded locals approached. Tamraz jumped behind a boulder, his heart pounding so loudly he thought the searchers must hear it. He held his breath until they passed by.

Toward dusk, Tamraz emerged from his hiding spot and stole toward a valley. Voices arose from the darkness. Three teenage girls appeared. The airman moved into view and flashed the Churchillian "V" for victory signal. The gesture seemed to confuse the girls. Apparently, Yugoslavian teens did not watch Allied newsreels. Still, they did not look hostile or frightened. "Partisans?" Tamraz asked. "*Da!*" they exclaimed. One girl's eyes teared up. Tamraz let them hug him. Then the oldest beckoned him to follow.

The girls led him to their farmhouse, where a boy of about six greeted them. The girls took Tamraz into the bedroom, sat him on the bed, and took off his heavy jacket. They brought bread, a glass of *slivovitz*, and a slice of pork cut from a smoked carcass suspended from the rafters.

Tamraz tested his languages. *Mama? Papa?* One girl understood. She drew her index finger across her throat. No wonder these poor kids were anxious to help. They fired up the woodstove and brought blankets and quilts. Tamraz spent the night comfortably.

The next morning a man with a red star on his cap arrived. "*Zdravo*," he saluted. Tamraz returned the salute. *Wait here*, the soldier seemed to say, and departed. The next day, a party of Partisans came to guide him to town. Before he left, Tamraz cut away part of his parachute and gave it to the girls. They hugged him and cried as he took his leave.

Tamraz reunited with his crewmates in Drvar. Spotting Fred Sherer, he wheeled and punched the much larger, very surprised man in the face. "He stole my parachute!" screamed Tamraz. Blood separated them. "Let's have none of that," drawled the Texan. "We all made it." Tamraz stood down. Sherer had merely grabbed the wrong chute in his haste.[10]

■   ■   ■

Around midnight, Partisans collected the airmen and guided them to Drvar's railroad station, where they would board a train for the already overcrowded gathering point at Sanski Most. A group of twenty Partisan soldiers gathered around a campfire near the antique train. Bottles passed. One of the men squeezed a concertina, and others sang along. Some danced in the glow of the flames. The airmen warmed themselves by the fire.

Tamraz surveyed the train. Its half-sized, wood-fed engine belonged in the previous century. Attached were a few flatcars and a single boxcar. The main cargo seemed to be cigarettes, but one flatcar was stacked with woven bags covered by a tarpaulin. White granules flecked off the sides. A lone soldier swigging a bottle of *slivovitz* stood guard.

Tamraz turned to Warren LaFrance, who was usually up for shenanigans. "Let's go get some sugar," he suggested.

"Are you nuts?" LaFrance protested. "They'll kill you if you get caught."

Undeterred, Tamraz fashioned a sack from his parachute remnants. He moseyed up to the sentinel, drew out his harmonica, and played a simple ditty. Fascinated, the guard put down his bottle and beckoned for the instrument. Tamraz coyly resisted. The guard repeated his motions more urgently. Tamraz relented and edged next to the flatcar. As the guard blew into the mouth organ tunelessly, the airman felt behind his back, raised the tarp, and slipped his pocketknife blade into a sack. A pound of white granules filled his improvised bag. Tamraz eased it into his jacket and pulled the tarp back down.

Tamraz retrieved his harmonica and returned to the campfire. "Did you get it?" breathed LaFrance.

"Yeah," said Tamraz, offering him a pinch as proof.

LaFrance tasted it. "You dummy!" he hissed. "That's not sugar. It's salt."

Tamraz's face fell. He regretted risking his life for a pound of salt, as if dying for sugar made more sense. He need not have lamented, however. Salt was one of the rarest and most precious commodities in Yugoslavia, far more prized than sugar. His ill-gotten stash would serve him well during the long odyssey ahead.[11]

■   ■   ■

After a few hours, the eleven airmen boarded the boxcar, and the train started down the line. They arrived in Sanski Most in the early morning hours of December 31. Gene Cogburn was confined to the hospital with his broken leg. The rest of the crew was escorted to the already overcrowded attic of the courthouse on the town square.

David Blood's bull voice boomed as he entered the room. Bob Dean could not believe his ears. He had first encountered his fellow Texan during training. Then they had improbably bumped into each other on Vis. Now here was Blood again, big as life, reappearing in remote Sanski Most. "Oh my God!" exclaimed Dean. Was this bigmouth going to haunt him the entire war?[12]

■   ■   ■

The Partisan commandant, Despot Dusan, could not have been pleased either. Too many Americans with too much money were already consuming too many resources and breaking too many rules. Here were eleven more mouths to feed, eighty-four in total now. On the other hand, one of the new men was a physician; maybe he could help at the hospital.

Captain Johnson, who began the day as a tourist and had never commanded any group beyond his five-man medical team, had become the highest-ranking American officer in Sanski Most. He intended to take charge.

CHAPTER 16

At the Mercy of Friends

A s 1944 closed, downed American airmen had been accumulating in Sanski Most for forty days with no end in sight. Transports had arrived overhead but failed to land on December 26, 27, and 28. Bad weather grounded the entire Fifteenth Air Force on December 30 and 31.

The poor weather prevented airborne rescues across the rest of Yugoslavia as well. On January 1, 1945, the AAF issued a new bulletin to address the growing issue:

> In recent weeks a number of circumstances have arisen which have made it extremely difficult, if not impossible, to evacuate forced landed airmen from Jugoslavia [sic] by air. This means that such airmen must, under certain circumstances, walk under Partisan escort to points on the coast from which they can be evacuated by sea.... These same circumstances which make difficult the evacuation of airmen hinder the supplying of Allied missions in Jugoslavia. Therefore, airmen cannot expect to be supplied with clothing or arms by these missions

up to the same standard as was possible in the summer months.

Reports have been received that certain airmen have been insubordinate while in the custody of Allied missions. Such an attitude is a poor return for the assistance which has been given so freely to hundreds of stranded airmen. All concerned must understand that if they expect to be assisted in their return to their units, they must obey the instructions of their helpers regardless of rank or nationality.

The weather forecast for the next several days offered no hope of improvement. The airmen in Sanski Most were on their own, even as tensions with their Partisan hosts mounted daily.[1]

■　　■　　■

Dr. Johnson toured the Partisan hospital in Sanski Most soon after he arrived. The conditions were appalling. Severed limbs littered the halls. Cow-eyed, barefoot nurses routinely reused bloody bandages without so much as a rinse.

The injured airmen were glad to see an American doctor, but he could do little without his medical bag. Gene Cogburn's fractured leg threatened gangrene. If it got worse, Johnson would have to amputate, and the anesthesia was gone. Scotty Stewart's leg looked nearly as bad.

Johnson marched over to Commandant Despot Dusan's office with undisguised disgust. What kind of a hospital did he run? What kind of doctors allowed such conditions? The hospital staff must follow his protocols from now on. Everything must be thoroughly cleaned. Moreover, as the ranking AAF officer, he was entitled to private quarters.

Dusan turned Johnson away. The last thing he needed was another American irritant.[2]

■   ■   ■

Tom Tamraz discovered that many of the merchants in town spoke his third language, Turkish. He bought a *torba*—a single-strapped haversack—a cooking pot, and blue stationery.

When nature called, Tamraz visited the indoor latrine on the second floor of his building. Frozen dung clung to the walls. He was squatting over one of the two holes when the stout but pretty blonde barber sauntered in wearing gun belts and grenades. She saluted, parked her rifle, dropped her drawers, and crouched next to him. "*Odakle si?*" she asked. "Where are you from?"

"Chicago," blurted Tamraz. They made small talk. She finished her business, saluted again, and departed with a neat "*Dobar Dan*" ("Good day.") Tamraz stood agape.[3]

■   ■   ■

The irksome Captain Johnson and the rest of the Blood crew seemed to be the last straws for the Partisans. Prices had risen so high that only the Americans could afford to buy food.

On New Year's Eve, someone approached Archy Roper with a startling rumor: the Partisans intended to send the able-bodied airmen to the coast, partway by train. The idea sounded absurd. Roper's rail trip from Srnetica, less than twenty miles away, had taken eleven hours—and that was before the recent snowfalls. The Adriatic lay a hundred miles beyond. Bosanski Petrovac had recently fallen to the Germans. The path did not seem safe, especially for a large group of lightly armed men untrained in ground combat.

Before long, Commandant Despot Dusan summoned the Americans for a talk. The airmen walked uneasily through the falling snow to the town square. This could not be good.

The commandant explained the situation as Lt. Michael, the English-speaking Partisan who had escorted Herky Marrone and Jim

King into town, translated. Food was growing scarce, and prices were rising. The townspeople were complaining—too many airmen, too small a town. The Americans must go.

The plan, the commandant continued, was for the able-bodied evadees to board the train the next day. They would ride about eighty kilometers, nearly halfway to the Adriatic. Trucks would carry them the rest of the way to Split.

The Americans grumbled as the meeting broke up. Most of them had previous experiences with the railroad, none of which inspired confidence. Everyone wanted to go home, but not this way. Waiting for transports made more sense.

Major Milbanke had driven his jeep away to Grabovnica on an undisclosed errand, so Captain Tregidga now served as the senior British agent in town. A month before, Tregidga had been stationed at Bugojno, the southern terminus of the railway. He knew the territory. It was very unlikely, he told the airmen, that any trucks would meet them there. The terrain was too rugged. The airmen would have to hike to the coast through heavily forested mountains. There would be virtually no food or shelter along the way. The plan was a pipe dream, but he had no authority over the commandant.[4]

■   ■   ■

After the meeting, Tregidga returned to his cottage with Corporal Davis, his radioman. Tom Stack and Henry Rinna, who had befriended Davis during their train ride into town, tagged along. They called Bari at their daily scheduled time, 3:00 p.m.

Tregidga told headquarters the situation was critical. The Partisans were forcing the airmen to undertake a quixotic journey to the coast. The plan would surely end in disaster. Could Bari send planes today?

No, Bari replied. Italy was socked in by cloud cover. They would try tomorrow, weather permitting.

The last radio battery died even as the transmission ended. Their power had been used up during the several broadcasts of the past week. The cold did not help.

Tregidga had been afraid of this. Without Major Milbanke's jeep, he had no means of recharging the batteries. If Tregidga did not contact Bari at three o'clock tomorrow, headquarters—per protocol—would assume the mission was overrun or otherwise compromised. Even if planes were on the way, they would be recalled on the assumption that the landing field was not secure.

There was one hope: the British had liberated an American-made generator from the Russians, but someone had gummed up its insides by greasing them with butter. Maybe the airmen could fix it. Rinna, a radio operator, said he would give it a try.

The first step was to clean out the butter. He and Tom Stack disassembled the works and wiped each component with gasoline-soaked rags. Dusk fell, and they brought out flashlights and candles. After several hours, their frozen hands had reassembled the pieces. They wound a cord around the lawnmower-style starter and cranked it. Nothing happened. The motor would not catch.

Then Stack remembered a high school lecture on the art of combustion. First the fuel, Father Buckley had insisted, then the spark. Currently, the spark preceded the fuel. Rinna and Stack took the components apart again and filed down the spark plug point. They reassembled the generator and pulled the starter cord again. Fuel came, then spark. It caught.

Jubilant, they called Tregidga and Davis into the room. A satisfying *pockita-pockita* greeted them. The British agents beamed. Pleased with himself, Stack turned the motor off. "No!" cried the others. How did he know it would start again?

Stack had realized his mistake even before they spoke. He pulled the crank again. The generator started up. He kept it going while Davis fetched the batteries.

Tregidga insisted that Stack and Rinna stay and celebrate New Year's Eve. He broke out biscuits and a fifth of twelve-year-old scotch. The woodstove glowed. Davis found the BBC on the radio. Splendid music blared, including the plaintive "White Christmas." At midnight London time, Big Ben tolled the chimes. Londoners let out a roar. Four voices in Yugoslavia joined in.

Another bottle of scotch remained, but the men decided they'd better sober up for tomorrow's radio transmission. They capped the evening with a breakfast of Spam, powdered eggs, and strong coffee.[5]

■   ■   ■

In town, the Partisans prepared a party to celebrate the New Year and the airmen's departure. It would be held at the hall where Bartusch, Hirschfield, and Rosenthal had been honored a month earlier.

Hedy, the oldest of the four sisters who socialized with Keith Owens and his roommates, dropped by their abode with her friend Dorisha to invite them to the party. Owens, Herky Marrone, Jim King, Dick Kelly, Bill Otway, and Bill Rainey decided to warm up for the festivities with some *rakija*. Owens poured out jiggers and passed the glasses around. They inhaled the shots. Everyone gasped, eyes popping, as their mouths went numb. Wow, the stuff was foul. Undaunted, Owens toasted each of his friends with a shot, and they set off for the party. He was stumbling drunkenly by the time they reached the hall. Marrone pulled him up short. "Don't go in there," Marrone urged. "You don't want the girls to see you like this." Owens was in no condition to argue and headed home. He vomited midway.

The party started with gusto. Half the Americans attended, as did dozens of townspeople. Male and female Partisans dotted the scene, armed to the teeth as always. Someone started playing a concertina. A circle formed to dance the *kolo*, a Slavic folk dance.

The pretty blond Partisan who had met Tamraz in the indoor outhouse coaxed him onto the floor. Everyone put their hands around each other's waists and began a clockwise movement. The circle reversed, and the steps became more intricate. Tamraz kept up as best as he could.

Larry Rosenthal wished for a piano. Man, he would have torn the place up. He and Bartusch were not drinking. Bartusch was too sick with dysentery to think about it. Rosenthal liked beer, and there was none to be had. He asked a teenage Partisan girl about the German machine gun she carried. She pointed the nozzle at the ceiling and fired a burst. Plaster showered down. No one took notice. The girl led him by the hand to the *kolo*. After a time, she asked him to come home with her. Rosenthal thought he had better not.

Herky Marrone's would-be paramour, Darinka, came after him again. He never knew if she would kiss him or kill him. This game of living dangerously had grown old. Grateful he would be leaving tomorrow, he dodged her as best he could.

The room thickened with raucous laughter, cigarette smoke, and twice-breathed air. *Slivovitz* and *rakija* flowed. Joe Sedlak and Bernie Button stood side by side with glasses in their hands. "Chug-a-lug," Button sang. "Drink, chug-a-lug, chug-a-lug, chug-a-lug it." Sedlak downed his glass with a tilt of his head. Across the way, Joe Foto traded savage drinks with his crewmates.

Mike Yaworsky, David Blood's radio operator, had grown up speaking Ukrainian. He toasted his hosts with a phrase universal in the Slavic world: "*Na zdorovie*." "To your health."

"*Na zdorovie*," they replied. It was nice to see a polite American.[6]

Not all the airmen were so well-mannered. Young William Lane, still mourning the death of John Wolff and his other crewmates, became drunk and made a scene. A displeased Partisan officer ordered him out. His friends hustled him away.

Stanley's men did not mingle with the crowd. Stanley never drank, and Darrell Kiger did not like the stuff on hand. Forrest Smalley, however, became roaring drunk. Stanley spied him yelling at Don Baker, their copilot. *What could he have against Baker?* wondered Stanley. *He's one of the nicest guys on the crew.*

Before anyone could react, Smalley pulled a knife and waved it at Baker. Smalley's bitter eyes darted. The crew gathered about. "Put the knife down," they told the crazed man. "What's wrong with you?" Smalley ignored them.

Stanley pulled out his .45 and leveled it. That got Smalley's attention. "Put the knife down," repeated the pilot. A flicker of awareness registered in Smalley's glaucous eyes. Ed Seaver stood closest. "Give it to Ed," ordered Stanley. Seaver reached over and gingerly took the knife, and everyone let their breath out. They surrounded Smalley and escorted him away.

Stanley wondered if he would have pulled the trigger if Smalley had attacked. He holstered his gun, almost wishing for a drink.[7]

Meanwhile, the party continued unabated. Hedy and Dorisha danced with their American friends. Goofy Clarence Martin frolicked with an older woman named Yulekitza, who looked sturdy enough to toss him over her shoulder.

At last, the party broke up into the pitch-black night. Boisterous airmen felt their way through the stygian darkness. A muted *clip-clop* came from somewhere down the snow-covered street. The hoofbeats stopped. Bob Dean found himself face to face with a giant, threadbare horse—close enough to kiss. His crew erupted in woozy hilarity. Fortunately, their quarters stood nearby, and they stumbled off, their sides aching from laughter.[8]

■   ■   ■

The next day dawned with the first clear sky in memory. Stanley's crew prepared to travel while Forrest Smalley nursed his hangover. He did not remember brandishing his knife at Baker. It was a court-martial offense, but Stanley let it go.

As he had thrice before, Stojan Ubarić, the Stanley crew's bushy-bearded host, bid goodbye by kissing each of them on both cheeks. He handed Stanley a letter addressed to relatives in Trenton, New Jersey. Stanley promised to mail it when he could.

Bernie Button happened by the commandant's office. Dusan was dispensing a severe reprimand to Clarence Martin and his would-be paramour, Yulekitza. She had spent the night in jail after fighting with another woman over Martin. Martin emerged from Dusan's office wearing his Mortimer Snerd smile. "*Zdravo!*" saluted Button.

"*Gravo!*" replied Martin nonsensically.

Not long afterwards, Tom Stack and Hank Rinna arrived at the office to urge the commandant to hold the 11:00 a.m. train. They had reestablished contact with headquarters, and transports might arrive later in the day. The open skies meant they would have no trouble landing. Tregidga would radio Bari at three o'clock to confirm.

The commandant received the news with equanimity. He agreed to delay the departure until three o'clock, but no longer. One way or the other, the airmen must leave today.

Stack and Rinna returned to their quarters. "Where the fuck have you been?" asked Sig Piekarski. They replied with a chorus of "Auld Lang Syne." Piekarski, Lane, Hodgeman, and Kidder gazed at them incredulously. Were these guys drunk? "We contacted Bari," Stack and Rinna explained. "The planes might be coming!" No wonder they felt giddy.

The commandant accompanied Stack and Rinna when they returned to Captain Tregidga's quarters for the three o'clock transmission. Headquarters had mixed news: bad weather in Italy had grounded the Fifteenth again, but good flying conditions were predicted. The transports could fly again soon.

The commandant had heard promises like that before. The bottom line was that planes were not on their way. Three failed rescue attempts were enough—the Americans must go.[9]

■　　■　　■

Sixty-some airmen gathered at the train station on the town square. Twenty or so others were excused as being too sick or injured. Dr.

Johnson stayed behind to tend to them. Harry Carter avoided the journey too, perhaps as Stewart's caregiver. He thought the endeavor to be foolish and hopeless. In any case, he was unabashedly trying to remain MIA long enough to go home.

It was Monday, market day again. Some crews, including Bartusch's and Eldridge's bunches, stocked up on boiled eggs, apples, and bread for the journey. Tom Tamraz packed his haversack with his parachute, walnuts, and his ill-gotten salt. The temperature had plunged, so Marrone and Owens took the precaution of buying knit wool sweaters.

The Americans boarded three boxcars, while Partisans and civilians climbed aboard two flatcars. Several bore luggage containing their remaining possessions. A few women wore Muslim veils.

Lt. Michael, the sinewy English-speaking Partisan who would lead the expedition, bore a smoked lamb. Other Partisans carried raw carcasses on their backs. Loaves of bread clunked on the boxcar floor like stones. The train's fireman and the engineer clutched a squealing pig. Tamraz concluded the train was well-provisioned.

The train inched forward. After a few feet it stalled and ground to a stop. The engineer built up steam and tried again. Gradually, they rumbled off.[10]

Thirty minutes later the train stalled again, already out of fuel. Partisans jumped off flatcars with saws and axes in hand. Rail fences became the first victims. Meanwhile, snow was shoveled into the boiler. The train started but stopped after another half hour. The process repeated into the night.

Sometimes the Americans disembarked to stretch their legs or relieve themselves. At one point, Joe Sedlak leaned against the boxcar as he took care of business. His hand stuck to the metal handle and had to be pried off. He did not make that mistake again.

The grade steepened as the wind and snow mounted. The airmen huddled around the tiny potbellied stoves at each car's center, but most of the tepid heat escaped between the slats of the boxcar walls.

At midnight the train stopped for the night. Herky Marrone guessed they had traveled twenty miles. Like most of the others, he remained sleepless. The airmen estimated the temperature to be like it was at twenty-five thousand feet—below zero. It was too cold and crowded to lie down.

Keith Owens, standing in another car, had picked a bad day for a hangover. Some of the airmen took turns on the floor. The more talented among them dozed upright. Joe Sedlak's feet felt like blocks of ice inside their gunnysacks. He stomped them to keep the circulation flowing. Life seemed to ooze from his body. He feared if he slept, he would never wake up.[11]

■   ■   ■

Overnight, the moisture escaping from the airmen's bodies condensed and froze, sheathing the boxcars in a coat of ice. It was just as well: the veneer prevented the wind from whipping through. And it could have been worse—the flatcar passengers had made do with no shelter at all.

The fireman kept his boiler going all night to prevent it from freezing. Partisans scoured the countryside for more wood, aided by a few Americans. Tom Tamraz took one side of a two-man saw but found himself out of sync with his partner and quit. An old woman approached and screamed at the Partisans confiscating her fence rails.

Around 9:00 a.m., the little train chugged off again. The snow deepened, derailing a flatcar, and the Partisans righted it using planks as levers. The engine tooted and crept along cautiously.

Archy Roper, Hixon Eldridge, and their crewmates hunched together and shared their store of food. Others gnawed at the rock-hard bread. Emil Horak cut a slab of lamb with a handmade knife he had bought in town. The Partisan next to him took the blade with the meat and passed them along. After the lamb made the rounds, Horak asked the Partisan to return the knife. The man protested, spreading his arms wide in an offer to be searched. Horak waved him off; he would not risk an incident by frisking him.

Griping, always a soldier's prerogative, became the airmen's main occupation. Why had the Partisans forced them into this harebrained scheme? They could have waited another day or two. It was only a matter of time until the planes arrived.

The locomotive's wheels spun slower as its cowcatcher pushed against the deepening drifts. *Choo-choo-choo*, cried the tiny smokestack.

It was no use. The little engine couldn't.

Snowflakes mounted against the train's undercarriage. Partisans and airmen piled out and hacked away with picks and shovels, but soon realized the effort was hopeless. The track led uphill. They could not shovel their way across the Dinaric Alps. They must retreat before they became snowbound. The trip had been for nothing—and it was forty miles back to Sanski Most.

The train built up steam and headed in reverse. At least gravity was on their side now. A few hours later they came to a halt at the spot where they had spent the previous night.[12]

■   ■   ■

Few slept, despite their exhaustion. Owens dozed for about two hours. Marrone went sleepless for the second night in a row.

The day opened to bright sunshine. Transports might fly into Sanski Most today to pick up the wounded, and they might have been able to fly the snowbound men out, too, if they had stayed there. To add to the airmen's troubles, Lt. Michael informed them that the train had run out of fuel overnight and the engine had frozen. Another locomotive was on its way, but it would take time.

Several men collected wood for the ride back while they waited. Some climbed up slopes, chopped down trees, and let gravity topple them toward the train. Bartusch and Stanley pitched in.

Tom Tamraz had been wrong about the food supply—the Partisans had not brought nearly enough. A party of them went off and returned carrying wild goats on their backs. Soon they rigged up an oil drum as a stew pot. Someone handed Bartusch a tin cup full of stew. An eyeball bobbed inside. He wasn't that hungry. Joe Foto was, however; he did not like it, but he ate it.

The spare engine arrived at 2:00 p.m. Once enough logs were stockpiled, the engineer decided he needed more water and backed the engine down the line. The airmen wondered why he didn't just use snow. They had never seen such a fouled-up operation.

Hours later the locomotive returned, and they set off again. The going was even slower than before. Eventually, someone realized the load was too heavy. The Partisans unhooked the frozen engine and the third boxcar, while the passengers crowded into the remaining two cars, nose to nose.

After a third sleepless night for the passengers, the engine broke down completely. Lt. Michael told the airmen they might as well walk the rest of the way. Perfect, they thought. A fubar ending to a fubar trip.

The Americans traipsed the final six miles through deep snow. They reached town tired and hungry but glad no planes had come during their absence. Maybe they would try later.

At three o'clock Captain Tregidga contacted Bari again. HQ regretted that transports had been available, but no fighter escorts. Maybe tomorrow.[13]

■   ■   ■

The commandant was not pleased. After feeding the Americans at the soup kitchen, he herded most of them back into the courthouse attic for the night. Archy Roper and the rest of Eldridge's crew wished they had returned to their kindly Muslim hosts. Somehow Stanley's men escaped to Stojan Ubarić's cottage. Keith Owens, Bill Rainey, Bill Otway, and Bob Mitchell slipped out to visit Hedy and her sisters, who insisted they stay the night.

Rumors flew that the commandant would send the Americans out on that rinky-dink train again as soon as it was fixed. Would the Partisans really try that crazy, failed scheme again? What should the airmen do if they did? Foto wanted to give it another try, but most were ready to revolt.

Bartusch, Rosenthal, Sedlak, and Horak entered the courthouse attic. They had met with the commandant, who had laid down new rules. The Americans were forbidden to buy goods, drink *rakija*, or speak to women. They were confined to the hotel until further notice. They could not even visit the hospital.

Partisan guards stood outside their door. The airmen were no longer exactly guests.[14]

CHAPTER 17

Pulling Rank

The next morning, Keith Owens and his friends awoke unaware that most of their fellow Americans had been placed under guard at the hotel. The girls of the house fixed a pot of surprisingly good coffee. They washed and almost felt human again.

Outside, discouraging gray clouds drooped into the surrounding mountains. Owens and Carey Rainey headed uptown to see what was happening. Around 11:00 a.m., a Partisan directed them to the bath-house for delousing. Something must be up—nobody had told them to clean up before.

Every walking airman was being rounded up. They arrived in groups, stripped in the freezing anteroom, and passed into the showers. The Partisans stoked the boilers to the boiling point. After washing, the airmen reentered the unheated anteroom, dried off as best as they could without towels, and waited for their clothes to arrive from being steamed in barrels. Marrone could not remember ever feeling more uncomfortable.

At last their clothing arrived, slightly less lousy than before. As they dressed, Dr. Johnson entered and called them to attention. He announced that three C-47s and a fighter escort would make another rescue attempt at dusk—about 3:00 p.m. Captain Tregidga had again begged headquarters for transports. The Partisans had threatened to expel the airmen again today if they did not come. Amazingly, Bari had agreed to send them.

It seemed too good to be true. Everyone hoped, though few believed. The commandant, however, appeared convinced. He released the Americans from captivity to prepare.

Owens went outside and gazed up at the sullen sky. The ceiling still looked too low. There was no reason to get excited. He and Rainey went over to the commissary and ate a bowl of thin soup before returning to tell the news to Bill Otway and Bob Mitchell. Then Owens walked back to the city center for a haircut. He would believe the planes were coming when he saw them.

That afternoon, the doubtful host of airmen started out for the airfield once again. Partisans helped the sick and wounded from the hospital. George Earll hobbled along. The group stopped halfway to the field so their return walk would be shorter.

The sound of aircraft engines emerged from overhead. Everyone peered upward into the purple twilight. A C-47 with markings from the 51st Transport Squadron swooped through a break in the overcast. Whoops and hollers filled the air. The planes were landing! After all this time, and after all the failed attempts, the planes were finally going to land! Herky Marrone thought they looked as beautiful as angels. It felt like a dream to Sam Spomer.

In town, Owens sat serenely in his barber's chair. Dick Kelly and Al Goodling scurried by. "The planes are here!" they cried. Owens dashed off behind them.

Everyone scrambled toward the field. Flaming oil drums lined the runway. Partisans stood by with lids in case the enemy showed up and the fires needed to be doused. They had tried to tramp down the snow with little success. Rows of foot-deep fluff remained. The airmen wondered if the transports could land—and take off again—under such conditions.

Captain Tregidga supervised as Corporal Davis cranked away at their Eureka radio. Jene Hirschfield, Emil Horak, Joe Sedlak, Tom Stack, and Hank Rinna stood nearby. Bob Bartusch and Larry Rosenthal organized the men into groups: the wounded would leave first, and the rest would depart in order of earliest arrival without distinction of rank. Unknown to them, the HALYARD rescues had been prioritized the same way in Chetnik territory.[1]

The lead plane plunged over the fence bordering the field. Its wheels slapped the snow, bounced, and hit again. Downy powder spewed from the propellers. The pilots nodded knowingly—the white stuff wreaked havoc on depth perception.

The C-47 settled to a rest among a mob of whooping airmen. Its door opened, and cartons of cigarettes rained into the throng. The other C-47s followed with little trouble. Their crews disembarked and stretched their legs. They might have been about thirty—old men to Bernie Button.

Nine P-51 Mustangs circled overhead. The airmen recognized the sound of their engines. No enemy fighters would dare interfere while they were around.

Henry Wunderlich joined the crowd. Keith Owens appeared at the edge of the field, bringing up the rear.

Crewmen attached a pair of ramps to the wide double doors of one plane and rolled out a jeep, a present for Captain Tregidga. The two other planes unloaded tons of supplies. Two passengers, Partisans who had recovered from their wounds in Allied hospitals, pitched in.

Major Bruce C. Dunn, the transport squadron commander, yelled for quiet and addressed the group. The planes, he declared, could only carry twenty-two men each, sixty-six in total. He would return for the rest. Eighteen of the eighty-four airmen would have to remain. Any volunteers?

Stanley spoke up. *If you're coming back tomorrow*, he said, *my men will stay behind*—except for the injured Ed Seaver and Sam Spomer, of course. None objected. Stanley's crew had been shot down twice, and they were in no hurry to give the enemy a third chance.

That made eight less to carry. Ten others would have to remain. David Blood and Captain Johnson realized their crew had arrived last. They did not like the sound of things.[2]

■   ■   ■

Furtive moonglow peeked through the clouds. The transport pilots itched to get back in the air.

The first transport's crew prepared to stack stretchers three deep against the hull. Scotty Stewart, John Elmore, Andrew Jay, Harold Wamser, Herbert Eldridge, and Gene Cogburn were hauled aboard by litter bearers supervised by Dr. Johnson. Harry Carter boarded to attend to Stewart. He was one of the longest-tenured airmen in town anyway. The less critically wounded, including Red Braun, Willis Hodgeman, Ed Seaver, Sam Spomer, and the mysterious airman with the British accent filled the jump seats lining the walls. Stanley said goodbye to Seaver and Spomer and asked Seaver to let the crew's families know they were alright.

A few ragged girls tugged at George Earll's sleeve, begging for his watch. He waved them off and someone helped him onto the plane. Just being aboard gave him a sense of relief. Gene Dennis sat next to him. The senior nurse from the hospital tucked a colorful rug over them. Earll pulled out his remaining escape kit money and pressed it into her hand. She shook her head. "Buy supplies for the wounded," he insisted. She relented and accepted with gratitude.

The sick and wounded were loaded. There was room for a twenty-second man. "Go ahead," said Rosenthal to Bartusch. "I'll take the next one. See you in Bari."

Bartusch climbed aboard and closed the door. The twin engines revved—they had never been shut off—and the transport taxied away trailing snow dust. It gained speed and lifted off well before the edge of the field. The pilots took note: the plane clearly could have taken more men. The C-47's robust six-thousand-pound cargo capacity was common knowledge. They could do the math in their heads: sixty-two men remained on the ground, thirty-one per airplane, allowing nearly two hundred pounds for each of them. The remaining airmen fell well within the weight limit.[3]

Rosenthal and others pressed Major Dunn. Couldn't he take more than twenty-two men per plane? He insisted he could not.

Perhaps the major had the twenty-two-paratroops limit for C-47s in mind. If so, he forgot that airborne troops carried eighty pounds of arms and equipment apiece, adding nearly a ton to the weight the planes had to transport during parachute drops.

With the wounded gone, the earliest arrivals would board the second plane. The longest tenured remaining men were Rosenthal and Hirschfield, plus the Stewart and Dean crews.

Captain Johnson wanted no more of this adventure. He pressed forward with Blood hulking behind as enforcer. Rosenthal blocked their way. Everyone had agreed they would leave in order of arrival. Blood, Johnson, and the rest of their crew had come last.

"I'm a captain," declared Johnson. "I'm ordering you to stand aside."

"Rank has not mattered here for over a month," insisted Rosenthal. "First in, first out."

Blood shouted over Johnson's shoulder, "I've got a bad knee!"

"So what?" someone called from the crowd. "I've got a bad ankle."

"That ankle's not a knee," countered Johnson. Apparently, he had learned so in medical school.

Rosenthal placed his hand on his holster. "You son-of-a-bitch," he yelled. "Shut the hell up! You're not even supposed to be here."

Threatening a superior officer with a weapon was a court-martial offense, but if Major Dunn heard Rosenthal over the drone of the engines, he pretended not to. He just wanted to get off the ground, and this was taking too long.

A chorus of airmen chimed in, many slinging epithets. Only Blood supported Johnson, and his bullying would not be enough.

Johnson and Blood stood down.

Rosenthal waved the remaining members of the Dean and Stewart crews aboard. Jene Hirschfield joined them. Harry Hoogeveen raised his eyes skyward and thanked God.

Satisfied that the situation was under control, Rosenthal entered the aircraft. Herky Marrone and Jim King boarded as well. The plane shut its doors and took off. As with the one before, it needed only half the field to become airborne.

For the first time, Marrone felt sure he would survive the war. He had spent hundreds of hours in the air without a problem. This time the mixture of elation and relief overwhelmed him. He retreated aft to get sick.[4]

■   ■   ■

Even as the second plane disappeared into the night, the sound from the P-51s faded. The top cover was gone.

Bob Kidder had traded his GI shoes to a Partisan for calf-high, stiff, hobnailed riding boots. They would make good souvenirs, and he could pick up another pair of decent shoes in Italy. The third C-47's navigator greeted him warmly. They had been friends during training.

Airmen started to board: Dick Kelly, Bob Mitchell, Bill Otway, Keith Owens, and Carey Rainey from the Blank crew; Archy Roper and the others from the Eldridge crew; and Ted Keiser, the lone member of his crew in town. Henry Wunderlich boarded with his buddy Jules Levine. Before he entered the plane, Wunderlich paused, pulled out his .45, and tossed it to a Partisan. The man beamed like a kid on Christmas morning. Tom Stack, Hank Rinna, and Sig Piekarski followed them aboard.

Bob Kidder, Leo Wilensky, Al Champi, Joe Foto, Ed Kutch, and Jack Mulvaney took seats in the rear next to a stockpile of C and K rations. Everyone relaxed. Some broke out cigarettes. They could not wait for clean clothes and some good Army chow.

The bitter smell of engine exhaust wafted about. Dr. Johnson stepped through the plane door, shadowed by David Blood. He pointed at the first four men he saw: Bob Kidder, Jack Mulvaney, Ed Kutch, and Joe Foto. He addressed Foto.

"Sergeant," declared Johnson, "you are going to have to get off the plane."

"What do you mean?" stammered Joe.

"I've got injured men I want to put on it."

"You're not hurt!" someone protested.

"I need to tend to the wounded," retorted the doctor blithely. This was obviously absurd, as anyone who might have needed medical care during the flight to Italy had already departed on the first C-47. David Blood, Mike Yaworsky, and Warren LaFrance—the men whom Johnson wanted to place on the plane—showed no signs of injury.

Nevertheless, an order was an order. The four men exited the plane. Johnson plopped into Foto's seat, while David Blood took Kidder's place, snarling contentedly. LaFrance and Yaworsky slid into the other spaces.

Captain Tregidga stood nearby. "Captain, can't you do anything?" Foto implored.

"I'm not in your army," replied the SOE man. "I can't help you."

Leo Wilensky and Al Champi glumly emptied their pockets and handed their remaining escape kit money to Foto, Kutch, and Mulvaney. Foto did not have GI shoes, so Champi took his off and gave them to him. They were a little large, but better than nothing.

Tom Tamraz did not have a .45 pistol. He asked the crew chief for his, but the man refused. He also implored the copilot, but received the same answer. The copilot stepped past Kidder to enter the plane. "It's alright," he counseled. "We're coming back tomorrow anyway."

Don Baker pointed to the pile of rations in the back. "How about leaving us some of those?" he asked.

The major refused. "They're for an emergency."

"What do you think this is?" retorted Baker.

Others shouted too. "There's room for more! Didn't you see how the other planes took off?"

The major unbuckled his .45 and placed his hand on its handle. It seemed a day for .45s. He ordered the men outside to close the doors and back away. They obeyed. Before long, the plane lifted off as easily as the others.[5]

■   ■   ■

The eighteen remaining airmen were left with their thoughts. Foto could have departed on the first plane if he had allowed himself to be hospitalized for his bad ankle. Stanley hoped he had done the right thing when he volunteered his men to stay behind.

Kidder realized he could have asked his navigator buddy for a seat up front, out of sight from Johnson and that vicious son-of-a-bitch Blood. Why had a flight surgeon gone on a combat mission anyway?

Lewis Baker and Wilmot "Gibby" Gibson had not fully recovered from their injuries—Baker from his flak wound and Gibson from a bullet through the stomach. Doctor Johnson was aware of their afflictions but left them behind, taking the uninjured Yaworsky and LaFrance with him instead. None of it made sense.

And the transports could have carried all the stranded airmen if the major had just allowed them aboard. He could have at least shared some rations.

Snow began to fall. It was a long, long walk back into town.[6]

■   ■   ■

The second plane out of Sanski Most, the one mostly filled with the Stewart and Dean crews, arrived at Bari after an uneventful hour and a half flight.

The Fifteenth Air Force had established a procedure for processing evadees returning from the Balkans. Each plane was greeted by an officer who cautioned them not to speak to anyone about their experiences until they had been debriefed by an intelligence man. Then they trucked to the Twenty-Sixth General Hospital in Bari, a nice, modern building constructed by the Italians during the Mussolini era.

The airmen faced their delousing with stoic equanimity. Everyone scrubbed with strong soap, and every crevice was sprayed with DDT. Despite the indignity, Italy seemed like heaven. They donned fresh uniforms and ate canned beans and hot dogs. To Bernie Button, it might as well have been steak. Even the flush toilets seemed luxurious.

There was only one problem: the men from the first plane had not yet arrived.[7]

■   ■   ■

Gene Cogburn, lying on a stretcher in the missing transport, started to worry. As a navigator, he knew how long the flight to Bari should take. They had left Sanski Most two hours ago, and a thunderstorm raged outside. Meanwhile, the pilots had made no preparations to land.

Scotty Stewart was concerned, too. The transport's crew did not seem to know what they were doing. To die this close to safety after all he'd been through . . .

Cogburn asked the terrified flight engineer what was wrong. "We're lost," the man admitted. "Our crew is new to Italy. We don't know the procedures. Bari is socked in by a storm, so they sent us to another field. We couldn't find it. Now we don't know where we are."

Fortunately, there were twenty-two experienced airmen on board, including several pilots and navigators. The flight engineer helped Cogburn to the radio table where he called Big Fence, the Fifteenth Air Force's radar control center. "What's our location?" he asked.

"You've overshot the airfield," they replied. "You're over the southern Apennines, below the peaks. You'd better climb."

Big Fence gave a heading to Taranto. That field turned out to be weathered-in as well. Big Fence redirected the transport back toward

Bari, where the storm had ebbed. The aircraft landed at last, with little gas to spare. George Earll and Gene Dennis flipped a coin for the colorful rug their nurse had handed them. Earll won.

The plane transporting Dr. Johnson and David Blood had already arrived. Its ride had been rough, too. To avoid overwhelming the hospital, these men were processed at the Twenty-Second Replacement Depot. Their old clothing was confiscated and burned, including the beautiful wool sweater Keith Owens had recently purchased in the Sanski Most marketplace.[8]

■   ■   ■

The next day, each repatriated airman faced interrogation by an intelligence officer. Bartusch reported that six of his crewmen had bailed out over Austria and were likely captured. Tom Stack carried the news that John Wolff, Andrew Wozar, and Sam Butler had been killed despite Wolff's heroic attempt to save them. Hixon Eldridge and Archy Roper diplomatically testified that the five crew members who had abandoned their ship without orders had "decided [it was] necessary to bail out" over unsecured territory.

Several men offered tips for future bailouts. Many cited the importance of good footwear, especially GI shoes. Harry Carter and Sylvester Brown tried to alert the AAF that the airstrip at Sanski Most was available for emergency landings. They hoped the information might avert tragedies like the one that had killed John Wolff and his men.

The airmen also filled out forms reporting their lost equipment. Henry Wunderlich reported his pistol was gone. A lieutenant in the quartermaster's office asked what had happened to it.

"I gave it to the Partisans," replied Wunderlich. He figured he had done the right thing.

"You gave it to the Partisans?" barked the lieutenant "That's U.S. government property! You have no authorization to give it away!"

"They'll do more with it than I will," offered Wunderlich.

The lieutenant absorbed that for a moment. "Okay," he decided. "I can fix it so the cost doesn't come out of your pay. But spread the word. You really shouldn't have given it away." Wunderlich decided he should have just told the man he lost it.

Clarence Martin rebelled in his own way. Purposely or not, he fouled up every form he filled out. The clerks made Martin revise his reports at every station.

Captain Johnson's report unintentionally admitted he had no medical justification for ousting four men from the transport and replacing them with his friends. "Bombardier (Gene Cogburn)" he reported, "broke left leg—only injury sustained by crew."[9]

■　　■　　■

Everyone also faced medical evaluations. Henry Wunderlich, who had declined to eat meat while in Yugoslavia, returned in good condition. Archy Roper had drunk water only when it was treated with halazone tablets and was healthy as well. Most of the others suffered from dysentery. Several had lost significant weight. Harry Hoogeveen had dropped from 160 to 130 pounds.

George Earll did not feel well but found the examining doctor to be unsympathetic. "You look like hell," he conceded. "I suppose you've been drinking that *rakija*." Still, he refused to admit Earll to the hospital. When Earll's urine turned black and his skin and eyes became yellow, the Army finally hospitalized him with hepatitis and jaundice.

Earll resumed corresponding with his beloved wife Patty. Her letters confirmed that his telepathic messages had reached her. She had not become overly concerned when the MIA telegram arrived because she could feel he was fine.

Ed Seaver had suffered compression fractures in two vertebrae. Red Braun's broken left wrist had healed improperly and needed to be rebroken and reset. Like Earll, Braun had contracted jaundice. Willis

Hodgeman was hospitalized due to his stomach rupture and bronchial pneumonia.

Gene Cogburn's shattered leg was operated on by an Army doctor who had been chief of orthopedic surgery at the Mayo Clinic. He recovered nicely after several months of convalescence.

Others had contracted illnesses or sustained injuries undetected in Sanski Most. Joe Sedlak was diagnosed with a hernia. Ted Keiser had picked up a roundworm. Jimmie Ingram, Bob Dean's copilot, had walked around on a broken ankle for six weeks.

Not all wounds were physical. Larry Rosenthal and Jene Hirschfield were on rest leave in Capri when Hirschfield punched his fist through a window. Rosenthal took Hirschfield to the resort's hospital but shipped out before his friend recovered. They never met again.

Harry Carter and Joe Sedlak stood at Scotty Stewart's side when the doctors removed his cast. His leg was black from infected lice bites. The first step was treating the infection. Then the surgeons operated, rebreaking the leg and setting it with a metal plate and six screws.

Carter remained ensconced with Stewart while he healed. Carter had lost fifty pounds to dysentery and needed to recuperate anyway. In March, their original copilot, James Michalaros, and their navigator, William Craven, were killed in separate combat incidents. Stewart and Carter considered themselves lucky in comparison.

Once Stewart returned to the States, he took part in two bond-raising tours. Still on crutches, he spoke of his experiences with the Partisans to rapt audiences. On the second tour, he befriended a fellow injured Harvard man, John Fitzgerald Kennedy. One of Kennedy's friends told Stewart that Kennedy had a bright political future. Stewart believed him.[10]

■   ■   ■

Back at their bases, nearly all the lost airmen learned their belongings had been sent stateside. Herky Marrone lacked not only his goods, but his money as well, because he had stashed it in his footlocker. Keith Owens discovered his camera, electric shaver, and shoes had been stolen.

Fortunately for Hixon Eldridge's crew, their old navigator, Bob Mann, had looked after their things. Mann had also informed their families that they had bailed out safely. Two of Eldridge's men, Gus Perrone and Joe Colasante, returned to base on January 14. The Germans soon confirmed the other missing crewmen had become their prisoners.

Five of Bob Bartusch's crewmen—Carl Bush, Cletus Kramer, Raymond Klapp, Robert Steele, and Paul Bergschneider—were also confirmed as POWs.[11]

Twenty-two men from the lost aircrews remained unaccounted for. Four men from Harry Blank's plane had disappeared: Blank himself, John Turk, Tom Koballa, and Bill Ceely. The whereabouts of the eighteen men left behind in Sanski Most were also unknown. Contrary to Major Dunn's promise, no transport had returned to pick them up. They had not been heard from since they were left behind.

CHAPTER 18

On the Home Front

Once the ICARUS mission contacted Bari in mid-December, the Fifteenth Air Force established the identity of the airmen then stranded in Sanski Most. They were no longer quite "missing." Nevertheless, no one blocked MIA telegrams from being sent or notified families that the men had found relative safety. Even when sixty-six of them were evacuated on January 5, 1945, the Army took three weeks to let their loved ones know they were safe. Similarly, the AAF knew the identities of the eighteen airmen left in Sanski Most by the transports but failed to notify their families.

Soon after the surviving members of the Wolff crew returned to their base, Bob Kidder's copilot, Jerry Scherzer, learned that Kidder was alive but stuck in Sanski Most. Scherzer wrote to tell Kidder's parents but mistrusted the censor's scissors and resorted to hints. "I'm sorry I didn't write sooner," he began, "but I've been waiting for the proper opportunity....I've been waiting for the heavens to smile down upon us and they have....Bob has been doing fine and is enjoying himself immensely....He's in the best of health but a little lazy when it comes to writing."

The Kidders could not make sense of the letter, nor could any friends they shared it with. Surely their son was missing in action. The MIA telegram said so, and Bob's letters had stopped. The family prayed, wrote hopeful letters among themselves, and waited.[1]

■   ■   ■

Mrs. Stanley's letter to Mary Alice Schmitz telling her that Charles was missing came as less of a shock the second time. If he had made it back before, she reasoned, he could do it again.

Still, the waiting was hard. Her letters bounced back from Italy stamped "Return to Sender." They seemed so final. Wouldn't the Army hold his letters if they thought he would come back?

Mary Alice and her family swung into action in the only way they knew how. Every night, her father, Frank Schmitz, led them in prayer with his rosary. At first, they knelt throughout the many "Our Fathers" and "Hail Marys." After a few days of sore knees, Frank decided it would be all right if they sat while they prayed. Now and then Mary Alice broke down in tears. Others joined her until they composed themselves and were able to continue.

Mary Alice's mother called on the cloistered Dominican nuns at the Monastery of the Rosary whenever she needed God's special help. These holiest of women spent their lives in perpetual adoration of the Lord. If asked, they would pray to the Blessed Virgin to intercede on Charles's behalf. Certainly Jesus, good son that he was, could not refuse a request from his mother.

Mrs. Schmitz and Mary Alice took a bus to the large stone monastery. Designated sisters acted as liaisons with the public. Mary Alice and her mother approached a pretty little nun wearing a white habit. She listened to their request with serenity. "He's all right," she responded, looking deeply into Mary Alice's eyes. "I know he's all right."

Mary Alice returned to school after the new year. Word spread around campus that her fiancé was missing. Everyone did their best to comfort her, but only her gym teacher, Miss Brewster, who had once performed missionary work in China, found the right words. "When I was a missionary," she explained, "there were times I was 'missing.' I knew where I was. I wasn't really missing. It was just that I couldn't communicate with the outside world. It might be like that with your boyfriend, so don't worry. You don't know anything yet."

This made sense to Mary Alice. Charles would find his way back somehow.[2]

■   ■   ■

The MIA telegrams had been delivered to the Stanley crew's next of kin in mid-December. The families reached out to one another and asked for news, but there was none to be shared. They spent the Christmas and New Year holidays wondering whether their loved ones were alive.

At last, on January 4, a letter arrived in the Stanleys' country mailbox from Major General Nathan Twining's office. Mrs. Stanley feared opening it until she remembered bad news always arrived in telegrams. The middle paragraph seemed hopeful:

> Interrogation of returning airmen reveals that the ship came off the bomb run with two of the engines feathered. The craft continued behind the formation until they reached Yugoslavia where the bomber lagged at such a distance that it was lost from sight.

Mrs. Stanley forwarded the letter to Mary Alice. Together they concluded the crew had likely bailed out safely and were either with the underground or prisoners of war.

Twining's letter prompted a second round of correspondence. Lurline Tweedale, Claude's mother, wrote to Mrs. Stanley, "Your boy, Lt. Stanley is the pilot and must be a very courageous man. He brought them through safely the first time and I know he will do it again." Anna Homol, Peter's mother, wrote that she almost hoped the boys were prisoners of war so they would not have to return to combat. Mary Alice's mother felt the same way.

Charles's mother agreed, though being with the underground sounded better. One detail preyed on her mind: Bette Plaisance, Bob's wife, had mysteriously failed to respond to their letters. Mrs. Stanley had no way of knowing that Plaisance, Stanley's original copilot, had avoided being shot down with the crew again because he was on leave in Capri. Plaisance learned the crew was safe in Yugoslavia just after Christmas. Nevertheless, he failed to notify their families. Instead, he casually mentioned the news in a letter to his wife Bette in California.

For weeks Mary Alice distracted herself by attending classes and working in the family store. At last, in mid-January, a postcard arrived from Bette. "Dear Miss Schmitz," she began. "If you haven't heard yet from Charles, this quotation from my husband's letter of December 27 should interest you. 'They are safe in Yugo & will return as soon as facilities permit. Weather is holding them back now.'"

Mary Alice cried with relief when she read the news. Charles must be with the underground. Still, she resented that the Plaisances had taken their time in relaying the good tidings. Bob Plaisance could have found the crews' addresses if he tried. Instead, he relied on his wife, who lived on the other side of the country, to spread the word. Bette sat on the news for a few days, then sent a penny postcard, the cheapest and slowest method of communication. Couldn't she have spent three cents on a regular stamp, or even four cents for Air Mail? Didn't the woman realize every day without knowing was torture for the loved ones of everyone on the crew?

The families exchanged yet another round of letters. It turned out that Bette Plaisance had ambiguously told Eleanor Cone, Leo's wife, that the crew was "temporarily safe in Yugoslavia." Did this mean they would be rescued soon? Or did danger lurk in the long term?

Despairing of getting any more details out of Bette Plaisance, Stanley's mother wrote directly to Bob in Italy. No response came.[3]

■   ■   ■

Ed Seaver and Sam Spomer returned to base on January 7. Both immediately informed their parents they had returned safely. Neither mentioned the fates of the other crewmen, perhaps from fear of being censored.

Ed's father, Hugh, sent a letter to Mrs. Stanley telling her that Ed and Sam were safe. The letter mystified her. None of the other families had reported their boys had come back. Maybe the guerillas had broken the crew up to hide them more easily. It happened all the time in the movies. But it was all so maddening. How did Ed Seaver and Sam Spomer get out of Yugoslavia without the others? And what was taking the rest of them so long to follow?[4]

CHAPTER 19

Bitter Logic

The morning after the planes departed from Sanski Most, the eighteen remaining Americans awoke to a foot of fresh, powdery snow. The clouds hung low. No plane would return today, despite Major Dunn's promise. Still, the airmen remained unruffled. A plane would surely come soon.

Lewis Baker was working on a letter to his mother—to be sent upon his return to Italy—when word arrived that the Partisans might send them out by train a second time. "None of us are in good enough health to go through that again," he wrote. "I hope we don't have to do it." Neither he nor Gibby Gibson had recovered from their old wounds. Joe Foto's sprained ankle had not healed. Foto, Jack Mulvaney, and Ed Kutch suffered from colds. Half the men were ill with dysentery. No one had recuperated from the previous attempt by train, and they had not even caught up on their sleep.

Minutes later the rumor was confirmed: the Partisans would expel the remaining Americans immediately. The decision was beyond understanding. Sanski Most could support a mere eighteen airmen for a few more days. Regardless, the Americans had no choice but to go.[1]

■   ■   ■

The airmen gathered their belongings once again. Stanley and Sherer rolled up their parachutes. Leo Cone and Darrell Kiger roped wine-colored carpets across their backs like quivers. Gibby Gibson lugged two runners, one under each arm. Tamraz stuffed his *torba* with his parachute, walnuts, and ill-gotten salt. He understood why Kutch and Cone carried rugs—they could also serve as blankets. Yet why would Gibson, the smallest man among them, burden himself with useless runners? This was no time for souvenirs.

Several Americans were unarmed. Bob Kidder had given his .45 to Sig Piekarski, who in turn had traded it to a Partisan for an exotic-looking long barreled pistol. Joe Foto, Ed Kutch, and Jack Mulvaney had not been issued .45s for their flights. Fortunately, the Stanley and Blood crews still carried theirs. One never knew what trouble might brew on the trail.

Kidder regretted swapping his GI boots for the hobnailed pair. Stanley's Oxford shoes seemed inadequate for the snow. Fred Sherer had his GI shoes plus one flight boot. The other had been lost during his jump.

Their outerwear was lice-ridden but warm. Most of the airmen wore alpaca-lined leather flight suits. Stanley, Cone, and Scherer sported green, alpaca-lined, cotton B-15 jackets with faux fur collars.

Lt. Michael—the capable English-speaking Partisan who had headed the failed attempt to get to the coast—would be in charge again. He bore a light carbine. Leather strings tightened high goatskin boots against his calves.

Eight Partisan enlisted men would escort them, including a teenager and an ursine oldster who looked tough as a flak jacket and twice as dense. Due to his size, ill temper, and hirsute appearance, the airmen dubbed him "Bigfoot." Two other Partisans, a captain and his aide, would accompany the party part of the way. The lean captain was decked out in a full uniform—a rarity among the Partisans—but no overcoat. He jealously clutched a beautiful leather valise. The Americans assumed it contained important dispatches.[2]

■   ■   ■

Less ceremony accompanied the farewells this time. An eviction was not something to celebrate, after all. The only person who seemed sorry to see them go was old Stojan Ubarić, whose smacks on the cheeks had become all too familiar. Stanley still bore Ubarić's letter to his relatives in Trenton.

The group dreaded this journey even more than the previous one. The snow had deepened and the temperature had dropped. On the bright side, there were fewer mouths to feed, and a pack horse was carrying provisions for them this time.

The train *choo-chooed* off. The Americans paced the boxcars, stomped their feet for circulation, or huddled around the ineffective stoves. A few swastika-marked crates pilfered from the Germans served as chairs. Periodically, the train paused to take on wood and water.

An hour after dusk, the train halted at a junction near Srnetica. They had traveled forty miles—a better pace than the last time—but the snow was already knee-deep. Steep mountains loomed ahead. The train could not go much further without becoming snowbound. Lt. Michael detached the cars and sent the locomotive off to Drvar, where a larger engine with a snowplow was stationed.

The airmen spent the night in the boxcars. Ed Kutch and Leo Cone rolled themselves up in their rugs. Those with parachutes wrapped themselves in nylon. The close quarters allowed only half of them to lie down, so they slept in shifts. Lewis Baker stayed up all night feeding the fire.

Come morning there was nothing to do but wait and try to stay warm. The cold flayed their nerves. The snowy scenery looked prettier than a Christmas card, but nobody ventured outside except to relieve himself. Gibby Gibson, suffering a bad case of the "GIs," dared the elements most frequently.

Meals consisted of broth, boiled cornmeal, a few bites from an animal carcass, and ersatz bread filled with wood chips. One wag quipped he could eat and pick his teeth at the same time. Fred Sherer bore his own leg of lamb and refused the soup. Joe Foto gladly ate anything available, including a hunk of fat that slid down his throat like a slippery eel. Calories were calories.

Another night passed. The airmen took turns sleeping again. This time even Lewis Baker dozed. Outside, persistent flurries added to the deep snowfall.

The Americans speculated that Lt. Michael had been forbidden to return them to Sanski Most. They would reach the coast or freeze to death in the attempt.[3]

■   ■   ■

By morning the snow had risen to the airmen's hips. Their food supply was depleted. The snowplow would not arrive soon, if at all. Lt. Michael decided they must advance on foot to the next settlement along the line, Potoci. Eight months before, Tito and his men had regrouped there after the famous German raid against Drvar.

They departed at 10:00 a.m. "Be careful of frostbite," Michael warned. "Cover your ears. Don't let snow in your shoes. Keep moving until we reach shelter."

Michael's reedy figure led the way through the waist-deep snow. The party followed single file. After a time, Michael dropped back and let other Partisans cut the path. Stanley tried to chip in but made little headway. The largest Americans—Al Buchholz, Bob Kolvet, Jack Mulvaney, and Fred Sherer—took turns, but even the former football players were no match for the hardy Yugoslavians. The airmen marveled at their strength and endurance.

For a time, Gibby Gibson carried his two narrow rugs on his shoulders. Eventually he weakened and gave them to anyone willing to carry them. Soon they were discarded altogether. Joe Foto felt grateful for Al Champi's shoes, but wished they were a size smaller. Snow filled their insides, and his frozen feet felt brittle as glass. Crystalline snowflakes nipped at their faces, then thickened. By dark the storm had developed into a full-blown blizzard.

Potoci proved disappointing. Its wrecked, abandoned houses offered no food and little shelter. The men cupped their eyes against the stinging wind to scan the adjacent mountainside. Halfway up stood four barely visible cabins. They looked lonely as lighthouses but would provide good vantage points for spotting enemy patrols.

The party slogged up to the huts. Eight Americans shambled into one cabin. Ten took another. The Partisans occupied the other two.

The huts had likely served as shelters for railway workers or shepherds. Each was a small, solid structure empty except for a pot-bellied stove. If the Partisans had hoped to find food here, they were disappointed. The sacks straddling the pack horse appeared empty.

The teenage Partisan came into the Americans' huts and started fires. Joe Foto took off his shoes and warmed his feet. In New Orleans, it was customary to tip the help. He searched his pockets and found a five-dollar bill. The boy accepted it gratefully. Foto had made him a rich man.

The men sacked out around the stove. Its heat radiated only the slightest distance, so that if an airman lay with his head toward the fire, his feet froze, and vice versa. Most of them alternated positions through the night as keening winds raked the cabin walls.

The blizzard raged into the next day. The Partisans' horse, tethered outside, whinnied in protest. The galumphing Bigfoot acted as the Americans' special keeper. Whenever he dropped by, Tom Tamraz and a few other wags amused themselves by insulting him while smiling warmly.

They could not play the same game with Lt. Michael, who spoke excellent English with a British accent. Michael enjoyed their war stories and tales of home. The taciturn Al Buchholz rarely spoke. Stanley was not a talker either. Instead, he sat on the floor listening pensively to the others.

Michael tried to explain the differences among the Partisans, Chetniks, and Ustashe, but the airmen understood little. A native of Zagreb, Michael praised its beauty and culture and claimed it far surpassed Belgrade. Stanley guessed he was Jewish, which would give him plenty of incentive to fight the Germans. He liked the garrulous lieutenant but wondered if the guy would ever shut up.

■   ■   ■

Toward evening, a Partisan brought large pots of stew to their cabins, to the surprise and delight of the Americans. They had eaten nothing all day and assumed the food was gone. The meat looked undercooked, but the airmen dug in. Tamraz was halfway through when he realized the horse outside had stopped neighing. He tried not to think about it as he continued his meal.[4]

The storm raged on for two more days. Meanwhile, the men shoveled paths among the cabins. The snow grew so deep that suffocation became a danger, so they cleared the windows for air. Eventually the meat and cornmeal ran short. Something had to be done.

The third evening, Lt. Michael informed the airmen that the captain and his aide would try to reach the next town, some fifteen kilometers away. The captain, he explained, must deliver his dispatches as soon as possible. He would send help if he got through. "That's crazy!" blurted Tom Tamraz. "It's too cold and windy. He's not dressed for it. It's dark."

"He must go," replied Michael. "Those messages are important."

Six feet of snow covered the ground. The venture appeared suicidal, especially for the coatless captain. The Americans went to sleep certain he and his aide would never make it.

A knock on the door awoke Tamraz at 4:00 a.m. The captain's aide entered, assisted by a comrade. The aide could barely walk due to frostbite. Lt. Michael followed them in and explained that the storm had forced the man to turn back. The captain had pushed on by himself.[5]

■   ■   ■

Michael reentered the cabin in the morning. "We're out of food," he announced. "There will be no breakfast. The storm has abated. We must try to make it to the next town."

"What about the frostbitten man?" someone asked.

"His right foot has turned black," Michael replied. "It needs to be amputated, but that's impossible here. We cannot help him. We must leave him behind."

The Americans understood his bitter logic. If they stayed where they were, they would all starve or freeze to death. They had to travel while they had the strength, and taking the man with them was out of the question. They could not carry him through the head-high snow.

Guilt haunted the Americans as they pulled their things together. The sooner they left, the better. Lewis Baker craved a cigarette. Joe Foto cut the hem of his trousers, stuffed the material down into his oversized boots, and tied them tight. He would not expose his feet to the snow again.

Ready to depart, the airmen paused for a last look at the doomed Partisan. His stoic eyes betrayed no emotion. No one could find the words. They took their leave silently.

Lt. Michael produced a canoe paddle and propelled himself forward to break the trail. The Partisans and the Americans followed, wading through the sea of white as though it were surf. The going was hell. Before long even the hardy Slavs looked bushed. Fricative breath wafted from their mouths. Every two hundred yards, the lead man gave way to the next and dropped to the end of the column. The Americans pitched in as they could. Perhaps they shouldn't have teased Bigfoot—he carried his weight and more.

At first, they followed the railroad tracks. A telegraph wire ran alongside waist-high due to the high snow. They used it as a guideline, pulling themselves forward with their arms. Eventually they veered off into the mountains. They climbed for hours, straining against the tide of rising white. Each step met with stubborn resistance. Stanley thanked God for the muscle he had gained on the Burma Trail at Maxwell Field.

Joe Foto spotted a distant farmhouse below in a valley. Smoke drifted from its chimney. "I'm going down there," he called to Michael. "I can't go on."

"If you do, you'll die," the lieutenant cautioned. "You'll never make it back up." Michael reached into his pocket and gave Foto two Benzedrine pills—amphetamines—he was saving for an emergency. Foto tramped on.

Soon Gibby Gibson collapsed in the snow. "This is as far as I'm going," he moaned. The dysentery-wracked man had soiled his long johns, and his legs would not carry him.

Fred Sherer helped Gibson shed his underwear. He dressed him again, pulled him to his feet, and slipped his arm under his shoulder. "Let's go," Sherer ordered.

Gibson moved his legs as best he could. He had been slight to begin with, and now illness and starvation had reduced him to a mere wisp. If only Captain Johnson had let him board the transport and left the mammoth David Blood behind.

They spotted a figure in the snow as they approached the crest of a ridge. It was the captain's frozen body. The Partisans relieved him of his dispatches and moved on. Burial was out of the question. If they did not make it to shelter by nightfall, they would all share his fate.

They reached the summit near dusk. A dozen Partisans awaited them there, including a short, stout woman festooned with a gun belt across her shoulder. They likely sought the captain's dispatches.

Stanley topped the rise and let his pulse slow. Despite the cold, his sweaty undershirt clung to his back. Ahead the slope tapered downhill.

Lt. Michael addressed the leader. *"Zdravo! Bilo gda je prtina?"* "Any snow path?" There was. They followed it downward, stumbling on frozen hoof imprints hidden beneath the snow.[6]

■   ■   ■

Several more days of hiking passed. The way stations—Prekaja, Rore, and Medena Selista—lay about fifteen kilometers apart, a full day's hike given the snow. The men's single-file line spread out, the better to survive if a German patrol or aircraft happened upon them.

Afternoons—when Allied fighters patrolled the skies—provided the safest times to walk.

At each hamlet, the troupe dispersed into available homes, sometimes to the resentment of the inhabitants. Most houses were simple one- or two-story structures with dirt floors. Women cooked on open fires doubling as the sole source of heat. The airmen, Partisans, and men of the house ate first. The womenfolk took the leavings. Once they understood the routine, the Americans consumed only enough for subsistence. Piles of straw served as beds, and lice attacked ferociously. The airmen avenged themselves by picking them off and casting them into the fire.

The airmen encountered no small children. Stanley wondered if the locals were hiding them. At one stop, a man offered to have some Americans sleep with his teenage daughters. Whether this was for warmth or another purpose was unclear. Either way, the airmen declined.

Whenever they entered a settlement, Tom Tamraz cried out *"Bilo jaja (yaya)?"* "Any eggs?" If the villagers had any, or more rarely, offered a chicken, they retorted *"Koliko?"* "How much?" Tamraz then negotiated a price. His stolen salt and scraps of material from his parachute provided better bargaining power than his gold-backed dollars.

Five days after leaving the cabins at Potoci, the party reached Glamoč. Though the Partisans had occupied the city since 1942, tensions still ran high with its mostly Serbian inhabitants. The airmen's beards had grown too long for comfort. Fearing an incident, Lt. Michael arranged shaves for the airmen and kept them under wraps until they left in the morning.[7]

■   ■   ■

It took them the whole next day to reach another hostile town, Livno.

Livno, a much larger city, sat on a picturesque hillside beneath a towering gray cliff streaked with rivulets of ice. Thickly spaced, multistory structures with faded red roofs bore the scars of battle. The city had changed hands several times during the war. Anytime the Fascists regained control, Ustashe terror squads moved in and committed mass acts of torture and murder.

Several ethnic Germans still lived in the city. They yelled taunts at the passing Americans. Albert Buchholz translated. "Germany is winning the war! Join us! America and Germany should be friends." George Benedict suspected some of them might be enemy agents.

Lt. Michael escorted the airmen to the homes of their unwilling hosts. He left Stanley, Leo Cone, Gibby Gibson, and Tom Tamraz with a seething, middle-aged Croatian woman. As he departed, Michael pointed to his eye and ran his finger across his neck. For a moment, Tamraz wondered why Michael had not used his English. Then he realized Michael wanted their hostess to understand he had given them the warning.

Tamraz slept with one eye open. Near dawn, he awoke to the clicking of a spinning wheel. Noticing he was awake, the woman spat tobacco near his head. Tamraz tried to go back to sleep, but she did it again for emphasis. Likely the swarthy Assyrian looked like a Moslem to her.

She served a bowl of bland cornmeal for breakfast. As they picked at the horrid stuff, she strip-teased a hardboiled egg and ate it with relish. The Americans hid their envy.

Every time Allied aircraft flew over the city, the woman grabbed some bread and wine and bolted out the door. She would not return for hours, a welcome relief. The airmen figured she had suffered from too many German bombing raids. They did not know the AAF had bombed Livno seven months before, and that perhaps she had good reason to resent the Americans.

There was no toilet paper—or even newspaper—so the airmen used Kuna, as they had along the trail. One day Bigfoot found Stanley, Cone, Gibson, and Tamraz crunching up Kuna. When he asked what they were doing, Tamraz explained they were breaking up the fiber so it would make softer toilet paper. Bigfoot declared they were "*lud*"—crazy—and went away. Later, they discovered that used Kuna had disappeared from the outhouse. Either Bigfoot or their sourpuss landlady had taken it. Either way, it was okay with them.

A pair of Partisan policemen arrived one afternoon, grabbed Gibson, and started screaming in his face. Tamraz intervened. Gibson, the MPs explained, had defecated off the main bridge in town, an affront to the dignity of the landmark. Tamraz convinced them that Gibson suffered from uncontrollable diarrhea. They moved off, grumbling to themselves.

Another time, the airmen visited Lt. Michael at his encampment and engaged the Partisans in a friendly contest of marksmanship. No one, not even the well-trained gunners, could match Lt. Michael's skill with his carbine. A Partisan offered to trade his Walther 6 mm pistol for Stanley's .45. Stanley agreed, reasoning the soldier could put the large-bore gun to better use than he could.

When it was time to move on, Lewis Baker felt too ill to travel. His left midsection had cramped badly during the last leg of the trip, and now he had a fever. The men feared pneumonia. Joe Foto felt sick too and was in no hurry to return to duty, considering Dr. Johnson had cheated him out of the plane ride to Italy.

A few of the officers asked Tamraz, the best linguist of the group, to remain behind and look after Baker and Foto. Tamraz agreed to stay. He did not feel well himself. Gibby Gibson decided to travel onward despite his dysentery. Running into the MPs again might be bad for his health.

Lt. Michael and his men would not accompany the airmen the rest of the way. They had passed into the jurisdiction of another Partisan corps. As he bid them farewell, Michael pressed an envelope into Stanley's hands. The letter was addressed to his parents, who had somehow escaped Yugoslavia and lived near Bari. Stanley promised he would deliver it. It was the least he could do for the man who had cheerfully and capably guided him across eighty miles of frozen wilderness.[8]

■   ■   ■

The fifteen airmen departed the next morning with two fresh Partisan guides. For hours they plodded through a deep snowfall. Midway, a whiteout storm erupted. After ten miles they reached their shelter for the night, a log hut at the foot of a high, rocky escarpment.

The cabin lacked a fireplace or stove. There was barely room for everyone to lie down. Stanley landed on a low, wooden bench. Before long, he realized he had made a mistake. The dirt floor would have been hard and cold, but not as frigid as the sub-zero air. For the first time, his parachute and flight clothes failed to provide enough warmth. He spent a sleepless night on the bench as the blizzard raged on.

At dawn, everyone stirred, moaning and cursing. It had been the coldest night of Stanley's life. A foot of snow had piled up, and more was falling. The sooner they climbed the ridge, the better.

Ed Kutch, sick and numb with cold, decided that scaling the cliff in his condition would be too risky. He found his way back to Livno by himself.

The rest clambered up the deep slope. Wind and snow flayed the rocks. The men's freezing hands and feet slipped against the crystalline ice, and the higher they rose, the more dangerous the ascent became. Trails of breath escaped into the crisp, snowy air. The airmen were accustomed to great altitudes, but not to heights so immediate and jagged. They tried not to look down.

At last their rubbery legs achieved the summit. Below, silent fir trees dotted the white, undulating valley. They had conquered a two-thousand-foot precipice. Solemnly, they turned and descended the other side.

Not far along the trail, they came across a dead horse half-covered in snow. It reminded them of the frozen Partisan captain and the frostbitten man they had left behind at Potoci. Their turn might come next; it was better not to think about it.

Everyone kept their thoughts to themselves until they reached Sinj six hours later. The city was the loveliest yet, but there was no time for sightseeing. Nightfall approached, and a train would depart for Split momentarily. As they rushed to the station, Bob Kidder caught the rhapsodic scent of fresh bread. It smelled of civilization.

This train was not a "little engine that could" like the others. It was a full-sized, coal-driven, ten-wheel locomotive with real passenger cars, another sign that they were nearly home free. The Partisans had restored its operation on January 6, the day the airmen set out from Sanski Most. The Americans doubted Commandant Dusan had known it was operating when he expelled them.

The train chugged away as soon as they boarded. Burnt-out tanks with German, Italian, and NDH markings passed in the gathering dusk. Gradually, the wooded hills of the interior gave way to the sweeping gray crags of Dalmatia.[9]

■   ■   ■

They disembarked in Split not far from the crescent-shaped harbor. The once-busy port had supported forty-four thousand people before the war. Now it sheltered only a few fishing boats and the occasional Allied supply ship. Starvation had stalked the city's streets for months, and dozens of residents had died, including several who committed suicide due to hunger.

The Partisan escorts delivered the fourteen airmen to a large structure near the waterfront. Another Partisan greeted them with a simple "*Zdravo.*" His fresh, gray uniform indicated his importance. He led them up an outdoor staircase to a balcony abutting two entrances and rapped on the right door several times, but no one answered. An airman shouted from the rear, "Why doesn't the dumb son-of-a-bitch try the other one?" The Partisan turned, shot the man a sour glance, and knocked on the left entrance.

Naval Lieutenant (j.g.) Timothy Pfeiffer opened the door. He greeted the airmen and introduced them to their guide. He was Vedran Jihovy, Pfeiffer's translator. He had understood the airman's insult perfectly well.

Pfeiffer's mission—along with the half-dozen other OSS men in Split—was to funnel supplies from the port to the interior, to keep his ears open for intelligence, and to assist the U.S. fliers escaping from the hinter-lands. Evadees slept on the floors because the mission's cots had been donated to the local Partisan hospital. Pfeiffer repeatedly begged Bari for supplies—not just for Split, but for the other missions in Yugoslavia as well.

Pfeiffer and Jihovy provided twenty-two twelve-ounce cans of U.S. Army C-rations to their new guests. The fourteen gathered around a large table and dug in. Since the tin cans' labels had long since fallen off, each got potluck. After weeks on the trail, the stuff tasted like a gourmet dinner. Bob Kidder's corned beef hash surpassed the finest sirloin. Fred Sherer thoroughly enjoyed his cold pork and beans. Stanley judged his vegetable-beef soup to be the best meal he ever ate.

Captain James Goodwin, the OSS agent who had aided the Keiser crew's escape, had lingered in Split recovering from an ear infection. Now he entered the room with a request: "When you reach Bari, get word to Colonel Kraigher. We need food, underwear, socks, shoes, and cots. The rations you just ate were from our personal supply."

As the sun sank low over the Adriatic, Pfeiffer summoned a British crash boat to take the fourteen airmen to Vis. They walked the short distance to the stone wharf and awaited the boat's arrival with five other evadees. "Be ready," urged Pfeiffer. "Snipers infest the hills. The captain will want to depart as quickly as possible."

The crash boat arrived with a flourish, slapping cold seawater at them. Darrell Kiger scrambled on first, and the rest hustled behind. They were barely aboard when the motor roared and the craft raced off. Kiger swore he heard gunshots trailing in the din.

The vessel smacked viciously against the choppy waves. Soon several of the airmen hung their heads over the sides, and a few lost their recent dinner. Bob Kidder made his way to Lt. Watson, the square-jawed Scotsman manning the helm. "Kind of rough, isn't it?" remarked Kidder, hoping the skipper would do something about it.

"Aye, a bit," he replied. No relief came until they reached port.

At Vis, they were shown to their quarters. Cots and wool blankets served as bedding. The British offered them tins of ham and loaves of French bread for sandwiches.

Bob Kidder wanted just one thing—a real toilet. When he found the facilities, however, he discovered the john was a "stoop-to-poop" like the ones in Sanski Most. His cot also disappointed. He was so used to sacking out on the ground that he could not get comfortable. In the end, he slept on the floor.

In the morning, the airmen walked past the wrecked bombers lining the airstrip and boarded the C-47 that would carry them home. Soon they were airborne, and relief mixed with uncertainty. The plane was flying them to safety—but it might also be transporting them back to combat and their doom.[10]

■　　■　　■

They faced the obligatory delousing with DDT in Bari. Their clothing from the trail was burned. After showers and shaves, they donned new uniforms. Somehow Leo Cone and Darrell Kiger saved the carpets they had lugged across Yugoslavia.

Then came the medical evaluations. Each airman had lost at least twenty pounds. Darrell Kiger had dropped thirty-five pounds and suffered from snow blindness. The doctors hospitalized Don Baker for raw feet and dysentery.

Intelligence officers debriefed them. Bob Kidder emphasized that the transports could have carried them to Italy on January 5. George Benedict and Gibby Gibson reported the airstrip at Sanski Most was available for emergency landings. Stanley passed the word that the mission in Split needed supplies.

Jack Mulvaney carried the word that crewmates Ed Kutch and Joe Foto had stayed in Livno with two others, Lewis Baker and Tom Tamraz. The four of them straggled into Bari eleven days later, having been trapped in Livno for some time due to a raging blizzard.

The day after his return to Italy, Mulvaney dashed off a letter to his mother. He apologized for his poor handwriting and grammar, writing, "my nerves are a bit shaky." "I have to stop writing soon and settle myself," he continued. "The reason for my condition is that I had to walk about 120 miles over mountains in about 6 feet of snow and I'm just worn out."[11]

■   ■   ■

Similarly, Stanley wrote to his mother and Mary Alice at his first opportunity. His other priority was to deliver Lt. Michael's letter to his parents. The family had not received word from their son in years. They greeted Stanley with open arms and fed him a fabulous meal.

After a few days, Stanley and his men returned to their base, where bad news awaited them. Leo Cone's father had passed away while he was missing. Weeks later, more ill tidings came: Forrest Smalley's brother, a Marine, had been killed on Iwo Jima.

Seaver and Spomer had been awarded Purple Hearts, as had Bob Plaisance due to his ankle injury. The rest of the crew were now offered the same medal. Everybody accepted but Stanley, who thought he did not deserve it.

All worried that they would return to war. No one wanted to be shot down a third time. Soon, however, they learned they would all be sent stateside. Stanley did not understand why and was afraid to ask. He was still unaware that the criterion for being relieved of combat duty was forty-two days. If he had not volunteered the crew to remain behind when the transports flew out of Sanski Most, they would not have qualified. Their long, arduous hike across Yugoslavia had bought them their tickets home. Ed Seaver and Sam Spomer were going stateside too, due to their injuries.[12]

One other piece of news welcomed them, perhaps the most gratifying of all: on the morning of January 23, the briefing officers at Pantanella had delivered a special announcement. Blechhammer, as well as the oil refineries at Odertal and Oświęcim, had fallen to the Russians. Witnesses speculated the airmen's cheers could be heard all the way to Bari.[13]

■   ■   ■

Perhaps the brass paid attention to the airmen's debriefings. Sylvester Brown, Almondo Champi, Jules Levine, Leo Wilensky, Henry Wunderlich, and, later, Joe Foto, reported Captain Johnson's ugly behavior at the Sanski Most airstrip. Dr. Johnson's bomb group banned flight surgeons from flying combat missions soon afterward. In addition, the AAF listed the airfield outside Sanski Most as being useful "for crash landings" in its Weekly Escape Bulletin. It remained on the list until the end of the war.

Nevertheless, due to the Russian advances, the town no longer lay on a path between key targets and AAF bases in Italy. The Russians also made airfields in Hungary available for emergency landings. Only a few more crews took refuge in Sanski Most over the next few months. Perhaps it was just as well. In February, Captain Tregidga reported that the Partisans had become "unruly and hard to get along with."

A crippled B-17 attempted an emergency landing outside of Sanski Most on April 1. Seven crewmen died in the crash, while the pilots and two enlisted men were taken into town. There they joined Lt. Colonel Hugh A. Griffith, the commander of the Forty-Eighth Fighter Squadron, who had crash-landed his P-38 near Prijedor. The five airmen were flown out on April 5. They became the final U.S. evadees evacuated from Sanski Most during the war.[14]

CHAPTER 20

Far from Over

The Stewart and Dean crews—plus Bartusch, Rosenthal, and Hirschfield—had lingered in Yugoslavia for over six weeks, long enough to be sent home. The failure of the rescue efforts had qualified them. If the December 26 attempt had succeeded, they would have returned to combat.

The balance of the sixty-six airmen who came back from Sanski Most on January 5—except for Dr. Johnson and those who were severely injured—began flying missions after a period of recovery. For them, the war was far from over.

■　　■　　■

Frederick Coe and his copilot, Dale Hoffman, had returned to Italy on December 28. Coe spent three weeks in the hospital before he resumed flying. Henry Wunderlich and Jules Levine rejoined his crew after they were flown out of Sanski Most. A month later, flight engineer Jack Mulvaney, having returned from his hike across Yugoslavia, resumed flying combat missions with them as well. Coe and his men decided to fly as often as possible to finish their tours.

On February 22, they set off for their seventh mission in ten days, a raid against a rail junction in Worgl, Austria. Weather broke the formation up over the Adriatic. Six planes, including Coe's, headed through the Brenner Pass toward their first alternate target, Merano, Italy.

Dick Baldwin, Coe's navigator, called to warn him they were just five minutes from some flak emplacements. Surely the lead navigators had made a mistake. Couldn't Coe divert around them? "We can't," replied Coe. He could not leave the formation unless the plane was crippled. Those were among the last words Coe ever spoke.

The flak guns embedded on the mountainsides opened fire from virtually point-blank range. The lead bomber took a direct hit and caught flame. A few parachutes blossomed as the plane screamed downward.[1]

■   ■   ■

Henry Wunderlich sat in the tail turret of Coe's B-24J unaware of the tragedy unfolding ahead. Shells burst all around, shaking the plane violently. They felt unusually close. His first mission had taught him to wear a backpack-style parachute in the turret. *Good thing*, he thought.

A strange shudder reverberated through the plane. Before Henry could react, waist gunner Ed Brown banged him on the back. "Let's go!" he yelled. Wunderlich turned and saw Brown leap through the hatch. Everyone else in the waist had already jumped.

The plane fell into a death spiral, its right wing ablaze. Wunderlich swung his body out of the turret and fought toward the escape hatch. The B-24 disintegrated around him as he seized the door jam and cast himself out. He pulled the rip cord and his chute thwacked open. Moments later, he landed standing up in deep snow, a feat he would never have thought possible. His backpack parachute, with a larger canopy than a chest pack, had served him well.

Wunderlich heard a German voice as he released his chute. A half-dozen Wehrmacht soldiers approached with rifles aimed at his heart. They were led by an *Unteroffizier*, a non-commissioned officer roughly equivalent to a sergeant in rank. The airman raised his hands in surrender.

"*Haben Sie Pistol?*" asked the *Unteroffizier*.

"*Ya*," replied Wunderlich.

"*Gibt Sie es Mir*" ("Give it to me"), he demanded.

"*Nein*," Wunderlich answered. It did not seem to be a good idea to reach into his jacket for a gun with all those guns pointing at his heart.

The *Unteroffizier* grasped his meaning. "*Wo ist?*" ("Where is it?") he inquired.

"In my jacket," Wunderlich responded in English.

The *Unteroffizier* stepped forward, tugged at Wunderlich's jacket zipper, searched inside, and found the .45.

"*Ach!*" he cried. "*Ist Kanone!*" German pistols had a smaller caliber. The soldiers pressed in to admire it. Wunderlich resisted the urge to explain it to them. *Shut up*, he reminded himself. *These men are not your friends.*

As his captors marched him off toward Merano, Wunderlich reflected on how narrow his escape had been. His precaution of wearing his chute in the turret, plus Ed Brown's tap on the back, had saved his life.

In town, the soldiers locked Wunderlich in the city jail. Wunderlich knew he was in trouble as soon as he spotted the SS men manning it. His guard happened to be a well-educated pre-med student who spoke English better than Wunderlich spoke German.

"What are they going to do to me?" asked the airman.

"They are planning to execute you," replied the youth blandly. "They're that way, you know." Wunderlich could expect no help from him.

The airman tried speaking German to the guard on the next shift. Perhaps the language would harvest some sympathy. "Did they find my plane?" Wunderlich asked.

"*Ya*," the jailor replied.

"Is everybody alive?"

"*Nein. Drei Mann tot.*" Three were dead. Wunderlich wondered if the other crewmen had been captured. If so, he guessed he would not see them. The Nazis would keep them separate, the better to break their spirits.

"There's a big problem with you," the lad volunteered. "The Luftwaffe says you are going to the Dulag Luft at Oberursel for interrogation, and the SS wants to execute you."

The Luftwaffe won the argument, but the price was a grilling by the SS. The interrogator flashed Coe's identification card and Hoffman's ID bracelet before Wunderlich's eyes, searching for signs of grief or shock. He found none. Before long, a gray-clad officer claimed Wunderlich and escorted him away. How ironic, the airman mused; he owed his life to the Luftwaffe.

To compound the irony, the AAF soon became the greatest threat to Wunderlich's life, as U.S. fighters strafed his train several times before he arrived at Oberursel.

After three days of softening in solitary confinement, Wunderlich was led into a room to meet his interrogator, an *Unteroffizier*. "There isn't anything we don't know about you," he began in perfect, British-accented English. He read details of Wunderlich's life from a dossier, including the elementary schools he had attended as a child. The Germans could only have received such detailed information from one source—Wunderlich's Bundist grandfather.

"In many ways," the *Unteroffizier* continued, "you are a traitor. Your grandfather is a member of the Nazi Party." He recited Andrew Ostermeier's membership number in the Bund.

"I'm not a traitor," Wunderlich insisted. "I was born in the United States. You told me I was born in Buffalo, New York. That makes me an American. I am not a German."

"And if the cat has kittens in the oven," the *Unteroffizier* asked rhetorically, "I suppose they are biscuits?" Wunderlich smiled.

The interrogator moved on. "Tell me about the crew on a B-24," he continued.

"Well," Wunderlich replied, "there are ten gunners and two scorekeepers."

The *Unteroffizier* rose and delivered a ferocious slap. Wunderlich had gone too far. From then on, it was strictly name, rank, and serial number. Soon the German gave up, and Wunderlich was transferred to nearby Dulag Luft Zwei, in Wetzlar. The camp had first been used as a processing center for new prisoners. Now it served as a mini-stalag in the overwhelmed German POW system.

The camp *Kommandant*, Oberleutnant Becker, greeted Wunderlich's group with a clichéd but effective speech. "For you the war is over," he declared in English. "Stay put behind the barbed wire and you will probably get to go home. Do not be stupid by trying to escape. Do you hear me? The war is almost over! If you get to the barbed wire you will be shot. If you get over the barbed wire, the dogs will get you. In any case, you will be caught."

"Here you are a prisoner," he continued. "In town, you are the quarry. You will be killed. Believe me. It has happened. And they do some horrible things. Just stay put."

Wunderlich knew the *Kommandant* was right. Hostile civilians had screamed at him during stops along his railroad trip through Germany. He was safer inside than out. The war was as good as won, so escape was pointless.

Conditions at the dulag surpassed those in the stalags. The camp's senior Allied officer, Colonel Charles W. Stark, had eased into a truce with the Germans. His men would not cause trouble. In return, the *Kommandant* granted concessions whenever he could.

As in other camps, however, food remained scarce. The prisoners would have starved without the parcels supplied by the Red Cross. Colonel Stark held a reserve supply in case his men were forced to evacuate.

On the morning of March 27, the dreaded evacuation order came. Before it could be executed, however, gunfire erupted nearby. By noon, the camp was liberated. The war was truly over for Wunderlich.

Later he confirmed that three men from his crew had been killed. Two of them were pilot Fred Coe and copilot Dale Hoffman. Coe's parents had received word that he was missing in action again in early March. Since he had gone missing and returned once before, they believed he could do so again. It was not to be. The posthumous Distinguished Flying Cross awarded to their son was small consolation. When his belongings were sent home, they found a poem written in his notebook:

> A little flower, a pleasant smile,
> And kind words said to me
> Mean more than long-drawn eulogies
> When life has ceased to be!

The third dead crewman was flight engineer Jack Mulvaney, who had likely been standing between the pilots when the flak hit. Mulvaney, one of the men forced off the final plane departing from Sanski Most by Dr. Johnson, had been a bulwark of strength during the long hike across the Dinaric Alps. The journey had caused him to be missing for a biblical forty days. If he had been gone for just two more days, he would have been sent home and survived the war.[2]

■   ■   ■

Tom Stack rejoined his bomb group two days after his flight back to Italy from Sanski Most. He wrote to his mother immediately, claiming the MIA telegram had been a "big mistake" while admitting he had "played hooky" during a raid to Poland. He also confessed he had flown combat missions, but withheld the news that John Wolff, Sam Butler, and Andy Wozar were dead. He also failed to tell her when he resumed flying a month later.

Stack could not put off telling his mother about his deceased crewmates indefinitely. The Army would notify their families, and condolences would circulate. Besides, he might go missing again. On February 24, he finally disclosed that Wolff, Butler, and Wozar had been killed and that he had reentered combat. "All I can do now for them," he wrote, "is hit back hard and often at the damnable enemy that caused their deaths."

Stack's fellow survivors from his crew returned to combat duty too, including Herbert Eldridge, who had lived to tell the tale of Wolff's crash landing. Over the next few months, they flew sorties to Klagenfurt, Weiner-Neustadt, Regensburg, Vienna, and Moosbierbaum—some of the most dangerous targets in the Reich. All felt the mental strain mount with each passing mission. Strangely, Herb Eldridge, who had suffered the worst physical injuries, held up the best.

Stack flew his thirty-fifth and final sortie on April 18. He resisted the impulse to wire the good news to his mother, fearing the telegram's arrival would lead her to conclude he was missing in action again. Instead, he let the postal service do the job.[3]

■   ■   ■

George Earll and Gene Dennis rejoined Herky Marrone's crew immediately after they recovered from their injuries. Marrone refused to fly with Gregg Cloos, the man they had caught stealing in Sanski Most, so they found a new waist gunner.

Marrone began drinking himself to sleep the night before every mission. Sometimes he awoke with a frightful hangover, but he always pulled himself together. After each flight, he would take his two-ounce whiskey ration, Earll's as well, and then a few more.

On March 15, the crew made a return visit to Moosbierbaum, the source of their previous bailout. Once again, they took hits over the target. One engine failed, and another sputtered.

Marrone crossed Yugoslavia with a heavy sense of déjà vu. Near the Adriatic he called Big Fence seeking guidance. They ordered him to make an emergency landing at Vis.

Navigator Allen Goodling guessed they needed an hour to cross the sea. The plane still had fourteen thousand feet of altitude. The pilot decided he would chance it, but he did not disobey orders lightly. "I'm sending but not receiving," he lied. "Keep an eye out for me."

Marrone reached the Italian coastline at four thousand feet and headed to the nearest airfield. The base, it turned out, hosted B-17s, not B-24s. Ground crewmen surveyed the damage. "I have enough problems fixing B-17s," complained the chief. "I don't need any B-24s."

"I don't care if you ever fix it," retorted Marrone. He and his crew hitched a ride home.

In April, they were flying over the Adriatic again when the forward section filled with smoke. Gene Dennis, the nose gunner, called in a panic asking for permission to bail out. "Hold your position until we find out what's wrong," ordered Marrone. It was suicide to parachute into the sea anyway. Soon Allen Goodling fixed the problem by unplugging a malfunctioning radar set.

Everyone forgot the incident but Dennis, who inexplicably resented that Marrone had not let him jump to his death in the Adriatic Sea. On V-E Day, he got drunk and accosted Marrone. "Lieutenant Marrone, I'm going to kill you!" he cried. When Dennis charged, Marrone floored him with one punch and left him in the mud to sober up. It was a strange way to end a war.

The next day, Dennis apologized and asked whether Marrone intended to press charges. "Hell no," Marrone reassured him. "I've been drunk myself."[4]

■   ■   ■

Not long after Hixon Eldridge and Archy Roper started flying missions again, they spotted Gus Perrone and Joe Colasante wandering around their base. Eldridge immediately reported that the pair of them had bailed out without orders and refused to fly with them again.

Perrone and Colasante had been found by Partisans, transferred to Russian hands, and sent to Romania by train. In Bucharest, they became quartered at the same hotel the Stanley crew had passed through after being shot down in October.

The other three missing men from Eldridge's crew paid a heavy price for bailing out prematurely. Barker Houghton and Eugene Quinn were vaguely aware that they had not heard a bailout signal but followed Charles Fribley and the others out anyway. On the ground, locals led them to a supposed safe house with ten other airmen, a crew from the Ninety-Eighth Bomb Group. Soon German soldiers burst through the door and took them captive. The locals had betrayed them for a price.

Eventually, Houghton, Quinn, and Fribley were interned at Stalag Luft I near Barth on the Baltic Sea. Their compound lacked running water and recreational and mess halls. Over time, coal and food grew scarce, and sanitation disappeared. Vermin infested the barracks.

Stanley Schwartz, the captured Jewish bombardier from Ted Keiser's crew, was also interned at the stalag. In April, the Germans segregated the Jewish POWs from the rest. A rumor spread that Hitler had ordered their execution. Fortunately, Schwartz's fake dog tags labeling him as a Christian spared him from the segregation. Soon, however, fears grew that the Nazis would exterminate the POW population in general.

Later in April, the *Kommandant*, Oberst (Colonel) von Warnstedt, informed the camp's senior POW officer, Colonel Hubert Zemke, that the stalag was to be evacuated in the face of the Russian offensive. Zemke understood immediately that a forced march would mean the death of many undernourished prisoners. Refusal, however, might mean mass executions, beginning with Zemke and his staff.

Zemke called for a vote among his senior officers, who opted to stay put. Zemke notified the *Kommandant*, warning him that he and the high command would be held responsible for any loss of life. Everyone nervously awaited the German reaction.

Time passed without any response from the Germans. At last, on May 1, von Warnstedt beckoned Zemke to his office for the final time. The once arrogant *Kommandant* announced, "The war is over for us." That night, he and his men fled westward.

Zemke's men felt the exhilaration of freedom as only those who have lost it can. The camp's loudspeakers played a BBC broadcast of the *Your*

Hit Parade radio program. To the delight of all, it counted down to the number one song, Bing Crosby's "Don't Fence Me In."

The next day, the first Russian troops arrived. The airmen tore down the fences with an abandon some likened to toppling goalposts after winning a football game. Six days later, V-E Day was enlivened by a ceremonial burning of the camp watchtowers.

Soon American transports landed near the camp. Per Zemke's directive, the British—who had been confined far longer than most Americans—were flown out first. The Americans' turn—Houghton, Quinn, Fribley, and Schwartz among them—came a few days afterward. Colonel Zemke, as he had promised, became the last man to leave the grounds.[5]

■   ■   ■

Upon his return from Yugoslavia, Tom Tamraz was confined to the AAF hospital in Bari. The doctors assumed he had dysentery like everyone else and prescribed medicine to bind him. It was exactly the wrong treatment for his constipation. Tamraz developed hemorrhoids so severe he needed surgery.

On April 9, Tamraz lay recovering from his second hemorrhoid operation when an ammunition ship exploded in the Bari harbor. More than 300 sailors and Italian laborers were killed, and over 1,600 men were injured. So much blood spewed on the hospital floor that the attendants had to squeegee it off. Tamraz was pressed into setting up tents for the wounded. The port remained closed until the end of the war.

Tamraz returned to his unit, but by now the missions were mostly milk runs in support of infantry units. His base celebrated V-E Day with a massive bonfire. Drunken revelers tossed empty fifty-five-gallon drums of aviation gasoline on the fire to watch their fumes blow them high into the air. Predictably, one of the drums landed on an airman, breaking his leg.[6]

■   ■   ■

Ted Keiser spent the remainder of the war ferrying B-17s around the Mediterranean theatre. Jim Martin, Ken Wheeler, and the rest of Keiser's crew returned to combat, except for the captured Stanley Schwartz.

Martin, whose brother was still confined to a conscientious objector camp, became increasingly pacifistic as the war dragged on. He felt glad that he had never fired his guns in combat.

Martin was flying a mission as a substitute ball turret gunner when a flak shell burst just below his plane. The rear took the brunt of the shrapnel. He hopped on the interphone. "Check the tail gunner," he yelled, "something hit back there."

A voice replied moments later. "He's been hit—bad."

Martin clambered into the fuselage to help. The tail gunner lay unconscious, his mouth frothed with blood—a sign he had been hit in the lungs. Another fragment protruded from his skull. Martin called the pilot. "You'd better reduce altitude," he suggested. "He needs oxygen."

The plane dropped lower and headed for Vis, but the gunner died before they touched down. Martin never learned the man's name.[7]

■   ■   ■

Four of Clarence Marshall's crewmen—Albert Hill, James Martino, LeRoy Nayes, and Jan Wroclawski—returned from their adventures on January 18. Wroclawski and Martino were sent home due to their injuries. Nayes returned to flying with another crew.

Albert Hill started flying with Marshall again after a short rest. Their first mission, on February 21, 1945, was a tough one against Vienna. Before they reached the target, their plane took three heavy-weight punches from nearby explosions. They lost an engine, a rudder malfunctioned, and gas sieved from the fuel tanks. Marshall dropped out of formation and headed for an emergency field beyond the Russian lines in Hungary.

Fortunately, the airstrip there featured a long, concrete runway, and Marshall had no problem landing. That evening, his Russian hosts feted his men and another stranded crew. An orderly kept everyone's vodka glasses full. An English-speaking captain regaled the airmen with war stories. He had once been a major, he declared, but was demoted when he ordered some cooks to be shot for their terrible food. "It got better after that!" he exclaimed.

The party continued all night, long after the Americans bedded down. In the morning, the Russian pilots took off for their missions still drunk.

Marshall and the pilot of the other aircrew decided to salvage parts from Marshall's plane to get the other, less damaged craft into the air. After two days of preparations, however, the base commander claimed he lacked permission to let them depart. Marshall wondered if the Russians wanted to keep the B-24, as they had nothing like it in their arsenal.

The next day a third U.S. bomber made an emergency landing at the field. Now there were thirty U.S. airmen present, too many to fit on a single plane. In any case, nobody was leaving until the Soviets let them.

After two weeks of Russian prevarication, Marshall received permission to take off. When he boarded the plane with thirteen others, they discovered it had been stripped of its armaments. Drunken Red Army pilots, the English-speaking captain explained, often attacked unfamiliar aircraft. The Russians did not want the B-24 to shoot them down. Marshall managed to fly back to Italy without incident. The rest of the airmen returned via Bucharest.

Back at the base, the flight surgeon asked Albert Hill how he felt about flying again. "The quickest way to get home," Hill replied, "is to get my missions in."

"No," the doctor countered, "I think you've had enough. We're going to send you home." Hill burst into tears. He had not realized how frayed his nerves were.[8]

■   ■   ■

Keith Owens of Harry Blank's crew was slated to return to combat on January 23, but bad weather precluded flying for nine days. Then his bomb group really went to work. They flew twenty-one missions in February alone, few of them milk runs.

Owens's closest call came over Vienna. As a radio man, he spent part of his time at his station and the rest manning a waist gun. Owens was kneeling in the waist throwing chaff out of the bomb bay when an explosion peppered the ship with shrapnel. Shards cut through the chaff box, but he escaped without a scratch. When Owens returned to his station, he discovered his desk had a new window—a hole as big as his head.

V-E Day came with Owens's original pilot, Harry Blank, and three of his crew—John Turk, Tom Koballa, and Bill Ceely—still missing in action. Owens figured if they had not returned by now, they never would.[9]

CHAPTER 21

A Terrible Blindness

*L*ittle *Butch II* had taken Harry Blank as far as she could. The plane
was nearly out of fuel and losing altitude. Everyone but the pilots
had bailed out. Blank tried to slide his seat back, but it was jammed. He
was pinned against the steering column. His only way to escape was to
push the yoke forward, but that would plunge the plane into a nosedive.
Copilot John Turk would have to pull it out of the dive while Blank
exited, and then Turk would jump. They had mere seconds.

Blank pushed the wheel and slipped from his chair. The B-24 plunged
as he climbed through the half-deck and leapt out the bomb bay. He
popped the chute and caught sight of an open canopy. It must be Turk.
An instant later Blank felt his silk catching some tree limbs. His weight
stretched them downward until they gave way and he landed awkwardly,
turning his ankle.

Blank gathered up his parachute, hid it under some brush, and
limped down the snowy, forested hillside. Before long an old, bearded
man approached. *"Englez?"* he inquired.

"No," replied Blank, "American."

The man smiled broadly. After a brief greeting, he led Blank to his tiny village. The codger introduced his clan and brought out a jug. Blank shook his head. "*Dobra*," his host insisted. Blank took a swig and gasped—the stuff tasted like aviation fuel.

Within a half hour the flight engineer, Tom Koballa, and the tail gunner, William Ceely, were brought into the hamlet. They wanted to wait for others to come in, but the old man was anxious to move along. Blank caught the word "Partisans" spoken among the villagers in a fearful tone.

Soon a guide led the airmen eastward, the opposite direction from Sanski Most. They marched for two days with only brief rests. At last, they reached a Chetnik safehouse on a hillside overlooking Banja Luka. There they found John Turk, who had arrived half a day earlier.

The leader of the Chetnik band promised the airmen that they would soon be taken to a Mihailović-held airfield and flown to Italy. The rest of their crew, he lied, had been killed by Partisans. He claimed it was a good thing his side had picked them up rather than the murdering Communists.

The four airmen hiked for a week. As they approached General Draža Mihailović's headquarters on the evening of December 27, they saw the unmistakable silhouette of American P-38s circling overhead. No doubt they were escorting transports. Rescue seemed at hand.

By the time they reached the airfield, however, the fighters were gone. So were the transports and nineteen airmen who had been sheltered in the Chetnik camp. The last three OSS agents from the HALYARD mission had departed with them. Blank, Turk, Koballa, and Ceely had missed their chance to be flown out by a mere hour.

The Chetniks quartered the airmen in a comfortable two-story log house. Guards manned the doors. Blank and his men were well treated, but they were not free to leave either. They were far too valuable. Maybe their presence would force the American mission to return.[1]

■   ■   ■

General Mihailović still hoped to secure enough ground in Serbia to sustain his eight-thousand-man army, collect more followers, and reorganize.

Months before, Lt. Colonel Robert H. McDowell of the OSS RANGER team had advised Mihailović to move his troops westward toward Slovenia and then Italy, where they might link up with the American Fifth Army. McDowell had also given Mihailović unauthorized and unrealistic assurances that the Allies would change their minds about him and furnish renewed aid.

Regardless, Mihailović deemed such a distant and large-scale migration to be too risky. Strong Wehrmacht and Croatian forces stood between him and Slovenia. The Partisan army would give chase, and his ill-equipped men would be caught in the middle.

Instead, Mihailović reached out to the Allies twice and offered to place his troops under their command. Twice they ignored him. Desperate for support from any source, the general finally realized he needed to broaden his base of support beyond ethnic Serbs. On January 3, 1945, he issued a call to all Yugoslavians to join his cause. He appealed to Croatians, Muslims, and non-Mihailović Chetniks to rally to his side. He ordered his troops to stop raiding Croat and Muslim villages for supplies. The pillaging continued anyway, and few recruits joined.

The condition of his hungry army declined. Typhus swept the ranks. Some discouraged Chetnik soldiers sold or traded their arms to the local populace for food.[2]

■   ■   ■

On January 7, 1945, two new Allied fliers joined Blank and his men in their solid log abode. Twenty-year-old Lt. Lawrence Zellman, an American P-38 Lightning pilot, had been flying his first mission when a gas leak forced him to bail out. Lt. Roy G. Cumming, a South African RAF pilot, had been shot down while attacking a railroad bridge near Doboj with his Spitfire. About the same time, an English-speaking major named Blagoyevitch, who claimed to have once been the royal ambassador to Denmark, became the liaison between the airmen and the Chetniks.

After a few days, the Chetniks allowed the airmen to reach out to the ACRU in Bari via radiograms (coded, radio-transmitted telegrams). They asked for a rescue by air, or failing that, a supply drop.

The ACRU replied that they could not drop supplies because the evadees' position was too close to the Germans. They also directed the airmen to ask the Chetniks to arrange a transfer to the Partisans and closed with a request: "ADVISE IF CHETNIKS ARE PREVENTING EVACUATION TO PARTISANS." The airmen scratched their heads. They would have to pass their reply through the Chetniks.

The airmen sent several more radiograms trying to establish their identities and begging the ACRU for help. They explained that they were in no condition to travel even if the Chetniks were willing and able to pass them to Tito's men. Most of the airmen suffered from injuries and dysentery. The Germans were far enough away that an airdrop would not fall into enemy hands. When these radiograms failed, Blank, Zellman, and Cumming bypassed HQ by sending messages directly to their units. Nothing worked.

Bari continued stalling all through February. No one there would admit to Blank and the others that sending a plane to Chetnik territory was a political impossibility. Headquarters continued to insist that they would have to find their way to the Partisans. The airmen knew this was infeasible. To them, Bari's dithering seemed inexplicable.[3]

■   ■   ■

Both the Chetnik and the Partisan armies remained inactive for weeks, bogged down by the severe winter. In mid-February, however, the Chetnik stronghold bustled with newcomers. Mihailović's troops had been joined by the other remaining Chetnik army in Yugoslavia, the Montenegrin force led by Pavle Đurišić. Five new American airmen entered camp with him.

Major Blagoyevitch, called "Blackie" by the Americans, guided the new group to the house where Blank, Turk, Ceely, Koballa, Zellman, and Cumming were quartered. The arrivals, overjoyed to see fellow Allied fliers, rushed forward to greet them. They stopped short, though, when Blank and his men seemed to recoil at their appearance.

"We're Americans," explained navigator Lt. James Inks, who later described the encounter in his book *Eight Bailed Out*. Inks and the others with him wore ragged Chetnik garb. All were bearded, gaunt, sickly, dirty, and lice-ridden. They might carry typhus.

"Jeez," exclaimed Harry Blank. "How long have you been out here?"

"Almost eight months," snapped Inks, pulling his five-foot-nine inch frame upright.

"Holy cow," said another of Blank's group. "What happened to you?"

"We've been through hell," stated the worn-out man.

"You…look it," was the awkward reply.

Inks and his ragtag band had expected a warmer welcome. A coolness settled.

"What unit are you guys from?" asked one of Blank's men. The answer for most of them was the 465th Bomb Group, but it was too late to be friendly. Inks and his men set their jaws as Blank's group caught them up to speed. A swift rescue seemed unlikely. The OSS liaisons had departed, and headquarters appeared to be indifferent to their plight.

Inks called out to Blagoyevitch, "Where do we go from here?" He did not ask to stay in Blank's log cabin, nor was he invited. Neither group offered to shake hands as they parted.[4]

■   ■   ■

Inks's men had bailed out on July 28, 1944, after an attack against Ploesti. Eight of the crew had been picked up by bearded men who

promised not to turn them over to the Germans but confiscated their
.45s anyway. The men claimed to be Chetniks who were not fighting
the Nazis, but were not their allies either. Their enemy was a man
named Tito. The Americans had never heard of him.

Entering the Chetnik camp, the airmen were introduced to Pavle
Đurišić, the tall, bearded commander of the Montenegrin Chetniks.
Earlier in the war, Đurišić had carried out several atrocities against Muslims while collaborating with the Italians. Eventually, the Germans captured him but later decided he could be useful to their cause. They released
him, armed his forces, and set him fighting against the Partisans in Montenegro. Now he commanded the strongest Chetnik army in Yugoslavia,
a force of about fifteen thousand combatants and civilian refugees.

Of course, the Americans knew none of this. To them, Đurišić
seemed to be a friend who carried himself with an air of pride and distinction. He promised to arrange their return to Italy and assigned a
young English-speaker to elaborate.

The Chetniks, the youth explained, were Royalists who had once
fought the Axis and received Allied supplies. After the Allies switched
all aid to the Partisans, self-preservation forced the Chetniks into an
alliance with the Germans. The airmen were not prisoners, however; the
Chetniks would get them to Italy somehow. Meanwhile, a pair of guards
would watch over them.

Weeks dragged by. The airmen debated whether they should escape.
They fell into two cliques—those who wanted to seek out Tito's men and
those who preferred to stay. Pilot Lewis Perkins and two others hoped
to get away. On September 15, they wandered off and stumbled into some
Partisans. They returned to Italy within a week.

A month after Perkins and his companions escaped, Sgt. Herbert
Martin, a tail gunner from the 454th Bomb Group, joined Inks and the
others remaining in Đurišić's camp. Shot down in May, he had been
missing long enough to have become proficient in Serbo-Croatian.

Disguised in Chetnik clothes, the airmen wandered freely about the
town near the Chetnik camp. They even frequented taverns patronized

by the Germans, who apparently viewed them as just a few more Slavic inferiors.

In December, the airmen grew tired of the broken Chetnik promises and tried to reach the Partisans. Within half an hour the Chetniks discovered their absence and rounded them up. The Partisans, the Chetniks scolded, would have killed them if they had found them.

The Germans and Đurišić's army had remained stagnant because they were trapped in the area by the Partisans, Allied aircraft, and "Floyd Force," a British artillery contingent. In November, however, Tito became alarmed by the size and success of Floyd Force and ordered it away. Realizing their good fortune, the Germans began migrating to the northwest. Đurišić followed, hoping to link up with Mihailović.

The German-Chetnik caravan stretched as far as the eye could see. Sparse vehicles supplemented a train of wagons, hand-pulled carts, and livestock. Occasionally, Allied fighters strafed them. At first, the Chetniks returned fire. They only stopped when the airmen told them more planes would come if they shot one down.

The Germans monopolized the rations. Desperate and starving, the Chetniks staged night raids against their supply trucks, posing as Partisans to divert suspicion.

The airmen suffered terribly. Inks urinated blood. His kidneys felt like he had gone twelve rounds with Joe Louis. Nose gunner Robert "Mac" McCormack ran a fever. Willard Griffin, the ball turret gunner, had been muscular and tan when he bailed out. Now he looked gaunt and gray. Floyd "Arky" Umfleet's cheekbones stuck out like they had been painted by Picasso.

After two and a half months on the move, the Chetniks split from the German column at Zvornik. Copilot Lloyd Aclin, sick and weary, believed the crew would starve without the Wehrmacht supplies. As the Germans veered off to the west, he separated himself from his friends. Before they could stop him, he shouted, "I am an American flier!" and surrendered to a surprised German MP. The remaining Americans hurried on, wondering if he would betray them.[5]

■   ■   ■

Harry Blank felt sorry for Inks and his men but was appalled when he learned they had traded away their clothes—even their priceless GI shoes—to avoid capture in the taverns they patronized with the Germans. They had signed so many chits—vouchers theoretically backed by the American government—that even the Chetniks would not take them anymore.

Relations between the two groups of airmen deteriorated. Mostly they argued over food. Blank's bunch carefully husbanded and rationed their supplies, while Inks's men never seemed satisfied with what they were given. To them, the Blank group hoarded the little available sustenance.

The issue came to a head when Inks discovered the Chetniks possessed blankets and rations left behind by the HALYARD mission. These goods, Inks and his men decided, were the property of the U.S. government and should be released to them.

Blank refused to make such a demand. HALYARD had given the wares to Mihailović for the benefit of his troops. The stuff belonged to them, not to any American who happened by.

Inks upped the ante by raising the issue of rank. Although he was a navigator and Blank was a pilot, both were second lieutenants. The one with the earlier date of rank had seniority, and Inks had been on the ground for seven months. He knew he must outrank Blank. There were, however, two other Allied officers in camp. Inks asked their dates of rank. Larry Zellman was a graduate of Class of 44-A. He outranked Blank, but not Inks.

Inks turned to Lt. Roy Cumming, the RAF pilot from South Africa. Cumming's date of rank came one month earlier than Inks's. He was the senior Allied officer in camp, even if he belonged to a different air force. Cumming promptly appointed Blank as his deputy. That settled the argument. The airmen would make no demands for the HALYARD supplies.[6]

■   ▦   ■

On February 19, 1945, a few days after the Inks group arrived in their camp, the Chetniks allowed them to transmit their own set of radiograms to Bari. Inks outlined his men's trials and physical woes and begged for help. If the ACRU could not send a transport, wouldn't they at least drop food, clothing, and medical supplies, especially typhus serum? The next day, Inks repeated his plea. He also requested that the airmen's families be notified of their safety.

Ten days passed without an answer. At last, on March 1, Bari asked Inks to confirm his men's identities and location. Inks provided the correct information. Major Blagoyevitch sent his own hopeful radiogram to Bari asking HQ to confirm that it intended to send transports.

Two weeks later, Cumming sent a radiogram directly to his squadron asking to be evacuated. They forwarded it to Fifteenth Air Force headquarters on his behalf.

At last, the Inks and Cumming messages convinced Colonel Kraigher, the ACRU leader, that he needed to act. On March 16, he radioed the head American delegate in Belgrade, Colonel Charles Thayer, to see if the Partisans would object to a supply drop.

Thayer negotiated a compromise. The local Partisan commander would attempt to evacuate the airmen. If he failed to succeed within the week, the ACRU would parachute the provisions.

Kraigher radiogrammed the stranded men to look out for a Partisan emissary. The Chetniks failed to relay the message to the airmen.[7]

Inks sent more pleas to HQ on March 18 and 23. He threatened that he and his men would escape without permission if they did not get help by April 7.

On March 30, Blank notified Bari that seven new fliers had joined the Chetnik camp. One of them was an RAF pilot, Flight-Sergeant Walter M. Monkman of Leeds. The others were Americans from the 460th Bomb Group led by Lt. Aelrod Gill, a bombardier. Blank also told

Bari that he had located a possible landing strip. Kraigher responded for the first time in weeks, asking for details.

Blank replied on April 2. The Chetniks would help prepare the airstrip if headquarters gave assurances the transport would come. Hopeful of a rescue by air, Inks allowed his self-imposed deadline for escape to lapse.[8]

■　　■　　■

Meanwhile, Đurišić and Mihailović contemplated their next move. They could not stay where they were. The Partisans would attack with the spring thaw.

Đurišić realized he had made a terrible mistake in joining Mihailović in Bosnia. The poor condition of Mihailović's soldiers distressed him. Despite their long march, Đurišić's army was in far better shape. If he had stayed in Montenegro, he might have headed south and surrendered to British troops in Greece. Being captured by the Partisans or the Russians meant certain death.

Đurišić wanted Mihailović to move northwest with him toward Slovenia, as the American OSS agent Robert McDowell had suggested months before. A few thousand Chetniks still persevered there. To Đurišić, linking with them seemed the only chance of survival, however slim. The Allied armies in Italy were advancing in that direction. Perhaps they would welcome the Chetniks as brothers-in-arms. If not, at least they would accept their surrender without reprisals.

Mihailović, however, still harbored his old pipe dream of finding an enclave in friendly Serbia and awaiting an Allied invasion. He doubted his army, even when combined with Đurišić's forces, could survive against the Partisan and Ustashe forces hindering their path to Slovenia.

According to the Partisan historian Milovan Djilas, a misinformation campaign duped Mihailović into believing conditions would be favorable in Serbia. Unknown to the Chetniks, the Partisans had captured one of Mihailović's radio operators. They sent spurious messages in Chetnik code that convinced him to turn toward Serbia, just as the Partisans wanted him to.

Regardless, Mihailović's hopes of an Allied change of heart grew ever more unrealistic. Tito formed a government in Belgrade on March 7. The Allies immediately recognized its legitimacy per their agreement at the Yalta Conference the month before.

Over time, the argument between Mihailović and Đurišić escalated. Mihailović commanded the Montenegrin to accompany him to Serbia. He alone had been named as supreme commander by the king, so disobedience was more than insubordination; it was treason. Đurišić refused. He would head for Slovenia. The two leaders argued so fiercely some feared they might come to blows.

Given Đurišić's intransigence, Mihailović had only two options: he could relent and join Đurišić in his journey to the west, or he could let Đurišić go on alone. In the end, Mihailović refused to abandon his Serbian dream but allowed anyone from his army who wanted to try his luck with Đurišić to depart. Đurišić's Chetniks soon set off. The captive Allied airmen were left behind with Mihailović.

Over the next several weeks, Đurišić's men forged a path northwest under constant attack by the Ustashe. In late April, the Ustashe and the Croatian Home Guard destroyed Đurišić's main force. The remnants were picked off or perished of hunger and exposure. Few reached Slovenia.

Eventually, the Montenegrin pro-Axis leader Sekula Drljević, working as an intermediary with the Ustashe, talked Đurišić into surrendering. The Ustashe disarmed and slaughtered Đurišić and his retinue. That part of the Chetnik army had been destroyed.[9]

■　　■　　■

Colonel Kraigher sent a final message to the Chetnik camp on April 11, instructing the airmen to evacuate to the Partisans. Again, the Chetniks intercepted the message.

General Mihailović and his remaining troops began their march toward Serbia during the night of April 12–13, 1945. Their prospects were bleak. The Ustashe loomed nearby. The Partisans controlled most of their path.

The Chetniks started west, but only to convince the Partisans and the Ustashe that they were heading to Slovenia. Then they circled southward into Ustashe territory, hoping to break through and turn east. The Chetnik troops, and the Allied airmen in their midst, walked through the day and all night as well. On the morning of April 14, they stopped to eat their first meal in forty-eight hours.

Mihailović had long taken a personal interest in the airmen. He had first met with Blank, Turk, Ceely, Koballa, Zellman, and Cumming on February 3. They were the first Allied soldiers he had seen since the HALYARD mission departed. Major Blagoyevitch interpreted their conversation. The general was most kind and seemed genuinely interested in their welfare. He visited them several times again in March while they hoped for an airdrop or a rescue.

Now General Mihailović came to meet with all eighteen airmen in his camp. He outlined his view of the political situation, claiming he was on the same side as Britain and the United States. They had forsaken him—and the stranded fliers—for ill-considered reasons. He promised to return the airmen to Italy as soon as possible.

Mihailović's soft-spoken dignity impressed his audience. He looked and acted more like a college professor than a guerilla commander. The things he said made sense to Inks and his men.[10]

The Chetniks set off again that evening. After a few days, they came upon the Ustashe lines and routed a small opposing force. Afterward, they paused to loot and burn Ustashe houses. Fires illuminated the countryside. The pillaging, the Chetniks explained, was retaliation for Ustashe atrocities against Serb villages.

Eventually Mihailović ordered an end to the mayhem, and his army marched on. At first the airmen refused to join them. The general personally intervened and convinced them the Partisans meant them harm. In addition, if the airmen left the Chetniks, they would be giving up their ability to communicate with Colonel Kraigher in Bari—even though he seemed to be ignoring their pleas for help.

Unknown to the airmen, Kraigher disagreed with the decision to leave them to their fate and had asked for permission to fly to Belgrade to discuss the issue. On April 18, he flew supplies there, perhaps as an excuse to argue his case with the Partisan high command.

As a practical matter, however, the question was moot by then. The Chetniks had moved far from the airfield during the delay. Rescue by air was impossible.[11]

■　　■　　■

On April 23, the airmen again asked Mihailović to transfer them to the Partisans. The general lied, saying that the Partisans were no longer nearby, but he promised he would hand them over when he could. He was, in fact, surrounded by Tito's men.

Two evenings later, Mihailović summoned the airmen to his campfire one last time. The general knew his army would soon be attacked by superior Partisan forces. This was likely his final opportunity to explain himself to the outside world.

Mihailović spoke in a soft, low, professional voice. He apologized for the way the evadees had been forced to live but noted he had not fared any better. Tomorrow his troops would pass through a valley. He would leave the Americans with a neutral family who would transfer them to the Partisans. Then he would continue south toward Split on the Adriatic coast.

This was disinformation meant for the Partisans' ears. The last thing he intended was to move his depleted army across the rugged, Partisan-held Dinaric Alps.

Mihailović presented his vision of geopolitics and the course of the war. Russia, France, and Britain had long sought to dominate the Balkans because of its strategic location between Europe and the Near East.

Tito had trained in Moscow and still served his masters there. When Germany first invaded Yugoslavia, the Communists had collaborated with the Germans while the Chetniks fought on. Tito joined the fight only after Hitler attacked the Soviet Union.

The currents of international power politics were strange, Mihailović observed, and the ways of supposed statesmen even stranger. He could not understand how the Communists turned Britain and the United States against their friends, the Chetniks. He called on the airmen to witness how the Partisans were using Allied weapons to fight their countrymen rather than the Germans. The Allies had forced him to join the Germans in a defensive alliance. Still, as some of the Americans here knew, he sabotaged and fought them whenever he could.

"That's right! That's right!" Inks shouted. Arky Umfleet and Willard Griffin chimed in. They remembered the Chetnik raids on German supply trucks during the long march, forgetting that starvation, not resistance, had been their motivation.

Everyone fell silent as Mihailović delivered his parting words: "Soon your people will know how terrible their mistake has been. It will not be long. The Germans are now breathing their last gasp, and sooner than you think they will give up. And then Stalin and his servant, Tito, will no longer need you. They will be strong then, and with what you have given them, stronger than the strength you lost by giving it to them, they will turn your strength upon you. Do not deceive yourselves that Communism and democracy can live side by side. The day has not yet come when the lion lies down beside the lamb.

"It will not be long. It will be sooner than you can at this moment conceive to be possible, that Stalin and Tito will turn upon you. I shall not be here then, for I shall not be here very long. I shall not be here long enough to see that I have been right. But I see it now and I know that I am right. And then, you, too, will know of your terrible blindness. But then it will be too late."

Mihailović rose. "I will say goodbye in the morning," he promised. "Now you must rest and pray for tomorrow." No one spoke as he walked off.[12]

■   ■   ■

The next day, Mihailović shook every airman's hand and presented each with a pre–World War I British half-sovereign, a nickel-sized gold coin with King George V's image stamped on it. He told them to use the gold to buy passage to Italy if they reached the coast. He apologized he could do no more. "Godspeed," he bade them, "to your homes and loved ones."

The airmen lined up and stood at attention as Mihailović mounted his horse and rode off to lead his once-proud army to its last stand.

As Mihailović had promised, a Chetnik major would guide them up a mountainside to a farmhouse owned by a neutral family. He introduced himself and shook the airmen's hands. Reaching Inks, he noticed his black onyx fraternity ring. "I'm a Phi Psi too!" he cried in perfect English. He bent over and whispered the secret password in Inks's ear. Inks had never been so flabbergasted in his life.

The Chetnik wanted the ring, so Inks traded it for a .38 pistol. "I die a Phi Psi to the last," the major exclaimed gaily, and they set off.

Distant fire erupted as they entered the designated farmhouse. The neutral family had gone into hiding—or perhaps they had arranged an ambush. The skirmish outside escalated. Each man had to decide whether to stay or move on.

Zellman felt too weak from typhus to go any farther. "I'm done," he announced. "I'm just going to wait and take my chances." Blank, Koballa, and the RAF pilot, Flight-Sergeant Walter Monkman, opted to stay with him. The rest moved on with the escorts.

Bullets whined about them. Some hit the farmhouse. The noise stopped until a blow knocked the door open, and a cross-eyed lad of about thirteen entered with another Partisan. The airmen threw up their hands. Blank wondered how the kid aimed his rifle as the boy frisked them.

The other fourteen airmen continued uphill. Soon they came under intense fire, and the major and the other Chetniks fled. The airmen, caught in the crossfire, hid in a gully and waited. A Partisan patrol found them and escorted them to the rear. Within minutes, Zellman, Blank, Koballa, and Monkman were brought in too.

A few captured Chetniks arrived with their hands tied behind them. The Partisans lined them up, had them kneel, and shot each one in the back of the head. An officer relieved Inks of his pistol and emptied it into a Chetnik youth. He grinned as the boy's body bounced with each shot.

The officer directed Inks and Zellman to carry a wounded Partisan soldier down the hillside to a medical team. A grenade had blown off half the man's scalp. He died nearly as soon as they arrived. Inks asked for the dead man's socks, and the doctor gave them to him without pause.[13]

The following day, the Partisans transported the eighteen fliers to their headquarters in Teslić. No one there knew what to do with them. After a week, the airmen lost patience and hopped a truck to Banja Luka. There Zellman, too weak to travel any farther, was admitted to a hospital. The next morning, everyone else hitchhiked to Brod. Eventually, the seventeen worked their way to Italy via Belgrade.[14]

■   ■   ■

After a few days in the Banja Luka hospital, Zellman felt somewhat better and decided to find someone who might help him. He walked around the town for hours until a jeep full of American soldiers came by. The officer in charge was not happy. He had come all the way from Belgrade looking for Zellman only to discover the airman had gone AWOL from the hospital.

Zellman lingered in Yugoslavia for nine more days. The Partisans released him only after he consented to an interview concerning his time with the Chetniks. When questioned, he carefully avoided implicating anyone who had helped him.

Lt. Lawrence Zellman finally caught a flight to Bari on May 20. He thus became the final American sheltered by the Chetniks to return to Allied hands. He had been missing 152 days.[15]

■   ■   ■

Meanwhile, Mihailović fought on toward Serbia. On May 10, his remaining forces found themselves on a cliff overlooking a tributary of the Drina River. The Partisans attacked as the Chetniks descended and crossed. An orgy of violence followed. Tito's orders were to "eradicate" the enemy. Already condemned to die, most Chetniks fought to the death. Mihailović and about five hundred of his men dissolved into the forests.

Mihailović hid until he was captured on March 13, 1946. He was tried and convicted of treason in a show trial and executed on July 17, 1946.[16]

Coming Home

M rs. Stanley and Mary Alice received Charles's letters announcing
his safe return on February 12, 1945. More good news followed:
he and the rest of the crew would be sent stateside.

With the crisis now past, Mrs. Stanley reflected on how she had been
comforted by her correspondence with the crew's family members. "Most
of the mothers wrote such warm, interesting letters," she confided to
Mary Alice. "Some of them seem to give Charles the credit for their sons
coming back alive. No doubt he used good judgment, but for my part
I'll give a Higher Power credit for the boys' safety."[1]

■ ■ ■

Late in February, Stanley, Don Baker, and Leo Cone boarded the
USS *Catoctin* for transport to the Unites States. Just two weeks before,
the ship had hosted the advance party for President Roosevelt's "Big
Three" meeting with Churchill and Stalin at Yalta. Roosevelt himself
had slept on board for a night. As a result, the *Catoctin* was well-stocked

with delicacies. Someone had to eat the stuff before it spoiled. Charles crossed the Atlantic happily regaining weight.

Even better, the ship reached port at the Philadelphia naval yard, not too far from his home in East Brady. Buffalo stood just a stone's throw beyond.

Meanwhile, Bob Plaisance—now the commander of his own crew—continued flying. On March 2, Plaisance was awarded the Distinguished Flying Cross for the October 13 flight past the Russian lines in Romania. General Nathan Twining, the head of the Fifteenth Air Force, pinned the medal on his chest. Apparently, Plaisance claimed sole credit for flying the *Fertile Turtle* to safety. Regardless, the AAF ignored Stanley's role as the aircraft commander responsible for the success or failure of the mission. He received no such medal.[2]

■   ■   ■

By the time Tom Tamraz recovered from his hemorrhoid surgeries, the war was nearly over. A few weeks after V-E Day, he passed into New York Harbor aboard a Liberty ship.

Forty-two years before, the beacon of freedom emanating from Lady Liberty's upstretched hand had bid Tom's father, Yohannon, welcome as he sought refuge from the religious persecution of the Ottoman Empire. Now Tom passed under the statue's mute gaze with his head held high. He had done his part to secure freedom for the huddled masses of Europe and beyond.

Tamraz mustered out of the service at Ft. Sheridan, Illinois. He was riding home on an elevated train in Chicago when two women, an older one and a younger one, passed by and took the seat behind him. Tamraz turned and exclaimed, "Don't you remember me? I'm back!" His sister hugged him while his mother broke out in tears. Everyone in the car dabbed at their eyes. It was a hell of a coincidence.[3]

■   ■   ■

Herky Marrone's first stop stateside was Brooklyn, where his girl-friend Jane lived. They spent three days getting reacquainted. Then he went home to see his family.

He arrived at the train station closest to Eldred, Pennsylvania, late at night needing a ride. His best bet was his sister and her husband, who owned a car and ample gasoline ration stamps.

Marrone's drowsy sister picked up the phone. "How would you like to pick up a tired and hungry soldier?" a voice said.

"Who's this?" she asked.

"It's Herk."

"It's not!" she insisted. "He's over in Italy."

"Like hell!" laughed Marrone. "He's in front of the Texas hot dog stand in Olean." He added a special incentive. "And make room for my wife!"

Herk's brother-in-law and sister delivered him home after midnight. The whole family gathered to greet the returning hero and his bride. There was no new wife, however. He had not even brought Jane from Brooklyn. The family would have killed him if they weren't so happy to see him. Everybody cried a little, and they listened to his adventures until dawn.[4]

■   ■   ■

Clete Kramer, liberated from the Black March by British troops, was processed at Camp Lucky Strike so quickly he didn't find time to write his parents.

Kramer had been reported missing in action six months before. His family had not been notified that he was captured, so his father gave him up for dead.

His mother, however, still hoped. On Sunday, May 13, she, her hus-band, and their four other children gathered to celebrate Mother's Day.

She had just finished a pre-meal prayer for Clete's safety when he walked through the door. It was a reunion none of them would forget.[5]

■   ■   ■

All the repatriated airmen—including those who had completed their tours—stayed in the Army pending the surrender of Japan. Even then, the vast bureaucratic task of discharging millions of soldiers delayed their return to civilian life. Meanwhile the AAF kept them busy.

GIs often quoted an old saying: "There's the right way, the wrong way, and then there's the Army way." The military had its own logic, even if it seldom made sense on the surface.

In Larry Rosenthal's case, however, the Army got it right. It assigned him to its Special Services Division in California, where the pianist became acquainted with several famous entertainers, including Danny Kaye. He even taught boogie-woogie to the famous classical pianist Jose Iturbi. The Army offered to promote him to captain, but Rosenthal mustered out to become a professional musician. Later he married his wife Ildiko, a refugee from the Hungarian Revolution, and founded a successful clothing manufacture business.[6]

■   ■   ■

World War II dramatically affected marriage rates while soldiers and sailors served overseas. In 1945 and 1946 marriages rebounded. The famous baby boom inexorably followed.

Charles and Mary Alice hoped to get married as soon as he returned from Italy, but practical considerations intervened. Mary Alice wanted to complete her spring semester of college. Then the Army sent Charles to be a B-25 instructor in Georgia.

Charles was finally released from the service in October 1945. He caught the first available train to Buffalo while Mary Alice and her family made the arrangements. The principal preparation was making a wedding dress from the parachute he had carried across Yugoslavia. Red Yugoslavian mud stained much of the nylon, so the seamstress cut it into strips and ran seams down each side of the gown to disguise its flaws.

Two days before the ceremony, the front page of Buffalo's morning newspaper, the *Courier Express*, featured an article entitled "Flier's Chute to Be Bride's Wedding Gown—Parachute Performs Double Service." The story and photo were picked up by wire services and appeared in newspapers across the northeast.

Several other airmen married their sweethearts that fall, including Powell Robinson. Herman Marrone did not marry Jane, his wartime girlfriend from Brooklyn. Instead, he found love across the street from his mother's house. In 1950, he married Joy Kelsey and eventually had two daughters with her.

Mevlida, the Muslim girl who helped Vlado Grozden render aid to Robert Bartusch, Jene Hirschfield, and Larry Rosenthal, later married a man who became the mayor of Sanski Most. She was murdered during the Bosnian Wars of the 1990s.

Claude Tweedale received a "Dear John" letter from his girlfriend while he was overseas. He remained a bachelor the rest of his life.

Ted Keiser and his wife, Ann, celebrated their seventieth year of marriage in 2012.[7]

■   ■   ■

With the war won, the airmen focused on new challenges. They went to school, built careers, and raised families.

Most returned to civilian life. Several, however, stayed in the AAF, including Robert Bartusch, Leo Cone, Calvin Jarnagin, Robert Kidder, Keith Owens, Woodrow "Tex" Riley, Mario Spaltro, John Turk, and Ken Wheeler. Although he never sailed around the world, Wheeler later fulfilled his nautical ambitions by becoming an ardent sailor and sailboat builder. Owens, who always enjoyed writing and kept a diary during the war, became the Seoul news bureau chief for *Stars and Stripes*.

Several of the airmen completed college on the GI Bill and went on to successful careers. William Clark became president and CEO of a major insurance company. Powell Robinson rose to be vice president of lending operations for a large bank. Scotty Stewart finished at Harvard and became a prominent business executive. Emil Horak became a CPA and rose to be executive vice president of a hospital. Conrad Teague became a physician. Ted Keiser built a prosperous dental practice. Darrell Kiger became a veterinarian. Clarence Byers became an engineer. Tom Stack finished law school and became a leading San Francisco attorney.

Soon after Henry Wunderlich graduated from the University of Buffalo, he fulfilled his ambition to fly by earning his private pilot's license—even before he received a license to drive an automobile. He became an avid recreational flier and later earned a commercial license.

Wesley Chester dropped out of the University of Georgia to take a job as postmaster of his hometown. He retired from the post thirty-nine years later and never regretted his decision.

Oklahoma State offered Joe Sedlak a full scholarship to return to playing football. He turned it down because his wife Marcella had delivered their first baby and he needed to make a living. He became a farmer instead. The team he would have played on won the 1946 Sugar Bowl game.

Other airmen developed into successful entrepreneurs. Bob Dean learned geology at Texas Tech and became a prominent oilman. Edward Kutch created a chemical company. Henry Rinna's bakery grew to employ over one hundred people. Archy Roper started a business with his father and an Army buddy. They eventually sold out to the NAPA auto parts chain for millions.

Some became tradesmen. Radio operator Jules Levine, always a tinkerer, opened a television and radio repair shop. Vic Melcher constructed houses. Tom Tamraz earned his living as a bricklayer and carpenter. He continued to work late into life and built his own house while he was in his seventies.

Others dedicated themselves to good works. Gene Cogburn counseled veterans for the American Red Cross. Leo Wilensky earned a law degree but eventually followed his passion for providing housing for the under-privileged. Jim Martin's wartime experiences turned him into an avid pacifist like his brother Paul. He taught history at an Oregon high school.

Combat veterans possessed a remoteness their loved ones usually let be. Ordinary people could not understand what they had seen and done.

The Army was not oblivious to the situation. In 1945, the AAF issued Manual 35-155-1, entitled "Coming Home." The returning soldier, the booklet counseled, might feel out of place. His experiences have changed him. The world had not stood still in his absence. He must readjust to civilian life just as he once adjusted to the Army. Often, he needed a new job. Bottled up anxieties might emerge unexpectedly. Hard work, exercise, recreation, and "getting back in the swing of things" could help these tensions. If those things failed, the Veterans Administration offered medical assistance.

The adjustment was more difficult than is generally appreciated today. World War II soldiers and sailors returned to a grateful nation, but few came back to parades. They were so ubiquitous they stood unnoticed, like trees in a forest. Many did not talk of their experiences for forty years or more, when the pain eased, and time made the need to pass on their memories more urgent. Others never relayed their stories to anyone.

Several of the airmen returned with mental and physical scars. "Red" Braun's left wrist never fully recovered, and he received a 10 percent disability from the VA. Harold Wamser's fractured tibia required surgery, and he spent the next seven months in Army hospitals. Herman Marrone experienced recurring nightmares for months, ripping his sheets in the night thinking they were his rip cord.

Former POW Barker Houghton suffered from such severe post-traumatic stress that the VA awarded him a 100 percent disability. Nevertheless, he led a long and productive life. He graduated from Bowdoin College and earned post-graduate degrees in education. He earned his living as a high school English teacher, an educational consultant, and a special education teacher.

James Martino checked in and out of VA hospitals for physical and psychological difficulties until he secured a job with the U.S. General Services Administration.

William "Carey" Rainey never recovered psychologically from his experiences in the war. He became an alcoholic and never held steady employment. He passed away at age fifty-nine.

Darrell Kiger had bailed out over Romania on October 13 and over Yugoslavia on his thirteenth mission. He became superstitious about the number 13 and never left his house on the thirteenth of any month. The jaundice he had contracted in the Army weakened his heart. Eventually, ill health forced him to retire from his veterinary practice. He died of a heart attack at age sixty-four.

Others who died too young to collect Social Security included Edward Atkinson (61), Sylvester Brown (51), Clarence Byers (63), William Ceely (42), Gene Cogburn, (62), Joe Dearman (42), Andrew Jay (64), POW Raymond Klapp (62), James King (55), Robert Kolvet (49), Clarence Martin (61), James Powell (52), George Schiazza (64), Ed Seaver (60), Mario Spaltro (44), Sam Spomer (59), POW Calvin Steinberg (62), James Stevenson (44), and Claude Tweedale (54).

Tom Tamraz lost track of his buddy Warren LaFrance. His fate is unknown.[8]

■　　■　　■

Not all the airmen returned alive. After the war, teams of American officers searched the Yugoslavian countryside for the remains of the deceased AAF airmen. When found, their remains were either returned to the United States or buried in military cemeteries overseas.

John Wolff's parents, Herman and Anna Wolff, had their worst fears realized in late January 1945 when they learned their son had been killed in action. Tom Stack and his mother Gertrude sent them letters praising John's heroism. Anna replied to Gertrude that "we lived ten years in that one month [after learning their son was MIA]—and then to receive that last telegram—we were really crushed. But John had said 'The only bad thing about a big bomber, Mother, [is that] I'm responsible for the lives of ten.' So he felt the responsibility and did his best—I really do not think he could have lived with himself had he survived and the gunners had died."[9]

John Wolff's body was finally laid to rest in Plot G, Row 2, Grave 60, in the United States military cemetery at Nettuno (Anzio), Italy. Andrew Wozar was buried in Grave 62. Samuel Butler's body was reinterred in his hometown of Philipsburg, Pennsylvania.

In 1948, Thomas Stack and the other surviving crew members sought a Congressional Medal of Honor for Wolff. After an investigation, the AAF awarded him a posthumous Distinguished Service Cross, the nation's second highest honor.

■   ■   ■

The families of Gordon Commander, Joseph DeRosa, Frank Dick, and Gus Sundquist spent months hoping and praying their loved ones were prisoners of war or stranded behind enemy lines. Eventually, the surviving crewmen reported that they had landed in a swamp and likely drowned. A team from the Graves Registration Detachment traveled to Yugoslavia and recovered the bodies of Joseph DeRosa and Gus Sundquist in 1947. Another body, likely that of Gordon Commander, was found nearby but could not be identified. DeRosa's grave is in Mt. Carmel Cemetery, Hillside, Illinois. Gus Sundquist rests in the Jefferson Memorial Park cemetery, McKeesport, Pennsylvania.

Frank Dick's widowed mother, Katherine, spent nearly two years of uncertainty before the Army informed her of her son's fate. Yugoslavian refugees had reported that an officer from the crew was killed by the SS. The story was confirmed by Calvin Steinberg's testimony that two SS men bragged to him about the murder. Frank Dick's body was never found. He and Gordon Commander are listed in the Tablets of the Missing at the U.S. military cemetery in Florence, Italy.

Austrian townspeople buried Zack Johnson, also murdered by an SS officer. His remains were later disinterred and identified through dental charts. By the time the investigation was completed in 1950, his father had been declared mentally incompetent by a court and was committed to a psychiatric hospital. Johnson's body was eventually reinterred in the Baltimore National Cemetery.

The bodies of Frederick Coe, Kenneth Dale Hoffman, and Jack Mulvaney were also recovered. Coe is buried at the Mound View Cemetery in Mount Vernon, Ohio. Kenneth D. Hoffman is buried at the Mountain View Cemetery, Longmont, Colorado. John J. Mulvaney is buried in the Florence American Cemetery.

The British had a similar process for recovering their war dead. The remains of Lt. C. G. Begg, the South African pilot whose parachute failed to open when he bailed out near Sanski Most, were reinterred in the Belgrade War Cemetery.

■   ■   ■

Charles Stanley Sr., the father of the author of this book, had traveled a long road. He had been a doe-eyed, fledgling aviation student when he met Mary Alice Schmitz. He realized his dream of becoming a heavy bomber pilot, saw aerial combat, and was shot down twice. He had proven himself in every way that mattered to him.

Mary Alice found the war had changed Charles profoundly. Before he entered combat, she had been able to draw him out of his shell. He returned home quiet, withdrawn, and sullen. Even on their honeymoon in New York City, she had trouble coaxing him out to see Broadway shows. Their in-person courtship had lasted only seven weeks, and the rest had been by correspondence. Maybe, she thought, she never really knew him at all.

They settled in Buffalo. Once he had aspired to become a commercial pilot. Now he wanted to lead a normal, productive life anywhere but in the air. He graduated magna cum laude with a degree in accounting on the GI Bill and worked for the National Fuel Gas Company for forty years.

On those winter days when two feet of that famous Buffalo snow had fallen overnight, he woke up an hour early so he could shovel his car out to be on time for work. Most others slept in or took the day off.

After he retired, he decided his bucket list would be to read the great works of literature before he died. He filled his house with books and read them all—four times.

Years into Stanley's retirement, his sons finally read the remarkable correspondence he had shared with Mary Alice during their courtship. Stanley himself never reread them. Mary Alice had divorced him long before, and their wartime romance was bitter to him now.

Yet the other memories—the ones of his training, his combat missions, and his adventures on the ground in Romania and Yugoslavia—flooded back from the recesses of his mind. He unerringly recalled thousands of details this author cross-checked against multiple sources. He was proven wrong only once, on a single point his psyche had rejected.

He could not remember that he, seventeen fellow airmen, and their Partisan guides had been forced to leave a frostbitten man behind in that lonely, snowbound cabin on a mountainside in Yugoslavia, probably to freeze to death. That story came from others. Stanley had completely erased the memory, though he never doubted it had happened.

Stanley remained unfazed when he learned that Bob Plaisance had been awarded the Distinguished Flying Cross for their flight to Romania. If the copilot had earned a DFC, certainly the pilot was due one, but Stanley was not interested in medals. The only thing that mattered to him was that every member of his crew had returned to safety both times they were shot down.

Nevertheless, Stanley was awarded another kind of medal in 2002, when Governor George Pataki pinned the New York State Conspicuous Service Cross on his chest. It was presented at the opening ceremony for the New York State World War II Memorial in Albany.

On Saturday, May 29, 2004, Stanley, his five children, and most of his thirteen grandchildren gathered in Washington, D.C., for the dedication of the World War II Memorial at the National Mall. The glorious, sundrenched day was enjoyed by all. Veterans signed autographs like rock stars. The only strain was that post-9-11 security checkpoints necessitated a two-mile hike to gain access to the festivities. Stanley could walk fine, but the family brought a wheelchair because a bout with pneumonia had weakened his heart. It was the only day in his life he used one.

The day after he returned to Buffalo, a heart attack struck him down. He faced his final trial alone. Still, he was blessed as usual. No doubt the end came quickly.

It seemed that the Good Lord had allowed him just enough time to receive the thanks of his country. That accomplished, he was called home at last.

AFTERWORD

For as long as I can remember, I knew my father was a bomber pilot during World War II. Evidence of it pervaded my childhood home. A yellowed photo of a B-24 graced the fireplace mantle. Old uniforms gathered dust in our closets. Vintage garrison caps lay in my parents' bedroom drawer, and I often borrowed one when I wanted to play soldier. Every autumn, my father dragged out his weather-beaten leather flight jacket to perform outdoor chores.

My siblings and I took all this for granted. Nearly every kid's father was a World War II veteran. Ours seemed no different, except for one thing. He was a bomber pilot who had bailed out twice, first over Romania and then over Yugoslavia. Our mother must have told us so, because he never spoke of it.

We also knew our parents had met during the war, and that their wartime letters sat in a box in our attic. Still, we ignored them. None of us wanted to read the lovey-dovey stuff our parents once wrote to each other. We felt even more so as adults after they divorced.

For too long, I ignored a clue that should have told me my father had done extraordinary things. During my high school years, I ran across Steve Birdsall's *Log of the Liberators*, a classic World War II book about B-24 crews. On a whim, I looked for my father's name in the index. To my surprise, it was there, along with a brief account of the second time he bailed out. My father was featured in a major historical work and did not know it! Yet when I showed the book to him, he displayed little interest other than to agree the story was roughly correct.

There seemed to be plenty of time to find out what had happened to my father during the war. Decades passed.

In 1999, when my father was seventy-seven years old, I finally examined my parents' correspondence—over 1,200 letters in all. Half of them related the story of a green Army Air Forces (AAF) cadet as he learned how to fly and transformed into a battle-hardened bomber pilot. The others conveyed the tale of the girl he left behind and the hardships she and her family endured on the home front.

The letters introduced me to my father as a young man. To my vast surprise, I learned my quiet father had once been quite garrulous. Like many in the AAF, he had had ample time between flights to write letters and seized these opportunities with relish. His voluminous correspondence presented a vivid, concise, and wryly humorous picture of life in the Army. Incapable of falsehood or bravado, he always portrayed himself in a self-critical and humble way. Somehow, he managed to convey wartime realities without unduly alarming my mother. Oftentimes, he subtly hid meanings between the lines to avoid the censor's mark.

The letters prompted me to ask my father about his wartime adventures. While his memory proved exceptional, his answers were necessarily limited to his own experiences. His curiosity became as piqued as mine.

The natural next step was to talk to his old crew, so I enlisted my brother Frank—a bloodhound when it comes to such things—to help track them down. We discovered that some of them had recently passed away. I had nearly started too late.

In the beginning, I had no intention of writing a book. The story of my father's first bailout provided fodder for family legend, or maybe a magazine article, but no more. It was only when I researched his second bailout that I realized he had participated in historic, yet previously unexplored, events.

I discovered that a dozen crews besides my father's had abandoned their crippled bombers over Yugoslavia in November and December 1944. Most of these airmen found sanctuary with the Partisan underground forces in a Bosnian town called Sanski Most, but retreating German forces surrounded the area, and the airmen became stranded there. The several efforts to retrieve them ranked among the largest-scale air rescue operations of that theater during the war.

My research had ventured into unchartered territory. Over four-fifths of the 2,500 Allied airmen downed in Yugoslavia during World War II were aided by Marshal Tito's Partisans. Nevertheless, the literature centered on the help provided by the Partisans' bitter rivals, the Chetniks led by General Draža Mihailović. Strangely, no work had yet been devoted to the far more significant assistance rendered by the Partisans. Despite the myriad histories devoted to World War II, the story of Allied fliers who bailed out over Yugoslavia during the war remained untold.

I set out to remedy the oversight.

Since I held a demanding job at the time, I knew I would not finish writing until after I retired. Instead, I focused on interviewing all the participants I could find. Over the next couple years, my father—and sometimes my brother Frank—accompanied me on trips to Ohio, Chicago, and Connecticut to interview veterans who has shared his experience.

We discovered one veteran just in time. Fred Scherer was dying of cancer. His family gathered to witness his reminiscences with my father and videotaped the interview for posterity. Scherer died less than six months later.

My father and I also traveled to Maxwell Field, Alabama, where he had trained as a cadet. The base is the site of the Air Force Historical Research Agency (AFHRA). We had ordered a few microfilms by mail but had not yet ascertained the identities of all the downed airmen. By good fortune, or perhaps Providence, my father was the one who happened upon the mother lode of the Escape Statements that documented their stories. I had never seen him so excited in my life.

In April 2004, I telephoned Herman "Herky" Marrone. He showed interest in the project, and we agreed I would soon visit him for an interview. A few weeks later, his daughter reached out to me. Marrone's heart had failed a few days before; his family considered my research to be so important they called me the afternoon of his funeral.

Bad luck, I thought, but the worst was yet to come.

The next month, my father died, stricken by a heart attack like Marrone, soon after he attended the dedication of the long-overdue World War II Memorial at the National Mall in Washington, D.C. It had not occurred to me his end might be so near. Deep in denial, I had ignored the signs of his declining health. I consoled myself that my father did not suffer long and that he died knowing I would someday tell his story.

I would not let him down, though the effort took much longer than I anticipated—twenty-three years from the beginning of my research to the publishing date of this book. My only regret in the writing of this book is that I could not finish it in time for most of the airmen to read it. It simply was not possible. The book would not have been nearly as good or complete, and perhaps would not have found a publisher, if I had been impatient and tried to put it out earlier.

After all, this book is written to honor these men by preserving their story for posterity. Its purpose is to tell current and future generations about their experiences—not just to relate their stories, but to present the spirit of the times in a way that captures how it felt to be a downed airman during World War II. I can only pray that my narrative is worthy of the material I uncovered. Hopefully, it was worth waiting for.

Finally, I'll add a note on the book's style. I don't believe that authors of history should invent dialogue. This book only uses quotation marks when the discussion is based directly on the airmen's statements or correspondence from the time, or when I completely believe the airman's recollections as recounted in an interview.

To me, one of the most interesting findings of my research was that these men were practically infallible in their memories, down to the words they had spoken more than fifty years before their interviews. This was especially true in moments of crisis, such as when they were preparing to bail out of their dying bombers. Adrenaline apparently burned these memories deep into their psyches. I have cross-checked their recollections countless times yet have rarely found contradictions or embellishments. If a veteran airman did not remember an aspect of his experience, he usually said so. These men did not seek glory. I knew many of them, and I know their kind. I trust them, and I think the reader should too.

Chuck Stanley
September 2021

ACKNOWLEDGMENTS

First and foremost, I thank the forty Lost Airmen who agreed to be interviewed for this project. It has been my great honor to get to know them and to tell their story.

Some of them were kind enough to review my writing. Richard "Ken" Wheeler, Seymour "Larry" Rosenthal, Joe Foto, George Earll, and Ted and Ann Keiser reviewed the chapters telling their stories. Henry Wunderlich preformed above and beyond the call of duty by reading the entire manuscript. All exhibited exceptionally keen memories and insights.

Several family members of deceased airmen were instrumental in the research of this book. Those who shared a wealth of material include Kristan Arrona (Herman Marrone's daughter), Harry Blank Jr., Tom Ceely, Jay Frederick Coe (Frederick Coe's nephew), Matthew Cogburn, Donald and Gordon Dick, Julie Dickerson (Claude Tweedale's niece), Larry Elmore, Bob and Terre Eldridge, Herbert Eldridge III, Robin Goralczyk (Lewis Baker's daughter), Timberlee Tamraz Grove (Tom Tamraz's daughter), Brenda Hoffman (Albert Hill's daughter), Julie Houghton, Johnny Jarnagin, Charles Kramer, Patricia Lazaroff (Richard Kelly's daughter), Ann Keiser, Michael Kiger, Charles Kramer, Barry Kutch, Diane Lipman (Jules Levine's daughter), Debby Martin (Jim's daughter and Paul's niece), Terry and John Mulvaney, Martin Otway, Henry and Ron Rinna, Lydia Schreiber (Sam Spomer's sister), Sharon Schwartz, Jeff Seaver, Terry Sedlak, Diane Short (Carey Rainey's niece), Thomas Stack Jr., Nancy Vogt (Albert Buchholz's daughter), Sharon Wheeler, Neal Wilensky, Vicki Wroclawski, and Fred Sherer's family, especially daughter Jeanne Gogolski. I apologize if I have neglected to mention others.

I am particularly indebted to Charlie Stewart, Charles "Scotty" Stewart's son, who anticipated my work by interviewing his father before he died and collecting other valuable oral narratives from Claud Martin, Joe Sedlak, Harry Carter, and Powell Robinson. He and his wonderful mother, the late Caroline Stewart, were very generous in sharing Scotty's materials.

Jay P. Tennies, director of the Eldred World War II Museum at the time of my research, shared a wealth of material donated to the museum by Herman Marrone.

Stephanie Coon at the National Archives in College Park, Maryland, helped me gain access to key Fifteenth Air Force and OSS records. The staff at the Air Force Historical Research Agency at Maxwell Field, Alabama, were also most helpful.

Milos Bojanic, a leading Serbian historian and a consultant for the Halyard Commission, critiqued the chapters dealing with Yugoslavian wartime history. His in-depth familiarity with his country during the World War II era and Serbo-Croatian sources on the subject were invaluable as I navigated these treacherous waters.

Jerry W. Whiting, historian of the 485th Bomb Group Association and author of several fine books—including *I'm Off to War, Mother, But I'll Be Back* and *Don't Let the Blue Star Turn Gold*—was kind enough to review the manuscript and offered useful corrections.

Lynn McCarty, the late historian of the 459th Bomb Group, was also most helpful.

Heather Flynn read the drafts and offered several edits and stylistic improvements. Michael Denneny and James O. Wade also reviewed the manuscript and provided valuable help. Mary Beth Baker did an excellent job editing the final draft.

My brother, Frank Stanley, helped me locate many of the Lost Airmen and accompanied my father and I during several interviews. He also proved to be an exceptional proofreader. My son Christopher Stanley helped catalog the early research.

Of course, all errors are mine alone.

APPENDIX—AIR CREW ROSTERS

Airman	Position
Bartusch, Robert J.	B-17 Pilot
Hirschfield, Jene H.	Copilot
Rosenthal, Seymour (Larry)	Navigator/Bombardier
Bush, Carl F. (POW)	Flight Engineer
Klapp, Raymond Cletus Jr. (POW)	Radio Operator
Steele, Robert E. (POW)	Ball Turret Gunner
Kramer, Cletus J. (POW)	Waist Gunner
Bergschneider, Paul B. (POW)	Waist Gunner
Johnson, Zack M. (KIA)	Tail Gunner
Blank, Harry A.	B-24 Pilot
Turk, John N.	Copilot
Mitchell, Robert P.	Navigator/Bombardier
Koballa, Thomas E.	Flight Engineer
Owens, Keith D.	Radio Operator/Waist Gunner
Kelly, Richard B.	Nose Gunner
Rainey, William C.	Ball Turret Gunner
Otway, William A.	Upper Turret Gunner
Ceely, William S.	Tail Gunner

Airman	Position
Blood, David A.	B-24 Pilot
Baker, Lewis	Copilot
Benedict, George E.	Navigator
Cogburn, Eugene D.	Bombardier
Sherer, Fred B.	Flight Engineer
Yaworsky, Michael	Radio Operator/Waist Gunner
Kolvet, Robert F.	Nose Gunner
Gibson, Wilmot M.	Ball Turret Gunner
Tamraz, Thomas	Waist Gunner
LaFrance, Warren	Tail Gunner
Johnson, James B.	Flight Surgeon
Coe, Frederick H. (KIA)	B-24 Pilot
Hoffman, Kenneth D. (KIA)	Copilot
Kutch, Edward F.	Navigator
Brown, Sylvester	Bombardier
Mulvaney, John J. (KIA)	Flight Engineer
Levine, Jules	Radio Operator/Waist Gunner
Wilensky, Leo	Nose Gunner
Champi, Almondo	Ball Turret Gunner
Foto, Joseph	Waist Gunner/Photographer
Wunderlich, Henry J.	Tail Gunner
Dean, Robert A.	B-24 Pilot
Ingram, Jimmie P.	Copilot
Button, Bernard R.	Navigator

Airman	Position
Byers, Clarence E.	Bombardier
Fetter, Eldon E.	Flight Engineer
Horak, Emil I.	Radio Operator/Waist Gunner
Atkinson, Edward N.	Nose Gunner
Hoogeveen, Harry J.	Ball Turret Gunner
Peterson, Earnest A.	Waist Gunner
Kidd, Frank M.	Tail Gunner
Martin, Clarence G.	Photographer
Eatman, Curtis I.	B-24 Pilot
Haynes, Charles A.	Copilot
Evans, William E.	Navigator
McGee, William T.	Bombardier
Pakes, Lamont M.	Flight Engineer
Powell, James P.	Radio Operator/Waist Gunner
Dearman, Joe R.	Nose Gunner
Wamser, Harold J.	Ball Turret Gunner
Hahn, Edward W.	Waist Gunner
Jay, Andrew	Tail Gunner
Eldridge, Hixon B.	B-24 Pilot
Roper, Archimedes M.	Copilot
Teague, Conrad B.	Navigator
Clark, William J.	Bombardier
Melcher, Victor H.	Flight Engineer
Perrone, Augustus B.	Radio Operator

Airman	Position
Braun, Richard R.	Nose Gunner
Houghton, Olin Barker (POW)	Ball Turret Gunner
Colasante, Joseph A.	Waist Gunner
Fribley, Charles W. (POW)	Waist Gunner
Quinn, Eugene T. (POW)	Tail Gunner
Keiser, Ted	B-17 Pilot
Griffith, Robert L.	Copilot
Wheeler, Richard K.	Navigator
Schwartz, Stanley L. (POW)	Bombardier
Charlesworth, Edmund T.	Flight Engineer
Hoffman, Paul S.	Radio Operator
Martin, James H.	Ball Turret Gunner
Spaltro, Mario M.	Waist Gunner
Chester, Calvin Wesley	Waist Gunner
Riley, Woodrow H.	Tail Gunner
Marrone, Herman	B-24 Pilot
King, James R.	Copilot
Goodling, Allen	Navigator/Bombardier
Topal, Albert H.	Flight Engineer
Earll, George O.	Radio Operator/Waist Gunner
Dennis, Gene R.	Nose Gunner
Seery, Raymond J.	Ball Turret Gunner
Cloos, Gregg N.	Waist Gunner
Stevenson, James H.	Tail Gunner

Airman	Position
Marshall, Clarence P.	B-24 Pilot
Jarnagin, Calvin E.	Copilot
Dick, Frank M. (KIA)	Navigator
Nayes, LeRoy M.	Bombardier
Steinberg, Calvin S. (POW)	Flight Engineer
Commander, Gordon L. (KIA)	Radio Operator/Waist Gunner
Wroclawski, Jan E.	Nose Gunner
Sundquist, Gus A. (KIA)	Ball Turret Gunner
DeRosa, Joseph M. (KIA)	Upper Turret Gunner
Hill, Albert G.	Tail Gunner
Martino, James J.	Photographer
Stanley, Charles E.	B-24 Pilot
Baker, William D.	Copilot
Cone, Leo F.	Navigator
Seaver, Edward C.	Bombardier
Smalley, Forrest L.	Flight Engineer
Kiger, Darrell G.	Radio Operator/Waist Gunner
Buchholz, Albert R.	Nose Gunner
Homol, Peter	Ball Turret Gunner
Tweedale, Claude	Waist Gunner
Spomer, Samuel J.	Tail Gunner
Stewart, Charles P.	B-24 Pilot
Boehme, Richard H. (KIA)	Copilot
Carter, Harry R.	Navigator/Bombardier

Airman	Position
Elmore, John H.	Flight Engineer
Martin, Claud E.	Radio Operator/Waist Gunner
Schiazza, George C.	Nose Gunner
Robinson, Powell	Ball Turret Gunner
Sedlak, Joe C.	Waist Gunner
Heim, Richard M.	Tail Gunner
Wolff, John K. (KIA)	B-24 Pilot
Kidder, Robert F.	Copilot
Stack, Thomas F.	Navigator
Lane, William H.	Bombardier
Piekarski, Sigmunt	Flight Engineer
Rinna, Henry J.	Radio Operator/Waist Gunner
Hodgeman, Willis E.	Nose Gunner
Eldridge, Herbert E.	Ball Turret Gunner
Wozar, Andrew J. (KIA)	Waist Gunner
Butler, Samuel L. (KIA)	Tail Gunner

SELECT BIBLIOGRAPHY

Government Sources

AAF Fifteenth Air Force Unit Histories, Air Force Historical Research Agency Microfilm Rolls, Maxwell Field Alabama.

31st Fighter Group, Roll Bo110A and Bo111.

301st Bomb Group, Rolls Bo208 and Bo209.

449th Bomb Group, Rolls Bo564, Bo565, Bo565, Bo567, and Bo584.

451st Bomb Group, Rolls Bo595 and Bo596.

454th Bomb Group, Roll Bo601.

456th Bomb Group, Rolls Bo603 and Bo604.

459th Bomb Group, Rolls Bo607 and Bo608.

461st Bomb Group, Rolls Bo609 and Bo610.

464th Bomb Group, Rolls Bo614 and Bo615.

465th Bomb Group, Rolls Bo616 and Bo617.

483rd Bomb Group, Roll Bo642.

484th Bomb Group, Roll Bo643.

485th Bomb Group, Rolls Bo643 and Bo644.

Air Crew Rescue Unit, Roll 25696.

Escape Statements, Rolls A6544, A6544A, B, C, and D.

Numerous Missing Air Crew Reports.

Army Air Forces Headquarters. "Coming Home," AAF Manual 35-155-1 (pamphlet), 1945.

Army Air Forces Headquarters, *Pilots' Information File*, November 1944.

Carter, Launor F., ed. "Psychological Research on Navigator Training." Army Air Forces, Aviation Psychology Program, Research Report 10. Washington, D.C.: Government Printing Office, 1947.

Consolidated Aircraft. *Flight Manual for B-24 Liberator*. Appleton: Wisconsin: Aviation Publications, 1988 (reprint edition).

Crawford, Meredith P., ed. "Psychological Research on Operational Training in the Continental United States." Army Air Forces, Aviation Psychology Program, Research Report 16. Washington, D.C.: Government Printing Office, 1947.

Dailey, John T., ed. "Psychological Research on Flight Engineer Training." Army Air Forces, Aviation Psychology Program, Research Report 12. Washington, D.C.: Government Printing Office, 1947.

Davis, Frederick B., ed. "The AAF Qualifying Examination." Army Air Forces, Aviation Psychology Program, Research Report 6. Washington, D.C.: Government Printing Office, 1947.

Freeman, Major Paul J. "The Cinderella Front: Allied Special Air Operations in Yugoslavia during World War II." Research Paper Presented to the Research Department of the Air Command and Staff College, March 1997.

Guildford, J. P., ed. "Printed Classification Tests." Army Air Forces, Aviation Psychology Program, Research Report 5. Washington, D.C.: Government Printing Office, 1947.

Hobbes, Nicholas, "Psychological Research on Flexible Gunnery Training." Army Air Forces, Aviation Psychology Program, Research Report 11. Washington, D.C.: Government Printing Office, 1947.

Kennedy, Robert M. "Hold the Balkans! German Antiguerrilla Operations in the Balkans, 1941–1944." Department of the Army Pamphlet 20-243, 1954. Shippensburg, Pennsylvania: White Mane Books, 2000 (reprint edition).

Leary, William M. "Fueling the Fires of Resistance: AAF Special Operations in the Balkans." Air Force History and Museums Program, 1995.

Melton, A. W., ed. "Apparatus Tests." Army Air Forces, Aviation Psychology Program, Research Report 4. Washington, D.C.: Government Printing Office, 1947.

National Archives (UK).

National Archives and Records Administration (U.S.).

North, Robert A. "Aviator Selection 1919–1977." Pensacola, Florida: Naval Aerospace Medical Research Laboratory, 1977.

U.S. Army. *The Officer's Guide.* The Military Service Publishing Company, July 1943 edition.

U.S. Strategic Bombing Survey (European War). *Summary Report.* Washington, D.C.: Government Printing Office, September 30, 1945.

Correspondence/Letters 1943–1945

Baker, Lewis (485th Bomb Group).
Button, Bernard (484th Bomb Group).
Chester, C. Wesley (301st Bomb Group).
Coe, Frederick (459th Bomb Group).
Dick, Frank M. (461st Bomb Group).
Earll, George O. (449th Bomb Group).
Griffith, Robert (301st Bomb Group).
Houghton, O. Barker (456th Bomb Group).
Kidder, Robert (454th Bomb Group).
Kutch, Edward (459th Bomb Group).
LaFrance, Warren (485th Bomb Group).
Marrone, Herman C. (449th Bomb Group).
Mulvaney, John J. (459th Bomb Group).
Quinn, Eugene (456th Bomb Group).
Plaisance, Robert (464th Bomb Group).
Schmitz, Mary Alice.
Seaver, Edward (464th Bomb Group).
Stack, Thomas (454th Bomb Group).
Stanley, Charles E. Sr. (464th Bomb Group).
Stewart, Charles (485th Bomb Group).
Tamraz, Thomas (485th Bomb Group).

Unpublished Diaries/Logs/Narratives

Baker, Lewis (485th Bomb Group).
Blank, Harry A. (451st Bomb Group).
Carter, Harry (485th Bomb Group).
Cogburn, Gene (485th Bomb Group).
Cone, Leo (464th Bomb Group).

Charlesworth, Edmund (301st Bomb Group).
Earll, George O. (449th Bomb Group).
Eldridge, Herbert (454th Bomb Group).
Haynes, Charles (465th Bomb Group).
Hodgeman, Willis (449th Bomb Group).
Hoffman, Paul (301st Bomb Group).
Johnson, James B. (485th Bomb Group).
Marrone, Herman C. (449th Bomb Group).
Martin, James (301st Bomb Group).
Mitchell, Robert (451st Bomb Group).
Nayes, LeRoy (461st Bomb Group).
Owens, Keith (451st Bomb Group).
Roper, Archy (456th Bomb Group).
Scherer, Fred B. (485th Bomb Group).
Stack, Thomas (454th Bomb Group).

Interviews Conducted by Charles E. Stanley Jr.—Airmen and Family Members

Baker, William (464th Bomb Group).
Bartusch, Robert J. (483rd Bomb Group).
Button, Bernard (484th Bomb Group).
Carter, Harry (485th Bomb Group).
Champi, Almondo (459th Bomb Group).
Clark, William (456th Bomb Group).
Charlesworth, Edmund (301st Bomb Group).
Chester, C. Wesley (301st Bomb Group).
Colasante, Joseph (456th Bomb Group).
Cone, Leo (464th Bomb Group).
Earll, George O. (449th Bomb Group).
Foto, Joseph (459th Bomb Group).
Griffith, Robert (301st Bomb Group).
Heim, Richard (485th Bomb Group).
Hill, Albert G. (461st Bomb Group).
Hoogeveen, Harry J. (484th Bomb Group).

Horak, Emile (484th Bomb Group).

Keiser, Ted R. (301st Bomb Group).

Kelly, Richard B. (451st Bomb Group).

Kidder, Robert (454th Bomb Group).

Kiger, Michael (son of Darrell Kiger, 464th Bomb Group).

Kramer, Cletus (483rd Bomb Group).

Mann, Robert (484th Bomb Group).

Martin, Claud (485th Bomb Group).

Martino, James J. (461st Bomb Group).

Owens, Keith (451st Bomb Group).

Plaisance, Robert (464th Bomb Group).

Possell, Leroy (465th Bomb Group).

Quinn, Eugene (484th Bomb Group).

Robinson, Powell Jr. (485th Bomb Group).

Roper, Archy (456th Bomb Group).

Rosenthal, Larry J. (483rd Bomb Group).

Scherer, Fred B. (485th Bomb Group).

Schwartz, Sharon (daughter of Stanley Schwartz, 301st Bomb Group).

Sedlak, Joseph (485th Bomb Group).

Stanley, Charles E. Sr. (464th Bomb Group).

Stanley, Mary Alice.

Stewart, Caroline.

Tamraz, Thomas (485th Bomb Group).

Wheeler, Kenneth (301st Bomb Group).

Wroclawski, Richard (son of Jan Wroclawski, 461st Bomb Group).

Wunderlich, Henry J. (459th Bomb Group).

Zellman, Lawrence (82nd Fighter Group).

Interviews by Others

Blank, Harry A. (451st Bomb Group)—by Elmer Wigley.

Eldridge, Hixon (456th Bomb Group)—by Captain Kyle T. Eldridge.

Evans, William Everett (465th Bomb Group)—dictated on tape.

Houghton, Olin Barker (456th Bomb Group)—by John Davis.

Marrone, Herman C. (449th Bomb Group)—by Greg Krupinsky.

Martin, Claud (485th Bomb Group)—by Charles P. Stewart III.

Martin, James (301st Bomb Group)—by Debby J. Martin.

Martin, Paul (Conscientious Objector)—by Debby J. Martin.

Robinson, Powell Jr. (485th Bomb Group)—by Charles P. Stewart III.

Sedlak, Joseph (485th Bomb Group)—by Charles P. Stewart III.

Stanley, Charles E. Sr. (464th Bomb Group)—by Lt. Col. Robert Van Hassln.

Stewart, Charles P. (485th Bomb Group)—by Charles P. Stewart III.

Wheeler, Kenneth (301st Bomb Group)—by EAA Air Venture.

Journals and Magazines

Bailey, Ronald H. "Made in America: Homegrown Hate." *World War II Magazine* 28, no. 6 (March–April 2014).

Callander, Bruce D. "The Aviation Cadets." *Air Force: Journal of the Air Force Association* 73, no. 11 (November 1990).

Griffin, Glenn R. and Jefferson M. Koonce. "Review of Psychomotor Skills in Pilot Selection Research of the U.S. Military Services." *The International Journal of Aviation Psychology* 6, no. 2 (1996).

Matteson, Thomas T. "An Analysis of the Circumstances Surrounding the Rescue and Evacuation of Allied Airmen from Yugoslavia 1941–45." Research Report Number 128, Maxwell AFB, Air War College, April 1977.

Trifković, Gaj. "The Yugoslav Partisans' Lost Victories: Operations in Montenegro and Bosnia-Herzegovina, 1944–45." *The Journal of Military History* 82, no. 1 (January 2018).

Newspapers

Ames Tribune (Iowa).

Brownsville Herald (Texas).

Chattanooga Times Free Press (Tennessee).

Courier Express (Buffalo, New York).

Buffalo Evening News (New York).

Corsicana Semi-Weekly (Texas).

Danville Bee (Virginia).

Denver Post (Colorado).
Edwardsville Intelligencer (Illinois).
Hartford Times (Connecticut).
The Herald (Randolph, Vermont).
Herald News (Massachusetts).
Herald Post (El Paso, Texas).
Indiana Evening Gazette (Indiana).
Morning Avalanche (Lubbock, Texas).
Mount Vernon News (Ohio).
Nashville Tennessean (Tennessee).
News and Observer (Raleigh, North Carolina).
Oakland Tribune (California).
Providence Sunday Journal (Rhode Island).
The Townsman (Wellesley, Massachusetts).

Books

Ambrose, Stephen E. *The Wild Blue: The Men and Boys Who Flew the B-24s Over Germany.* New York: Simon and Schuster, 2001.

Arnold, Henry H. and Ira C. Eaker. *This Flying Game.* New York: Funk and Wagnalls, 1943.

Beck, Earl R. *Under the Bombs: The German Home Front 1942–1945.* Lexington, Kentucky: University Press of Kentucky, 1986.

Bernstein, Arnie. *Swastika Nation: Fritz Kuhn and the Rise and Fall of the German-American Bund.* New York: St. Martin's Press, 2013.

Bowman, Martin W. *USAAF Handbook 1939–1945.* Mechanicsburg, Pennsylvania: Stackpole Books, 1997.

Carigan, William. *Ad Lib: Flying the B-24 Liberator in World War II.* Manhattan, Kansas: Sunflower University Press, 1988.

Catherwood, Christopher. *Churchill and Tito: SOE, Bletchley Park, and Supporting the Yugoslav Communists in World War II.* South Yorkshire, UK: Frontline Books, 2017.

Clissold, Stephen. *Whirlwind: An Account of Marshal Tito's Rise to Power.* New York: Philosophical Library, 1949.

Clodfetter, Mark. *Beneficial Bombing: The Progressive Foundations of American Air Power, 1917–1945*. Lincoln, Nebraska: University of Nebraska Press, 2010.

Cook, Ronald C. and Roy Conyers Nesbit. *Target: Hitler's Oil: Allied Attacks on German Oil Supplies 1939–1945*. London: William Kimber, 1985.

Crane, Conrad C. *American Airpower Strategy in World War II: Bombs, Cities, and Oil*. Lawrence, Kansas: University of Kansas Press, 2016.

Craven, Wesley Frank and James Lea Cate, eds. *The Army Air Forces in World War II, Volume Three, Europe Argument to V-E Day*. Chicago: University of Chicago Press, 1951.

Davis, Larry. *C-47 Skytrain in Action*. Carrollton, Texas: Squadron/Signal Publications, 1995.

Djilas, Milovan. *Wartime*. New York and London: Harcourt Brace Jovanich, 1977.

Dosenovich, The Very Reverend Father Volislav. *So Help Me God!* New York: Vantage Press, 1992.

Freeman, Gregory. *The Forgotten 500*. New York: Caliber, 2007.

Frka, Danijel. *Vis: The Last Hope: RAF Station Vis 1944–1945*. Zagreb, Croatia: Despot Infinitus Press, 2021.

Ford Jr., Kirk. *OSS and the Yugoslav Resistance 1943–45*. College Station, Texas: A&M University Press, 1992.

Fussell, Paul. *Wartime*. Oxford University Press, 1989.

Greentree, David. *Knight's Move: The Hunt for Marshal Tito*. Oxford: Osprey Press, 2012.

Hastings, Max. *Bomber Command*. New York: Touchstone, 1989.

Inks, Major James M. *Eight Bailed Out*. New York: W. W. Norton, 1954.

Isby, David. *C-47/R4D Units of the ETO and MTO*. Oxford: Osprey Publishing, 2005.

Jancar-Webster, Barbara. *Women and Revolution in Yugoslavia 1941–45*. Denver: Arden Press, 1990.

Jernigan, A. Jack. *Selecting the Best: World War II Army Air Forces Aviation Psychology*. Bloomington, Illinois: 1st Books, 2003.

Keim, Albert N. *The CPS Story: An Illustrated History of Civilian Public Service*. Intercourse, Pennsylvania: Good Books, 1990.

Kraemer, Richard H. *The Secret War in the Balkans: A World War II Memoir*. Bloomington, Alabama: AuthorHouse, 2010.

Kurapovna, Marcia Christoff. *Shadows on the Mountain: The Allies, the Resistance, and the Rivalries that Doomed World War II Yugoslavia*. Hoboken, New Jersey: John Wiley and Sons, 2010.

Leary, William M. *Fueling the Fires of Resistance: Army Air Forces Special Operations in the Balkans during World War II*. Ann Arbor, Michigan: University of Michigan Library, 1995.

Lepre, George. *Himmler's Bosnian Division: The Waffen-SS Handschar Division 1943–1945*. Atglen, Pennsylvania: Schiffer Military History, 1997.

Lindsey, Franklin. *Beacons in the Night: With the OSS and Tito's Partisans in Wartime Yugoslavia*. Stanford: Stanford University Press, 1993.

Lingeman, Richard. *Don't You Know There's a War On? The American Home Front 1941–45*. New York: Putnam's, 1970.

Maclean, Fitzroy. *Eastern Approaches*. London: Penguin Press, 1949.

Mahony, Kevin A. *Fifteenth Air Force Against the Axis: Combat Missions over Europe during World War II*. Lanham, Maryland: Scarecrow Press, 2013.

McConville, Michael. *A Small War in the Balkans: British Military Involvement in Wartime Yugoslavia 1941–1945*. London: McMillan, 1986.

McFarland, Stephen and Wesley Norton. *To Command the Sky: The Battle for Air Superiority over Germany 1942–44*. Tuscaloosa, Alabama: University of Alabama Press, 1991.

McManus, John C. *Deadly Sky: The American Combat Airman in World War II*. Navato, California: Presidio Press, 2000.

Meilinger, Paul S., ed. *The Paths of Heaven: The Evolution of Airpower Theory*. Maxwell Airforce Base, Alabama: Air University Press.

Miller, Donald L. *Masters of the Air: America's Bomber Boys Who Fought against Nazi Germany*. New York: Simon and Schuster, 2006.

Muirhead, John. *Those Who Fall*. New York: Random House, 1986.

Nichol, John and Tony Rennell. *The Last Escape: The Untold Story of Allied Prisoners of War in Europe 1944–45.* New York: Viking, 2002.

———. *Tail-End Charlies: The Last Battles of the Bomber War, 1944–45.* New York: St. Martin's Press, 2006.

Okerstrom, Dennis R. *The Final Mission of Bottoms Up: A World War II Pilot's Story.* Columbia, Missouri: University of Missouri Press, 2011.

Pavlowitch, Stevan K. *Hitler's New Disorder: The Second World War in Yugoslavia.* New York: Columbia University Press, 2008.

Perret, Geoffrey. *Winged Victory: The Army Air Forces in World War II.* New York: Random House, 1993.

Ramet, Sabrina P., ed. *The Independent State of Croatia 1941–45.* New York: Routledge, 2007.

Redzic, Enver. *Bosnia and Herzegovina in the Second World War.* London: Cass, 2005.

Roberts, Walter R. *Tito, Mihailović and the Allies, 1941/1945.* New Brunswick, New Jersey: Rutgers University Press, 1993.

Rochlin, Fred. *Old Man in a Baseball Cap: A Memoir of World War II.* New York: Harper-Collins, 1999.

Steinbeck, John. *Bombs Away: The Story of a Bomber Crew.* New York: Penguin Classics, 2009.

Thole, Lou. *Forgotten Fields of America: World War II Bases and Training Then and Now.* Missoula, Montana: Pictorial Histories, 1996.

Tillman, Barrett. *Forgotten Fifteenth: The Daring Airmen Who Crippled Hitler's War Machine.* Washington, D.C.: Regnery, 2014.

Tomasevich, Jazo. *The Chetniks: War and Revolution in Yugoslavia 1941–45.* Stanford: Stanford University Press, 1975.

———. *War and Revolution in Yugoslavia 1941–45: Occupation and Collaboration.* Stanford: Stanford University Press, 2001.

Vuksic, Velimir. *Tito's Partisans 1941–45.* Oxford: Osprey Press, 2003.

Waltry, Charles A. *Washout! The Aviation Cadet Story.* Carlsbad, California: California Aero Press, 1983.

Wells, Mark K. *Courage and Air Warfare: The Allied Aircrew Experience in the Second World War.* London: Cass, 1995.

Whiting, Wayne B. and Jerry W. Whiting. *I'm Off to War, Mother, But I'll Be Back*. Walnut Creek, California: Tarnaby, 2001.

West, Rebecca. *Black Lamb and Grey Falcon*. New York: Penguin Classics, 2007 printing.

Williams, Heather. *Parachutes, Patriots and Partisans: The Special Operations Executive and Yugoslavia, 1941–1945*. Madison, Wisconsin: University of Wisconsin Press, 2003.

Withington, Ted. *Flight to Blechhammer: The Letters of a World War II Pilot*. Brunswick, Maine: Biddle Publishing Company, 1993.

Zemke, Col. Hubert, as told to Roger Freeman. *Zemke's Stalag: The Final Days of World War II*. Washington, D.C.: Smithsonian Institution Press, 1991.

Bomb Group Histories

Grimm, Jacob L. *Heroes of the 483rd, Crew Histories of a Much-Decorated B-17 Bomber Group during World War II*. Warner Robins, Georgia: 483rd Bombardment Group Association., 2004.

Hill, Mike. *The 451st Bomb Group in World War II*. Atglen, Pennsylvania: Schiffer, 2001.

Hill, Michael D. and John R. Beitling, *B-24 Liberators of the 15th Air Force/49th Bomb Wing in World War II*. Atglen, Pennsylvania: Schiffer, 2006.

Hill, Michael D. and Betty Karle. *The 464th Bomb Group in World War II*. Atglen, Pennsylvania: Schiffer, 2001.

Hill, Sedgefield D., ed. *The Fight'n 451st Bombardment Group (H)*, 2nd edition. Paducah, Kentcucky: Turner Publishing Company, 2000.

McCarthy, Lyle, ed. *The Coffee Tower: The History of the 459th Bomb Group*. Paducah, Kentucky: Turner Publishing Company, 1997.

Members of the 449th Bomb Group Association. *Grottaglie and Home, A History of the 449th Bomb Group, Book III*. Paducah, Kentucky: Turner Press, 1997.

Ninety-Ninth Historical Society. *The Diamondbacks: The History of the 99th Bomb Group*. Paducah, Kentucky: Turner Press, 1998.

Schneider, Sam, ed. *This Is How It Was: The History of the 485th Bomb Group (H).* St. Petersburg, Florida: Southern Heritage Press, 1995.

Stern, Daniel. *483rd Bomb Group (H).* Paducah, Kentucky: Turner Publishing Company, 1994.

Turner, Damon. *Tucson to Grottaglie, A History of the 449th Bomb Group, Book I.* Collegiate Press, 1985.

———. *And This Is Our Story: A History of the 449th Bomb Group, Book II.* Collegiate Press, 1985.

NOTES

Chapter 1: The Making of a Pilot

1. Perret, *Winged Victory*, 249; Wells, *Courage and Air Warfare*, 102; Djilas, *Wartime*, 127; McFarland and Norton, *To Command the Sky*, 9.
2. Withington, *Flight to Blechhammer*, 18; Stanley letters, May 19, June 17, and July 4, 1943; Schmitz letters, August 5, 1943; Mary Alice Stanley interview, 1–4.
3. Stanley letters, June 22, July 4, and August 9, 1943.
4. Stanley letters, May 17, 1943; Schmitz letters, May 12, 15, 30, and July 22, 1944.
5. Jernigan, *Selecting the Best*, 385; Waltry, *Washout!*, 49–54; Arnold and Eaker, *This Flying Game*, 110; Carigan, *Ad Lib*, 70; Stanley letters, May 21 and 24, 1943.
6. Meilinger, ed., *The Paths of Heaven*, 212; Richard Overy, *The Bombers and the Bombed*, 144; McFarland and Norton, *To Command the Sky*, 27; Crane, *American Airpower Strategy in World War II*, 21–25; Clodfetter, *Beneficial Bombing*, 41–64; Randall Hansen, *Fire and Fury*, 38–39; Miller, *Masters of the Air*, 36–41; Perret, *Winged Victory*, 25–29; *Saving the Jews*, 297.
7. *Preflight: 44-A*, 14; *Preflight: 44-B*, 10–22; Stanley letters, June 27a and July 6, 9, 11, 14, 23, and 25, 1943.
8. Waltry, *Washout!*, 74; *Preflight: 44-A*, 9; *Preflight: 44-B*, 9, 18–19; Stanley letters, June 6, 19, 27a, and 28, 1943, and July 7, 9, 14, 18, and 21, 1943; Schmitz letters, June 18 and July 10, 1943.
9. Stanley letters, June 21, August 1, September 6, and October 7, 1943; Schmitz letters, October 23, 1943.
10. Schmitz letters, July 5, October 4, and 13, 1943, and February 23, 1944; Stanley letters, October 11, 1943, and February 11, 20, and 25, 1944.
11. Stanley letters, July 21, 1943, and January 4, 1944; McManus, *Deadly Sky*, 55–58; Ambrose, *The Wild Blue*, 77, 80; Carigan, *Ad Lib*, 40; Laura Hillenbrand, *Unbroken: A World War II Story of Survival, Resilience, and Redemption* (New York: Random House, 2010), 59–60; Tillman, *Forgotten Fifteenth*, 8.
12. Schmitz letters, February 23, 1944; Stanley letters, February 27, 1944.
13. Schmitz letters, February 26, 1944; Stanley letters, February 22 and 29, April 20, and May 1, 1944.
14. Buchholz interview, 1–3, 47; Lydia Schreiber letters, April 15, 2000; Michael Kiger interview, 1–4; Stanley letters, May 23, 24, and 27, 1944, and June 24 and 29, 1944.
15. Stanley interview, 36; Stanley letters, May 25, June 17, and July 11, 1944; *Lubbock Morning Avalanche*, July 12 and 14, 1944; *El Paso Herald Post*, July 12, 1944; Cone letters, August 17, 2000.
16. Stanley letters, August 3, 4, and 7, 1944; Schmitz letters, August 2, 7, 8, and 10, 1944.

Chapter 2: Shot Down Twice

1. Tillman, *Forgotten Fifteenth*, 17, 112, 130.
2. Stanley letters, October 8, 1944.
3. Air Force Historical Research Agency (AFHRA) Microfilm Reel B0614, 1424; Stanley letters, September 6, 14, 16, 25, and 28, 1944; Leo Cone notes.
4. AFHRA Microfilm Reel A6384, 192–96, 480; Reel B0616, 1443; Craven, *The Army Air Forces in World War II*, 281; Richard Overy, *Why the Allies Won*, 230–32; 464th Bomb Group, *Black Panther*, September 2004 and October 2005; Cook and Nesbit, *Target: Hitler's Oil*, 139, 146; *The United States Strategic Bombing Survey*, September 30, 1945, 8; Tillman, *Forgotten Fifteenth*, 82, 187.
5. AFHRA Microfilm Reel A6384, 480; Reel B0614, 1240–46, 1448; Buchholz interview, 11; MACR 9060; MACR 9133; Hill and Karle, *The 464th Bomb Group in World War II*, 100.
6. AFHRA Microfilm Reel A6544B, 299; Stanley interview, 8; Michael Kiger interview, 6; Cone's notes on the October 13 mission; Plaisance interview; "Lt. Seaver Describes Experiences," *The Herald* (Randolph, Vermont), November 9, 1944; Stanley letters, July 27, 1943, and March 28, 1944; Plaisance letter, October 25, 1944.
7. Mahoney, *Fifteenth Air Force Against the Axis*, 245; Plaisance interview; Stanley letter, November 14, 1944; *The Herald*, November 9, 1944; Michael Kiger interview, 7; Cone interview; Buchholz interview, 13.
8. AFHRA Microfilm Reel A6384, 40–41, 287; Reel A6386, 726; Reel B0615, 1244; Hill and Karle, *The 464th Bomb Group in World War II*, 100.
9. Mary E. Stanley letter, October 30, 1944; Mary Alice Stanley interview, 30; Schmitz letters, October 30 and November 1, 2, and 28, 1944.
10. AFHRA Microfilm Reel A6544B, 373; Reel A6544D, 176; Reel B0614, 1255–57, 1319; NARA Record Group 342, Entry 6, Box 15; Hill and Karle, *The 464th Bomb Group in World War II*, 106; Buchholz interview, 18; Kiger interview, 9–10; Cone notes from October 13 mission; Cone interview; Stanley letters of October 23, 25, 28, and November 21, 1944; Plaisance interview; Stanley interview, 13–16; Plaisance letters, October 25 and November 21, 1944.
11. Mary Elizabeth Stanley letter, November 15, 1944; Schmitz letters, November 1–28, 1944; Mary Alice Stanley interview, 27.
12. John S. Barker Jr., ed., *Flight of the Liberators: The Story of the Four Hundred and Fifty-Fourth Bombardment Group* (Rochester: Du Bois Press, 1946), 58–64; McCarthy, *The Coffee Tower*, 128; Leo Cone notes; Stanley letters, October 31 and November 1, 2 (V-mail), and 5, 1944, and July 4, 1945.
13. AFHRA Microfilm Reel A6385, 530; B0608, 549; Reel B0614, 1529–39, Reel B0616, 897; Hill and Karle, *The 464th Bomb Group in World War II*, 122, 124; Plaisance letter, November 21, 1944; Plaisance diary, November 22, 1944; Leo Cone interview; Stanley interview, 18–19, 33; Kiger interview, 11; Stanley letters, November 20 and 26, 1944, and May 7, 1945.
14. Hill and Karle, *The 464th Bomb Group in World War II*, 125–26; Stanley letters, November 24, 1944, and V-mail of December 1, 1944; "Lt. 'Eddie' Seaver Safe Again," *The Herald*, January 25, 1945.

15. AFHRA Microfilm Reel B0614, 1471–73; Reel A6385, 769, 811; Reel A6386, 541, 587; Reel B0616, 1064; Withington, *Flight to Black Hammer*, 92; Carigan, *Ad Lib*, 90–91; Steve Birdsall, *Log of the Liberators: An Illustrated History of the B-24* (New York: Doubleday, 1973), 246–49; William Baker interview; Stanley interview, 10; William Baker letter, January 16, 2000.

16. AFHRA Microfilm Reel B0615, 105–8, Reel B0616, 1069; Hill and Karle, *The 464th Bomb Group in World War II*, 127; *B-24 Liberator in Detail*, 56; Stanley interview, 41; Stanley letter, September 30, 1945.

17. AFHRA Microfilm Reel B0609, 421; Reel B0616, 1069; Reel A6544B, 857; Hill and Karle, *The 464th Bomb Group in World War II*, 127–28; MACR 10109, 10029, 10105; William Baker interview; William Baker letter, February 2000; Birdsall, *Log of the Liberators*, 246–47; Buchholz interview, 23; Cone notes on December 2, 1944, mission; *The Herald*, January 25, 1945; "Luck Brings Denver Flyer Home Alive," *Denver Post*, January 1945.

18. AFHRA Microfilm Reel A6544B, 1192; Cone interview; Michael Kiger interview, 8, 12; Buchholz interview, 24–27; *The Herald*, January 25, 1945.

19. AFHRA Microfilm Reel A6544B, 857; Escape Statement (SKP) 408, 1192, SKP 517; William Baker letter, February 13, 2000; Redzic, *Bosnia and Herzegovina in the Second World War*, 27–28, 214; Cone notes on December 2, 1944, mission; Stanley letter, June 28, 1945; Stanley interview, 10, 20.

Chapter 3: Churchill's Choice

1. Noel Malcolm, *Bosnia: A Short History* (New York: New York University Press, 1996), 48–49, 65–66, 151, 174; Tomasevich, *War and Revolution in Yugoslavia 1941–1945: Occupation and Collaboration*, 476–77.

2. West, *Black Lamb and Grey Falcon*, 54–55; Milovan Djilas, *Land without Justice*, quoted in Kurapovna, *Shadows on the Mountain*, 66.

3. Pavlowitch, *Hitler's New Disorder*, 13–31; Kurapovna, *Shadows on the Mountain*, 103–10; Tomasevich, *War and Revolution in Yugoslavia 1941–1945*, 47, 639–40.

4. Malcolm, *Bosnia: A Short History*, 177–79; Kurapovna, *Shadows on the Mountain*, 70; Redzic, *Bosnia and Herzegovina in the Second World War*, 119–32; Tomasevich, *The Chetniks*, 146, 170; Roberts, *Tito, Mihailović and the Allies, 1941–1945*, 39.

5. Tomasevich, *War and Revolution in Yugoslavia 1941–1945: The Chetniks*, 178, 184, 192–93, 606; Roberts, *Tito, Mihailović and the Allies, 1941–1945*, 23; Williams, *Parachutes, Patriots, and Partisans*, 60; Lindsey, *Beacons in the Night*, 115–16, 235; Kurapovna, *Shadows on the Mountain*, 73–75.

6. Tomasevich, *The Chetniks*, 148–49, 160, 168; Pavlowitch, *Hitler's New Disorder*, 62–63; Redzic, *Bosnia and Herzegovina in the Second World War*, 127, 134–38; Roberts, *Tito, Mihailović and the Allies*, 70.

7. Roberts, *Tito, Mihailović and the Allies*, 93; Pavlowitch, *Hitler's New Disorder*, 191; Kurapovna, *Shadows on the Mountain*, 97–98, 182; Tomasevich, *The Chetniks*, 197, 293–94.

8. Pavlowitch, *Hitler's New Disorder*, 170, 201–2; Williams, *Parachutes, Patriots, and Partisans*, 167, 182.
9. Tomasevich, *The Chetniks*, 365; Pavlowitch, *Hitler's New Disorder*, 192; Kurapovna, *Shadows on the Mountain*, 99; Maclean, *Eastern Approaches*, 390, 402–3.
10. Tomasevich, *The Chetniks*, 330–34.
11. Lindsey, *Beacons in the Night*, 272.
12. Jancar-Webster, *Women and Revolution in Yugoslavia*, 43; Roberts, *Tito, Mihailović and the Allies*, 260; Maclean, *Eastern Approaches*, 437–38; Tomasevich, *The Chetniks*, 370–74.
13. David Martin's *Web of Disinformation*, Michael Lee's *Rape of Serbia*, and Gregory Freeman's *The Forgotten 500* espouse the Communist conspiracy theory. Lindsey, *Beacons in the Night*, 340–41; Catherwood, *Churchill and Tito*, 39, 67, 129; Williams, *Parachutes, Patriots, and Partisans*, 247–48 refute their claims.
14. Fitzroy Maclean, *The Heretic: The Life and Times of Josip-Broz-Tito* (New York: Harper, 1957), 243; Ronald H. Bailey, *Partisans and Guerrillas*, 123–27; Kurapovna, *Shadows on the Mountain*, 194–97, 204; Thomas T. Matteson, "An Analysis of the Circumstances Surrounding the Rescue and Evacuation of Allied Airmen from Yugoslavia 1941–45," Research Report Number 128, Maxwell AFB, Air War College, April 1977, 13.
15. Roberts, *Tito, Mihailović and the Allies*, 214; Djilas, *Wartime*, 400; Ford, *OSS and the Yugoslav Resistance*, 99–100.
16. Ford, *OSS and the Yugoslav Resistance*, 117–18; Lindsey, *Beacons in the Night*, 242.
17. Roberts, *Tito, Mihailović and the Allies*, 265.
18. Lindsey, *Beacons in the Night*, 268–70. See AFRHA Microfilm Reel A6544D, 492, 494 for Col. Kraigher's account of the number of airmen and refugees rescued by HALYARD. The ACRU goods supplied to the Chetniks against orders do not appear in AAF records. Sources for these incidents include: Kraemer, *The Secret War in the Balkans*, 195–96 (August air drop); Ford, *OSS and the Yugoslav Resistance*, 133 (Christmas 1944 airdrop); Freeman, *The Forgotten 500*, 243–45, (supplies left behind by HALYARD). There were probably more such instances.
19. AFHRA Microfilm Reel A6544, 630, 644; Roberts, *Tito, Mihailović and the Allies*, 286, 308; Ford, *OSS and the Yugoslav Resistance*, 139–52.

Chapter 4: Following Tito's Footsteps

1. Craven and Cate, eds., *The Army Air Forces in World War II*, 646.
2. Robinson interview, 1–4; Robinson interview by Charlie Stewart, 2; *B-24 Combat Missions*, 113–14.
3. Carter interview, 5; Heim interview, 3; Carter-Sedlak-Martin interview, 15; Robinson interview, 7–8; Sedlak interview, 10; Stewart interview, 9.
4. Robinson interview by Charlie Stewart, 3–10; Robinson interview, 8–9, 11; Heim interview, 4.
5. AFHRA Microfilm Reel A6385, 160; Reel A6544B, 632–35; Reel B0643, 1785; Carter-Sedlak-Martin interview, 4; Claud Martin interview by Charlie Stewart, 2; Robinson interview by Charlie Stewart, 1–2.

6. Carter interview, 8; Carter-Sedlak-Martin interview, 10; Heim interview, 5; Martin interview by Charlie Stewart, 2; Robinson interview by Charlie Stewart, 2–3; Robinson interview, 11; Sedlak interview, 12–13.
7. Stewart interview, 10.
8. Carter-Sedlak-Martin interview, 6; Claud Martin interview, 2–3; Sedlak interview, 15.
9. Williams, *Parachutes, Patriots, and Partisans*, 166; Greentree, *Knight's Move*, 30–69; Pavlowitch, *Hitler's New Disorder*, 44; Redzic, *Bosnia and Herzegovina in the Second World War*, 205–7; Jancar-Webster, *Women and Revolution in Yugoslavia, 1941–45*, 52; Craven and Cate, eds., *The Army Air Forces in World War II*, 521.
10. Carter-Sedlak-Martin interview, 7; Sedlak interview, 15–16.
11. Stewart interview, 11–12.
12. AFHRA Microfilm A6544B, 630 (Wilkinson and Nye), 632–635 (Boehme, Powell, and Hill).
13. "Psychological Research on Pilot Training," 35–36; Carigan, *Ad Lib*, 47.
14. *B-24 Combat Missions*, 53; "Adriatic Island Succors Allied Airmen," *Torretta Flyer* (newsletter of the 484th Bomb Group) (Winter 1984), 27; Button interview, 8, 30–31; Hoogeveen interview, 9.
15. Carigan, *Ad Lib*, 12; Horak interview, 11; Button interview, 9, 17, 36.
16. AFHRA Microfilm Reel B0644, 1289–95; SKP 432; Carter-Sedlak-Martin interview, 15; Claud Martin interview by Charlie Stewart, 4; Robinson interview, 13; Sedlak interview, 18.

Chapter 5: Bombs Bursting in Air

1. Stephen E. Ambrose, *Citizen Soldiers: From the Beaches of Normandy to the Surrender of Germany* (Premier Digital Publishing, 2011), 291; McManus, *Deadly Sky*, 6, 186, 190; Crane, *American Airpower Strategy in World War II*, 88; Wells, *Courage and Air Warfare*, 27–28, 35.
2. Rosenthal interview, 2–9.
3. U.S. Army, *The Officer's Guide*, 353; Bartusch interview, 5–7.
4. Bartusch interview, 4, 25; Rosenthal interview, 8–10.
5. Bartusch interview, 3, 25.
6. Rosenthal interview, 5, 13.
7. AFHRA Microfilm Reel A6544B, 868; SKP 419, 887; SKP 397; Reel B0642, 1433; Grimm, *Heroes of the 483rd*, 77; Bartusch interview, 8, 11.
8. Bartusch interview, 7; Rosenthal interview, 14–16.
9. AFHRA Microfilm Reel A6544B, 868, 887; Stern, *483rd Bomb Group*, 44; Bartusch interview, 7, 12–13; Rosenthal interview, 16–17. The .50 caliber waist gun retrieved by the Partisans rests in the National Museum of Contemporary History in Slovenia.
10. Zack Johnson Individual Deceased Personnel File; MACR 9350.
11. Nichol and Rennell, *The Last Escape*, 114–165, 317–345; Tillman, *Forgotten Fifteenth*, 234–37; Bartusch interview, 5; Kramer interview, January 15, 2005.

Chapter 6: Stranded in Sanski Most

1. Dosenovich, *So Help Me God!*, 60–65, 117–123; Ivo Goldstein, "The Independent State of Croatia in 1941, on the Road to Catastrophe," in Ramet, ed., *The Independent State of Croatia 1941–54*, 22; Redzic, *Bosnia and Herzegovina in the Second World War*, 18, 122–26, 148–49; Kurapovna, *Shadows on the Mountain*, 301.

2. Associated Press articles, December 26, 1942, and May 16, 1944, quoting Partisan claims broadcast from Radio Moscow; Redzic, *Bosnia and Herzegovina in the Second World War*, 230–33.

3. AFHRA Microfilm Reel A6544A, 713–73.

4. Kraemer, *The Secret War in the Balkans*, 137; AFHRA Microfilm Reel 25696, 249, 307 (on ACRU airdrops and evacuations), 547 (on escape route as of November 8, 1944); Reel A6544D, 1059 (on closure of Sanski Most airfield and alternate route to coast). For other rescues see Reel A6544B, 198–200, 211, 214, 218, 258; Reel B0042, 1327–32, 1488–89; Reel B0601, 190–204; B0607, 1579–81, 1644–45, 1696, 1705; Reel B0615, 1248–52; Reel 0617, 142–47, 199.

5. AFHRA Microfilm Reel A6544B, 724–28; Reel A6384, 108; Reel A6386, 581; OSS cable from Huntington, December 9, 1944, NARA Record Group 226, Entry 136, Box 19, File J-3.

6. AFHRA Microfilm Reel B0644, 1289–95; Stern, *483rd Bomb Group (H)*, 44; Button interview, 22–26; Hoogeveen interview, 15; Horak interview, 12–19; Rosenthal interview, 19–23; Sedlak interview, 19.

7. Button interview, 20, 32; Joseph Foto interview, 10; Hoogeveen interview, 15; Horak interview 12–13, 16; Stanley interview, 22.

8. AFHRA Microfilm A6544B, 873; Stewart interview by Charlie Stewart, 13; Bartusch interview, 16; Rosenthal interview, 18, 23.

9. Stern, *483rd Bomb Group*, 44–45; Grimm, *Heroes of the 483rd*, 22; Rosenthal interview, 18–19; Sedlak interview, 27; Carter diary, December 2, 1944.

10. Carter diary, December 1 and 2, 1944.

11. Bartusch interview, 14, 17; Rosenthal interview, 21.

12. AFHRA Microfilm Reel A6386, 581; Reel A6544B, 868, Appendix B; Bartusch interview, 14; Button interview, 27; Martin interview by Charlie Stewart, 5; Stewart interview by Charlie Stewart, 13.

13. AFHRA Microfilm Reel A6544B, 1192; Baker interview, 3; Buchholz interview, 27–31; Cone interview.

14. AFHRA Microfilm Reel B0644, 1295; Carter diary, December 7, 1944; Buchholz interview, 31; Button interview, 24; Carter interview, 11; Cone interview; Horak interview, 15; Stanley interview, 22. For Lt. C. G. Begg's story, see National Archives (UK), File 54/44, "War Diary of the 5th Squadron (SAAF)," folios 31681-2 and File 54/185/3, folios 28871, 28880, 28911.

15. AFHRA Microfilm Reel A6544B, 868; Carter diary, December 8 entry; Button interview, 33.

16. AFHRA Microfilm Reel A6544B, 517, 868; Stern, *483rd Bomb Group*, 45; Carter diary, December 1–15, 1944; Carter interview, 10–12; Hoogeveen interview, 13–16; Horak interview, 13–19; Robinson interview, 13; Sedlak interview, 21–22.

17. AFHRA Microfilm Reel B0644, 1289–95; Button interview, 20, 28; Carter-Sedlak Martin interview, 24–25; Hoogeveen interview, 13; Horak interview, 14–17; Robinson interview, 13; Rosenthal interview, 27, 34; Sedlak interview, 21, 26; Carter diary, December 13 and 14, 1944, entries.

Chapter 7: Herky's Boys Get Downed

1. AFHRA Microfilm Reel B0584, 81; Turner, *Tucson to Grottaglie*, 97; Members of the 449th Bomb Group Association, *Grottaglie and Home*, 201, 409; Marrone interview by Greg Krupinsky, 5; Marrone undated narrative.
2. McManus, *Deadly Sky*, 15; Steinbeck, *Bombs Away!*, 24; Rochlin, *Old Man in a Baseball Cap*, 9.
3. Marrone interview by Greg Krupinsky, 2; Marrone letters, December 3, 1944, and January 7, 1945.
4. Marrone letter, January 10, 1945; Marrone narrative; Earll narrative, April 3, 2002.
5. AFHRA Microfilm Reel A6544B, 826; "Lt. James R. King Listed Missing over Yugoslavia," *Nashville Tennessean*, December 26, 1944; Earll narratives, April 3 and 21, 2002, September 27, 2004; Earll diary, December 11, 1944; Earll interview, 2; Marrone letter, January 10, 1945.
6. Members of the 449th Bomb Group Association, *Grottaglie and Home*, 42; Marrone diary, December 11, 1944; Earll narratives; Earll interview, 6, 10; Marrone interview, 5; Marrone letter, November 20, 1944; Earll letter, January 9, 1945.
7. MACR 10389; Earll narrative, April 3, 2002; Earll interview, 10–13; Earll letter, January 9, 1945.

Chapter 8: The Weakest Link Breaks

1. Wells, *Courage and Air Warfare*, 65, 93, 95; McFarland and Norton, *To Command the Sky*, 110–11; McManus, *Deadly Sky*, 301–2, 353. See also John Keegan's classic *The Face of Battle*.
2. Clark interview, 2; Mann interview, 13–19; Quinn interview, 1–3; Quinn letter, July 22, 1944; Roper interview, 1, 7–8.
3. AFHRA Microfilm Reel B0604, 1121, 1129; *The Townsman* (Wellesly, MA), December 8, 1944; Houghton interview by John Davis, 4–6; Houghton radio interview, December 24, 1944, 6.
4. AFHRA Microfilm Reel A6544B, 853–56, 993, 1085; Roper interview, 11–15; Roper diary, December 11 and 22, 1944; Clark interview, 3–4; "Oaklander Bailout Out over Balkans; 27 Days to Base," *Oakland Tribune*, February 5, 1945.
5. Roper and Earll diaries, December 13–15, 1944; Roper interview, 16–17; Earll narrative, April 3, 2002, 2.
6. Marrone diary, December 16–19, 1944.

Chapter 9: Point of No Return

1. Steinbeck, *Bombs Away*, 125; Wells, *Courage and Air Warfare*, 149; McManus, *Deadly Sky*, 331–32; Ambrose, *The Wild Blue*, 174.

2. Katherine Dick letter, August 3, 1943; Frank Dick letters, July 15, 1943, October 21, November 4, and December 9, 1944; MACR 8973; AFHRA Microfilm Reel A6544F, 399–433.
3. Gordon Commander, Frank Dick, Gus Sundquist, and Joseph DeRosa Individual Deceased Personnel Files.
4. AFHRA Microfilm Reel B0610, 953; 461st Bomb Group official history, July 25, 1944 (transcript available on the 461st BG Association website); Johnny Dale Jarnagin narrative; Nayes narrative; *B-24 Liberators of the 15th Air Force/49th Bomb Wing*, 85; Hill interview, 1, 8.
5. Martino interview, 1–6, 13; "Parachutes into Arms of Yugoslav Partisans," *Providence Sunday Journal*, April 1, 1945. Like Bob Dean and David Blood, Martino's pilot managed to take off again from Vis.
6. Nayes narrative; Hill interview, 10–11; Wroclawski interview; *Herald News*, September 8, 1971.
7. MACR 10676; AFHRA Microfilm Reel A6544B, 835, 1050–55; Hill interview, 4–5.
8. Ann Nesterik (Sundquist's sister), letter to Katherine Dick, July 26, 1945; Martino interview, 6–7; *Providence Sunday Journal*, April 1, 1945.
9. Hill interview, 4–5, 8.
10. Nayes narrative.
11. MACR 10676; AFHRA Microfilm Reel A6544B, 1050–55; Martino interview, 7–8; Hill interview, 4; *Providence Sunday Journal*, April 1, 1945; Nayes narrative.
12. MACR 10676 and AFHRA Microfilm Reel A6544B, 1050–55.
13. AFHRA Microfilm Reel A6544B, 1050–55; DeRosa Individual Deceased Personnel File; Nayes narrative.
14. AFHRA Microfilm Reel A6544B, 1050–54, 1066, 1102; NARA Record Group 226, Entry 136, Box 20; *Bergen Herald News*, September 8, 1971; *Providence Sunday Journal*, April 1, 1945; Nayes narrative; Hill interview, 8–11; Martino interview, 8–10.
15. MACR 10676; DeRosa and Dick Individual Deceased Personnel Files.
16. AFHRA Microfilm Reel A6544B, 835; Reel B0610, 953; DeRosa, Sundquist, Commander, and Dick Individual Deceased Personnel Files.

Chapter 10: Flying on Borrowed Time

1. Mahony, *Fifteenth Air Force Against the Axis*, 287; AFHRA Microfilm Reel A6385, 1519–20.
2. Blank interview by Elmer Wigley.
3. Robert Mitchell letter, November 2, 1999; Thomas Ceely interview; Martin Otway interview; Owens diary, November 3, 1944.
4. Blank interview, 10–11.
5. Blank interview, 11; Robert Mitchell letter, November 2, 1999; Owens diary, December 16, 1944.
6. Mahony, *Fifteenth Air Force Against the Axis*, 298; Hill, *The 451st Bomb Group in World War II*, 64; Robert Mitchell letter, November 2, 1999.
7. AFHRA Microfilm Reel A6544B, 879, 1125; MACR 10605; Hill, ed., *The Fight'n 451st Bombardment Group*, 204; Mahony, *Fifteenth Air Force Against the Axis*, 299; Owens diary, December 18, 1944.

8. MACR 10640; Blank interview, 12; Owens Interview, 3; Bob Mitchell, "Mission: Bomb Blechhammer Oil Refineries"; undated narrative by Keith Owens.
9. Blank interview, 12.
10. Mitchell, "Mission: Bomb Blechhammer Oil Refineries"; Keith Owens undated narrative; Owens interview, 5; and Owens diary, December 18, 1944 entry.
11. AFHRA Microfilm Reel A6386, 581; Reel A6544B, 838–42, 863–65; "Sgt. W.C. Rainey Back in Action," *Brownsville Herald*, January 26, 1945, 11.

Chapter 11: The ICARUS Mission Arrives

1. Henry Wunderlich interview, 2–3, 6–7, 17–18.
2. Wunderlich interview, 5, 8–13.
3. AFHRA Microfilm Reel A6385, 1519, and Reel B0601, 1106; McCarthy, *The Coffee Tower*, 145, 153; Wunderlich interview, 20; Joseph Foto interview, 1–7; Almondo Champi interview, 4, 12; Foto letter, November 25, 1944.
4. McCarthy, *The Coffee Tower*, 150–52, Joseph Foto, "My Thirteenth Mission," in the *Pathfinder*, the newsletter of the 459th Bomb Group Association, Spring 1998; Foto interview, 6; Wunderlich interview, 22.
5. Mahony, *Fifteenth Air Force Against the Axis*, 300; McCarthy, *The Coffee Tower*, 150–52.
6. "My Thirteenth Mission" by Joseph Foto; Champi interview, 6–7; Wunderlich interview, 25–26.
7. AFHRA Microfilm Reel B0607, 1399–1400, 1494–98; Reel A6544B, 861; Wunderlich interview, 25–26; Foto, "My Thirteenth Mission"; Joseph Foto interview, 7–13.
8. AFHRA Microfilm Reel A6544B, 726, 735; Reel B0042, 1175; Reel B0609, 813; Reel B0644, 1289–95; Freeman, "The Cinderella Front," 32–34; Rosenthal interview, 20–22; Kidder-Stanley interview, 33–34.
9. AFHRA Microfilm Reel A6544C, 99–105; Reel B0607, 1532–35; Haynes diary, December 26–27, 1944.

Chapter 12: A Conspiracy of Circumstances

1. Kidder-Stanley interview, 5; Robert Kidder letters, December 2 and 15, 1944.
2. Kidder-Stanley interview, 1–7; Kidder letter, December 9, 1944.
3. Henry Rinna Jr. note, January 22, 2014; Kidder flight log; Kidder letters, December 15, 1944, and February 14, 1945.
4. Thomas Stack letters, July 16, November 12, 23, and 25, 1944, December 14, 1994.
5. AFHRA Microfilm Reel A6385, 1519; Thomas Stack letter, July 2, 1969.
6. Thomas Stack letters, October 25, November 21, 1944, July 2, 1969; Hodgeman obituary.
7. Rinna family notes, January 2014; Lingeman, *Don't You Know There's a War On?*, 94–96.
8. AFHRA Microfilm Reel B6544B, 846, 1199; Reel B0601, 1110; Thomas Stack, "Wolff's Gang," 1969; Thomas Stack letters, July 2, 1969, February 17, 1971,

December 18, 1984, December 13, 1985, July 19, 1991; *454th Memories,* "Group Mission 170-A" by Thomas Stack; MACR 10686; Kidder-Stanley interview, 19–20.

9.   AFHRA Microfilm Reel A6544B, 1199; Rinna Casualty Questionnaire; Rinna application to the Caterpillar Society; Kidder email, May 31, 2001; Kidder-Stanley interview, 18–19.

10. AFHRA Microfilm Reel A6544B, 1199; MACR 10686; Thomas Stack letter, December 13, 1985; Kidder-Stanley interview, 21–22, 28, 39.

11. AFHRA Microfilm Reel A6544B, 846, 1199, 1208; Willis Hodgeman, "To Whom It May Concern" undated letter; Kidder letter, January 27, 1945; Kidder-Stanley interview, 24–34.

12. AFHRA Microfilm Reel A6544B, 1199; MACR 10686; *454th Bomb Group Bombing Missions and Related Stories,* Herbert Eldridge narrative, 74; Stack, "Wolff's Gang."

13. Kidder-Stanley interview, 21; Kidder letters, March 18, April 7, 1945.

14. NARA Record Group 342, Entry 6, Box 15, File 61; AFHRA Microfilm Reel A6544, 647.

Chapter 13: The Flying Shithouse and the Ghost Ship

1.   James Martin diary, August 28, September 10 and 23, 1944; Keiser interview, 8.

2.   Charlesworth interview, 7; Keiser interview, 6.

3.   1943 Selective Service Regulations, Section 622; Keim, *The CPS Story,* 81, 97; Paul Martin interview by Debby Martin, 2–4; James Martin interview by Debby Martin, 5–6; James Martin diary, September 6, 12, 13, 15, and October 4, 8, 13, 14, 1944.

4.   Wheeler interview by the author, 3, 14.

5.   Griffith letters October 1, November 19, and December 5, 1944; Griffith interview, 5; Keiser interview, 4; Chester interview, 10–11.

6.   AFHRA Microfilm Reel A6544B, 866; Wheeler log, December 18, 1944; Charlesworth interview, 10–11; Keiser interview, 4–14; Martin diary, February 15, 1945; Wheeler interview by EEA, 11; Griffith interview, 6; Wheeler interview by the author, 22–26; Chester interview, 23; Hoffman narrative, December 25, 1944.

7.   Keiser interview, 10; Wheeler interview by EEA, 11; Wheeler interview by the author, 26.

8.   Wheeler interview by EEA, 12–13; Wheeler interview by the author, 27–29.

9.   Martin diary, February 15, 1945; Chester interview, 15; Wheeler interview by the author, 29.

10. AFHRA Microfilm Reel A6544C, 55; Griffith interview, 7–14.

11. Martin interview, 9; Wheeler interview by EEA, 14; Wheeler interview by the author, 30–32.

12. AFHRA Microfilm A6544B, 108, 113, 149, 426, 482, 880; Reel B0609, 737–38; Roberts, *Tito, Mihailović, and the Allies,* 250; NARA Record Group 226, Entry 136, Box 29, Folder X-77; Wheeler interview by the author, 32–34; Wheeler diary, December 20; Hoffman narrative.

13. AFHRA Microfilm Reel A6544B, 866; Keiser interview, 14.

14. Keiser interview, 4; Sharon Schwartz interview.

Chapter 14: An Unmerry Christmas

1. Leary, "Troop Carriers Persist," in *Fueling the Fires of Resistance*; AFHRA Microfilm Reel A0981, 250–284; Roberts, *Tito, Mihailović and the Allies*, 286–94.
2. AFHRA Microfilm Reel B0607, 1494–98; Reel A6544B, 861, 868; Foto interview, 9; Hoogeveen interview, 15; Kidder-Stanley interview, 29–37; Roper interview, 18, 22; Marrone diary, December 20, 1944; Roper diary, December 24, 1944.
3. Earll interview, 7–17; Earll diary, December 16 and 28, 1944; Marrone diary, December 23, 1944.
4. AFHRA Microfilm Reel A6386, 581; Reel B0644B, 863, 1292; Stanley interview, 21.
5. Bartusch interview, 15–16; Foto interview, 12; Heim interview, 8; Kiger interview, 15; Sedlak interview, 22.
6. AFHRA Microfilm Reel B0607, 1495; Owens, Earll, and Roper diaries, December 25, 1944; Stack letter, January 8, 1945; Kiger interview, 15; Stanley interview, 22. For more on the airmen's contribution to the Battle of the Bulge, see Tillman, *Forgotten Fifteenth*, 211 and Craven and Cate, eds., *The Army Air Forces in World War II, Volume III, Europe*, 646.
7. Horak letter, December 25, 1944; Marrone and Roper diaries, December 25, 1944; Stack letter, January 6, 1945.
8. *Nashville Tennessean*, December 26, 1944; *Chattanooga Times Free Press*, December 25, 1944; *Ames* (Iowa) *Tribune*, December 22, 1944; Sedlak interview; Alice Schmitz letter to Charles Stanley, December 25, 1944; Mary Alice Stanley interview, 33; Mary Elizabeth Stanley letter to Mary Alice Schmitz, December 25, 1944.
9. AFHRA Microfilm Reel A0981, 272; Cone interview; Earll, Owens, Marrone, and Roper diaries, December 26, 1944; Stern, *483rd Bomb Group (H)*, 46; Rosenthal interview, 24.
10. Tomasevich, *War and Revolution in Yugoslavia*, 704; AFHRA Microfilm Reel A6544B, 868, 1289; Carter-Sedlak-Martin interview, 18; Roper diary, December 27, 1944; Roper interview, 22; Stern, *483rd Bomb Group (H)*, 46; Sedlak interview, 23–24; Wunderlich interview, 28, 31–33.
11. Jancar-Webster, *Women and Revolution in Yugoslavia*, 76; Carter-Sedlak-Martin interview, 24; Foto interview, 14; Marrone diary, December 22, 25, 26, 27, and 30, 1944; Marrone interview, 6; Owens diary, December 21–29, 1944; Sedlak interview, 22; Wunderlich interview, 31.
12. AFHRA Microfilm Reel A0981, 274–78; Reel A6544B, 1199; Marrone and Owens diaries, December 28, 1944.

Chapter 15: The Tourist Takes Charge

1. Dr. James Johnson narrative; Heim interview, 10; *Of Broad Stripes and Bright Stars*, Chapter 4.
2. Button interview, 29–31; Johnson narrative; Tamraz-Stanley interview, 28.
3. Johnson narrative; Schneider, ed., *This Is How It Was*, 265–66.
4. "The War Service of Eugene D. Cogburn," unpublished narrative by Eugene Cogburn, 7; George Benedict note, January 28, 1945; Johnson narrative; Lewis Baker diary, July 5, 7, 9, 18, August 21, 29, 30, September 3, 7, 17, and November 14, 1944.

5. Johnson narrative; Tamraz-Stanley interview, 21, 30–31.
6. AFHRA Microfilm Reel 6386, 76; Reel A6544C, 43; "The War Service of Eugene D. Cogburn," 7; MACR 10924; Tamraz-Stanley interview, 31–32.
7. Tamraz-Stanley interview, 34; Whiting and Whiting, *I'm Off to War, Mother, But I'll Be Back*, 103.
8. Sherer interview, 20–21; "The War Service of Eugene D. Cogburn," 8.
9. AFHRA Microfilm Reel A6544C, 43; Lewis Baker letter, December 31, 1944; "The War Service of Eugene D. Cogburn," 9.
10. Tamraz-Stanley interview, 37–43; Whiting and Whiting, *I'm Off to War, Mother, But I'll Be Back*, 104–5.
11. Tamraz-Stanley interview, 51–52.
12. Button interview, 30.

Chapter 16: At the Mercy of Friends

1. Mahony, *Fifteenth Air Force Against the Axis*, 310; AFHRA Microfilm Reel A6544, 655.
2. AFHRA Microfilm Reel A6544B, 1192; Button interview, 38; Heim interview, 17.
3. Tamraz-Stanley interview, 44–45.
4. AFHRA Microfilm Reel 25213, 23: Button interview, 32; Heim interview, 11–12; Roper diary, December 31, 1944.
5. Thomas Stack letters, March 14, 1945, December 13, 1985, July 19, 1991.
6. Bartusch interview, 18; Rosenthal interview, 27–29; Sedlak interview, 25; Tamraz interview, 44; Owens diary, December 31, 1944, January 1, 1945.
7. AFHRA Microfilm Reel A6544B, 868; Roper diary, January 4, 1945; Stanley interviews; Buchholz interview, 33–35.
8. Button interview, 36; Owens diary, January 1, 1945.
9. Button interview, 36; Marrone, Owens, and Roper diaries, January 1, 1945; Stanley interviews; Stack letters, December 13, 1985, July 19, 1991, May 17, 1993.
10. AFHRA Microfilm Reel A6544B, 869, 1193; Carter-Sedlak-Martin interview, 16; Foto interview, 10–11; Roper diary, January 1, 1945; Stanley letter, July 4, 1945; Tamraz interview, 43–44; Joseph Foto, "My Thirteenth Mission."
11. Marrone diary, January 1 and 2, 1945; Owens diary, January 1, 1945; Sedlak interview, 20, 28.
12. AFHRA Microfilm Reel A6544B, 868; Button interview, 36–37; Foto interview, 14; Hoogeveen interview, 12; Horak interview, 21–22; Marrone, Roper, and Owens diaries, January 2, 1945; Tamraz interview, 44.
13. Carter and Roper diary, January 3, 1945; Earll and Roper diaries, January 4, 1945; Bartusch interview, 19–21; Foto interview, 10–11. Estimates on the distance walked varied among participants. Six miles is the average.
14. AFHRA Microfilm A6544B, 864; Owens diary, January 4, 1945; Carter diary, January 5, 1945; Foto interview, 14.

Chapter 17: Pulling Rank

1. Carter, Marrone, Owens, and Roper diaries, January 5, 1945; Rosenthal interview, 25; "Luck Brings Denver Flyer Home Alive," *Denver Post*, January 1945; Kraemer, *The Secret War in the Balkans*, 196.
2. AFRHA Microfilm Reel A0981, 283; Reel A6387, 808; Reel A6544C, 43; Button interview, 29, 38; Marrone diary, January 5, 1945; Stanley interview, 23–24.
3. Bartusch interview, 21; "The War Service of Eugene D. Cogburn"; Earll narrative, April 2002; Earll interview, 18; Kraemer, *The Secret War in the Balkans*, 96; Davis, *C-47 Skytrain in Action*, 32. C-47s were known to carry over forty passengers during emergencies. See Kraemer, *The Secret War in the Balkans*, 188.
4. Isby, *C-47/RD4 Units of the ETO and MTO*, 12; Button interview, 29, 38; Heim interview, 17; Marrone narrative, 1947; Rosenthal interview, 25–26.
5. Whiting and Whiting, *I'm Off to War, Mother, But I'll Be Back*, 107; William Baker interview, 3; Champi interview, 10; Foto interview, 14–15; Joseph Foto, "My Thirteenth Mission"; Keiser interview, 22; Kidder letter, January 31, 1945; Kidder-Stanley interview, 33–34; Wunderlich interview, 24.
6. Kidder-Stanley interview, 33, 40.
7. AFHRA Microfilm Reel A6544, 195; Roper and Carter diaries, January 5, 1945; Button interview, 40.
8. "The War Service of Eugene D. Cogburn"; Earll narrative, April 2002; Owens diary, January 5, 1945; Stewart interview by Charlie Stewart, 14.
9. AFHRA Microfilm Reel A6544B, 846–49 (Stack), 853–56 (Eldridge), 859–62 (Brown), 887 (Bartusch); Reel B0042, 1175; Reel B0644, 1289 (Carter), 1296–99 (Johnson); MACR 10753; Button interview, 41–42; Wunderlich interview, 24.
10. Schneider, ed., *This Is How It Was*, 139 (Michalaros death); Carter interview, 10–14; Carter-Sedlak-Martin interview, 15–20; "The War Service of Eugene D. Cogburn"; Earll narrative, April 2002; Hodgeman, "To Whom It May Concern," undated letter; Hoogeveen interview, 16; "Oaklander Bails Out Over Yugoslavia—Walks 35 Days," *Oakland Tribune*, 1945 (Ingram); Roper interview, 19–23; Rosenthal interview, 28–30; Stewart interview by Charlie Stewart, 14–15; Wunderlich interview, 38.
11. Marrone letter, January 7, 1945; Owens diary, January 15, 1945; Mann interview, 17, 20; AFHRA Microfilm A6544B, 887; MACR 10372; MACR 10893; Colasante interview, 8; Roper interview, 16.

Chapter 18: On the Home Front

1. Scherzer letter to Kathryn Kidder, January 6, 1945.
2. Mary Alice Stanley interview, 32–34.
3. Eleanor Cone letter to Lurline Tweedale, January 6, 1945; Lurline Tweedale letter to Mary Elizabeth Stanley, January 8, 1945; Anna Homel letter to Lurline Tweedale, January 5, 1945; Mary Elizabeth Stanley letters to Mary Alice Schmitz, January 4, 12, and February 6, 1945; Mary Elizabeth Stanley letter to Mr. and Mrs. Tweedale, January 8, 1945; Robert Plaisance diary, December 27, 1944; Bette Plaisance letter to Mary Alice Schmitz, January 9, 1945.

4. "Lt. 'Eddie' Seaver Safe Again," *Randolph Herald* (Vermont), January 25, 1945; Mrs. Spomer letter to Mrs. Kiger, January 27, 1945.

Chapter 19: Bitter Logic

1. MACR 10698; Lewis Baker diary, January 6, 1945; Kidder-Stanley interview, 41; Tamraz interview, 44.
2. AFRHA Microfilm Reel B0607, 1494–98; Leo Cone interview; Foto interview, 11; Kidder-Stanley interview, 23, 42; Kiger interview, 16–17; Sherer interview, 29, 31; Tamraz-Stanley interview, 57.
3. Lewis Baker diary, January 8, 1945; Leo Cone interview; Foto interview, 11; Stanley letter, October 10, 1945; Tamraz-Stanley interview, 44.
4. AFRHA Microfilm Reel A6544B, 1192; Reel A6544C, 43; AFHRA Microfilm Reel B0607, 1494–98; Lewis Baker diary, January 12, 1945; Joseph Foto, "My Thirteenth Mission"; Foto interview, 10; Kiger interview, 15; Sherer interview, 24–25; Stanley letter, May 14, 1945; Tamraz-Stanley interview, 44–57.
5. AFHRA Microfilm Reel A6544C, 43; Lewis Baker diary, January 14, 1945; Tamraz-Stanley interview, 46–48.
6. AFHRA Microfilm Reel A6544C, 43; William Baker interview, 4; William Baker letter, February 13, 2000; Leo Cone's notes; Foto interview, 10; Kidder-Stanley interview, 43; Sherer interview, 25–27; Tamraz-Stanley interview, 45.
7. William Baker letter, February 13, 2000; Joseph Foto interview, 11, 18; Foto, "My Thirteenth Mission"; undated Robert Kidder letter; Stanley letter, September 6, 1945; Redzic, *Bosnia and Herzegovina in the Second World War*, 125, 214; *Wartime*, 293; Sherer log, January 17, 1945; Tamraz-Stanley interview, 51.
8. *Wartime*, 194–95; AFHRA Microfilm Reel A6544B, 1196–1204; Reel A6544C, 43; Sherer log, January 18–23, 1945; Lewis Baker diary, January 24, 1945; Foto interview, 17; Tamraz-Stanley interview, 48–60.
9. Joseph Foto interview, 13–17; Kidder-Stanley interview, 43–45, Sherer interview, 29–30; Stanley interview, 24; Tamraz-Stanley interview, 55; Maclean, *Eastern Approaches*, 357; NARA Record Group 226, Entry 136, Box 19, File J-3.
10. Frka, *Vis, The Last Hope*, 288; AFHRA Microfilm Reel B0616, 30 (465th BG evadee); Reel A6544B, 1161 (465th BG evadees), 1199, (Stanley Escape Statement); Reel A6544D, 1028–29 (Pfeiffer request for supplies); NARA Record Group 226, Entry 136, Box 19, File J-3, Cables NR 21, 31, 43, 53 from Pfeiffer to Lt. Orman Suker, Chief Y Section in Bari; NARA Record Group 342, Entry 6, Box 16, Extract file; William Baker interview, 4; Kidder-Stanley interview, 23; Kidder letter, January 31, 1945; Kiger interview, 18–19; Sherer interview, 30.
11. AFHRA Microfilm Reel A6544B, 1192, (Stanley), 1196–1200 (Benedict), 1199 (Kidder), 1201 (Gibson); Reel B0607, 1494–98 (Mulvaney); William Baker interview, 4; Leo Cone interview; Kidder-Stanley interview, 47; Kiger interview, 19–21; Sherer interview, 32.
12. William Baker interview, 4; Carter-Martin-Sedlak-Stanley interview, 28; Stanley letter, January 27, 1945; Stanley interview, 25; Tamraz-Stanley interview, 55–56.
13. AFHRA Microfilm Reel B0615, January 1945 summary.

14. AFRHA Microfilm Reel A6544, 678, 685, 694; Reel B0608, 1399; Reel B0609, 852–855. For other crews who later passed through Sanski Most, see Reel A1320, 624 and Reel A6544C, 115, 124, 666, 763.

Chapter 20: Far from Over

1. MACR 10698; "Lt. Frederick Coe Missing Again," *Mount Vernon News*, March 7, 1945; AFHRA Microfilm Reel B0608, 926–29.
2. MACR 12367; Wunderlich interview, 8, 22–23, 38–46; Frederick Coe notebook; John Mulvaney Individual Deceased Personal File.
3. Stack letters, January 6, 1945, February 24, 1945, March 14 and 17, 1945, April 18 and 27, 1945.
4. Marrone interview by Greg Krupinsky, 4–13; Earll interview, 7.
5. AFHRA Microfilm A6544B, 993; narrative by Fred Riley, 456th Bomb Group Historian, May 21, 2003; Colasante interview, 5–8; Perrone interview; Houghton interview, 9–11; Quinn interview, 10–13; Nichol and Rennell, *The Last Escape*, 248; Zemke, *Zemke's Stalag*, 28, 68–69, 75–85; Okerstrom, *The Final Mission of Bottoms Up*, 170; "Sgt. Barker Houghton Liberated from Camp," *Townsman*, (Wellesley, Massachusetts), May 1945.
6. Tamraz interview, 61–62.
7. Jim Martin interview by Debby Martin, 12.
8. AFHRA Microfilm Reel B0610, 1412–13; Hill interview, 14–20; Martino interview, 11–13; Nayes narrative, 7.
9. Owens diary, February 7, 1945.

Chapter 21: A Terrible Blindness

1. Blank interview by Elmer Wigley, 12–14. AFHRA Microfilm Reel A6544B, 418, 445, 463, and 466 show the Americans were brought out in a C-47, not a B-25 as claimed in Freeman, *The Forgotten 500*, 244.
2. Pavlowitch, *Hitler's New Disorder*, 254; Tomasevich, *The Chetniks*, 431–35.
3. AFHRA Microfilm Reel A1320, 443–47 (Cumming); Reel A6544C, 1112–14 (Zellman); Reel 25696, 361 (ACRU to Blank, February 27, 1945 re: Ceely identification), 374–75 (ACRU to Blank, February 8, 1945 re: Turk identification and proximity of Germans), 381–90 (ACRU to Blank; Blank, Cumming, and Zellman to units; and Blank to ACRU), 394 (ACRU to Ceely), 398 (Zellman to HQ), 401 (ACRU to Blank, January 11, 1945); Reel A6544D, 871–72 (Blank to Bari HQ, re: identification and proximity of Germans); Zellman interview. The Chetnik major's name is alternatively listed as "Blagovic," "Blagoyevich," and "Blankovic" in AAF records and Blank's account.
4. Inks, *Eight Bailed Out*, 198.
5. AFHRA Microfilm Reel A6544A, 817–18 (Perkins-Inks crew); Reel A6544C, 895 (Herbert Martin), 903–5 (Inks); Inks, *Eight Bailed Out*, 31–44, 50–59, 90–99, 116–122, 195–97; Pavlowitch, *Hitler's New Disorder*, 127; Freeman, "The

Cinderella Front," 37–39; Tomasevich, *The Chetniks*, 258–59, 430–34. The Germans flew Aclin to a POW camp near France where he was soon liberated.

6.   Blank interview by Elmer Wigley, 14–15.

7.   AFHRA Microfilm Reel 25696, 319 (Kraigher to Thayer, March 16, 1945), 320 (Blagoyevitch to Bari HQ), 324 (Kraigher to Inks, March 22, 1945), 326 (Thayer to Kraigher, March 19, 1945), 329 (Cumming to Balkan Air Force, March 12, 1945), 330 (Inks to Bari HQ, March 12, 1945), 333 (Kraigher to Inks, March 1, 1945), 335 (Inks to Bari HQ, February 20, 1945), 341 (Inks to Bari HQ, February 19, 1945); Inks, *Eight Bailed Out*, 202.

8.   AFHRA Microfilm Reel 25696, 315 (Blank to Bari, March 30, 1945), 317 (Kraigher to Blank, March 31, 1945), 323 (Blank to Bari HQ, April 2, 1945); Reel A6544C, 904 (Inks), 982 (Gill); Inks, *Eight Bailed Out*, 203.

9.   Pavlowitch, *Hitler's New Disorder*, 256; Tomasevich, *The Chetniks*, 440–44; *Wartime*, 447.

10. AFHRA Microfilm A6544C, 982 (Gill), 1112–14, (Zellman); Reel A6544D, 833 (Kraigher radiogram); Inks, *Eight Bailed Out*, 205; Pavlowitch, *Hitler's New Disorder*, 266; Blank log, March 5, 14, 16, and 29, April 13 and 14, 1945; Zellman interview, 8.

11. Inks, *Eight Bailed Out*, 203; AFHRA Microfilm A6544D, 793, 833.

12. Inks, *Eight Bailed Out*, 210–13.

13. AFHRA Microfilm A6544C, 1112–14; Inks, *Eight Bailed Out*, 213–14; Blank interview by Elmer Wigley, 17; Zellman interview, 9.

14. AFHRA Microfilm Reel A6544C, 895–91 (Martin), 903–5 (Inks), 925–29 (Blank); Inks, *Eight Bailed Out*, 204, 215–18; Blank interview by Elmer Wigley, 18. Inks claimed the airmen stayed with Zellman for ten days in his book *Eight Bailed Out*, but AAF records indicate they departed Banja Luka the day after their arrival, leaving Zellman behind. Zellman recounted being abandoned in his Escape Statement (AFHRA Microfilm A6544C, 1112–14) and in his interview, 9.

15. AFHRA Microfilm A6544C, 1112–14; Zellman interview, 9–10.

16. Pavlowitch, *Hitler's New Disorder*, 266–67.

Epilogue: Coming Home

1.   Mary Elizabeth Stanley letter to Mary Alice Schmitz, March 1, 1945.

2.   Plaisance diary, March 2, 1945; Stanley letters, February 6 and 8, July 20, and August 3, 1945; Stanley interview, 26–27.

3.   Tamraz interview, 63–64.

4.   Marrone interview by Greg Krupinsky, 14.

5.   Cletus Kramer interview, January 15, 2005; Charles Kramer interview, July 9, 2016.

6.   Rosenthal interview, 33–36.

7.   Lingeman, *Don't You Know There's a War On*, 92; *Courier Express*, October 25, 1945; Stanley interview, 31; *Edwardsville Intelligencer*, September 15, 1945.

8.   AAF Manual 35-155-1, "Coming Home"; McManus, *Deadly Sky*, Epilogue.

9.   Anna Wolff letter to Gertrude Stack, April 8, 1945.

INDEX